KEEPING THE HOME
FIRES BURNING

KEEPING THE HOME FIRES BURNING

ENTERTAINING THE TROOPS AT HOME AND ABROAD

PHIL CARRADICE

PEN & SWORD
HISTORY

AN IMPRINT OF PEN & SWORD BOOKS LTD
YORKSHIRE - PHILADELPHIA

First published in Great Britain in 2022 by
PEN AND SWORD HISTORY
An imprint of
Pen & Sword Books Ltd
Yorkshire – Philadelphia

ISBN 978 1 39900 441 1

Typeset in Times New Roman 11.5/14 by
SJmagic DESIGN SERVICES, India.
Printed and bound by CPI Group (UK) Ltd, Croydon, CR0 4YY

Pen & Sword Books Limited incorporates the imprints of Atlas, Archaeology,
Aviation, Discovery, Family History, Fiction, History, Maritime, Military, Military
Classics, Politics, Select, Transport, True Crime, Air World, Frontline Publishing,
Leo Cooper, Remember When, Seaforth Publishing, The Praetorian Press,
Wharncliffe Local History, Wharncliffe Transport, Wharncliffe True Crime and
White Owl.

For a complete list of Pen & Sword titles please contact
PEN & SWORD BOOKS LIMITED
47 Church Street, Barnsley, South Yorkshire, S70 2AS, England
E-mail: enquiries@pen-and-sword.co.uk
Website: www.pen-and-sword.co.uk

Or
PEN AND SWORD BOOKS
1950 Lawrence Rd, Havertown, PA 19083, USA
E-mail: Uspen-and-sword@casematepublishers.com
Website: www.penandswordbooks.com

Contents

Acknowledgements

First and foremost, heartfelt thanks to those men and women who were happy to talk to me about their experiences and allowed me to record them for posterity. Many of those individuals are no longer with us but their testimonies – reproduced here – remain a lasting tribute to their knowledge and skill. Their experiences are what makes the study of history such a compelling and fascinating process.

Raymond Humphreys and Joyce James, both of whom read the book in manuscript form and gave me invaluable feedback.

My son Andrew for his cartoon and drawings.

My darling Trudy, always there at my shoulder whenever I write. You gave me inspiration when you were alive; you give me reason to write on, even now. As General Custer said in one of Hollywood's dreadful adaptations of history, 'Walking through life with you has been a truly gracious thing.' The film was awful, the sentiment remains perfect.

My old friend and rugby-playing colleague Roger McCallum, not just for his skill with technology but also for his stories and memories. Joyce James spotted that I'd originally typed in 'fiend' rather than 'friend'. Thinking of all the thumps he gave me on the rugby field, I was tempted to leave the original.

Introduction

Raising and, perhaps more importantly, sustaining public morale, particularly at times of national crises like disaster or famine has never been easy. In the face of an epidemic or pandemic, perhaps in the wake of a flood or a tsunami, there are inevitable problems that have always been difficult to solve. War of any type or intensity is perhaps hardest of all potential problems to cope with. What engages one person may enrage another; finding the right level of intervention is a matter of skill and judgement.

The middle course is not always the best way. It can so easily become too lacklustre, annoying no one but pleasing no one either. Too dramatic and dogmatic can be equally as off-putting and how to find the right approach is often as much a matter of luck as judgement.

To make things worse, efforts to raise morale are often a series of moveable feasts – what works at one stage or point in time will not necessarily be effective at another. It may even be counterproductive. In effect, morale-boosting is a minefield that people enter at their own peril.

And yet, as the First World War demonstrated, it is an essential skill for any government or war machine that intends to emerge on the winning side of a conflict. Before the monumental conflict and killing fields of Flanders nobody in Britain had ever seriously considered an external or artificial boost to raising public morale. It was, government thought, something that would happen automatically. After all, hadn't Britain always fought a just and righteous fight?

There are so many elements in the morale issue – subliminal, official, overt and independent to name just a few. That is what makes any study of morale-raising such a fascinating topic.

It is doubtful that in the early days of the Great War the British military, hidebound and traditionalist as it was, had any concept of what might or might not raise or destroy the morale of soldiers:

> At the beginning of the war, a volunteer had to stand five
> feet eight to get into the Army. By October 11 the need for
> men was such that the standard was lowered to five feet five.
> And on November 5, after the thirty thousand casualties of
> October, one had to be only five feet three to get in.[1]

At the beginning of August 1914, the effect of rejection on men who measured an inch or so below the required norm would, at what was a time of great patriotism and enthusiasm for the war, have been hugely damaging. To be allowed into the army a few months later simply because height requirements had been lowered would surely have been equally as demoralizing, conjuring feelings of being second rate and not good enough the first time round – and so on.

The key word in the above example is 'lowered': standards had been lowered and would continue to be lowered. The poet Isaac Rosenberg was one of many who was initially rejected by the army because he was too short. The effect was debilitating. As he wrote: 'I think of getting … some manual labour to do – anything – but it seems I'm not fit for anything.'[2]

Rosenberg did, of course, finally find himself accepted by the army. He managed to get in as part the third element, the 'five-foot three brigade', but the effect of repeated rejection hardly did his self-esteem much good. He was, by most accounts, always a somewhat shoddy soldier.

Recruits did not need – or expect – to be molly-coddled but they did not want to be rejected out of hand purely because of their height. The question on the lips of many would surely have been, 'If I wasn't good enough first time around, why should I be good enough now?' Hardly ideal for the morale of a newly forming army.

Thankfully, the British government had a much clearer and more realistic view of morale than the high command of the army. Founding the War Propaganda Bureau in August 1914 was if not a stroke of genius then certainly a far-sighted expectation of what would be needed in the months ahead.

Of course, no one, apart possibly from Lord Kitchener, had any idea that the war would last so long. While the people of Britain were sure that the troops would be home by Christmas – and even Kaiser Wilhelm of Germany predicted it would all be over before the leaves fell from the trees – Kitchener was already warning the government that they should prepare themselves for a long and arduous campaign. That was one of the reasons he asked for volunteers for his new army.

Perhaps Asquith took note of Kitchener's warning, perhaps he had a sense of foreboding. As an extremely cautious man, it is more likely that he was simply trying to cover all bases. Whichever it was, the prime minister's decision to create a propaganda bureau was well timed. In the wake of crippling defeats and losses on land and at sea, the country would need to sustain the high level of morale it had achieved, almost by accident, in the summer and autumn of 1914.

For perhaps the first time in its history Britain would be forced to consider and develop the issue of morale. But morale-boosting, as we shall see, was not just a government-led initiative. It affected every single member of the British Empire and some of the more effective solutions to the problem came from entirely independent sources.

Prologue

Think propaganda and your mind invariably turns to the persistent outpouring of hate from Nazi Germany during the 1930s and 1940s. That was perhaps the low point of the art – and it remains an art, however it is used and accepted. Yet propaganda has been around a lot longer than the 1930s and has been employed for both good and evil by many regimes across the years.

Despite what many believe, Britain, good old-fashioned democratic Britain, has never been exempt from the power of propaganda. Indeed, it can be argued that the mighty British Empire, that vast conglomeration of territories on which the sun never set, was little more than a perfect example of propaganda. With all its rigid rules of place and position, its endemic notion of hierarchical racism, it was the greatest instrument of propaganda ever invented.

Throughout the nineteenth century, millions of Britons thrilled to the sound, the smell and the succour of Empire. They longed to be a part of it even though most of them were limited to cheering the Guards as they marched down the Mall and were destined never to get within a thousand miles of the exotic locations they dreamed of. More importantly, the public as a whole would never quite manage to question the ethics and the motivation that had brought the British Empire into existence in the first place. Forget money, lucrative trading opportunities and the exploitation of other people's rights, it was Britain's destiny to be seated at the top of the tree. After all, hadn't the Industrial Revolution turned the country into the greatest and most powerful nation in the entire world?

Throughout the century, backed up and emboldened by the hugely powerful dictate of 'Muscular Christianity', the British people gradually found new awareness of themselves. If that awareness manifested itself as belief in British supremacy, in British superiority and in the concept of a British Empire, then the key word has to be 'British'.

Isolated, physically and emotionally cut off from mainland Europe, browbeaten for too many years by a massive and inverted inferiority complex, the British people were eager to be part of the glory and glamour provided by their warlike and newly powerful government. Acquisition of overseas colonies was a natural progression. Pure propaganda if ever it was, albeit maybe on a rather subliminal scale.

Take it a stage further and listen to the strident Music Hall songs of the time. The Victorian music halls, by then the true opiate of the masses, provided music and words to thrill the nation. *Soldiers of the Queen* just about summed up the feelings of most of the population, men and women who would never wear a uniform in their lives.

Read the patriotic if historically inaccurate poems of people like Henry Newbolt and Bransby Williams: 'Play up, play up and play the game' as Newbolt declared; the strident if metrically flawed lines of 'There's a one-eyed yellow idol to the north of Kathmandu' and so on. Then you begin to see that there was no better way of promoting the concept of Empire and overseas conquest than to appeal to the barely suppressed emotions of the public.

All of which brings us to the outbreak of what was to become the most destructive war mankind had ever known. When, in the summer and autumn of 1914, it came to the very real possibility of British men taking up arms to defend a system and way of life they really did not understand, the result was a forgone conclusion. Fuelled by posters and slogans, by Music Hall lyrics that declared, 'We don't want to lose you but we think you ought to go,' the people of Britain flocked in their thousands to offer their bodies to the nation.

The real causes of the war – the world economic situation, the potential trade losses for any neutral nation (the USA excepted), the need to curtail German military and industrial expansion and so on – were lost in a welter of sentiment. 'Help defenceless little Belgium' was always a more appealing sentiment than 'Go to war and make us more money!'

Continual government use of propaganda during the First World War became the supreme masterpiece of manipulation and control over a willing people. It had to be. Otherwise, the number of casualties and the immense weight of inhumanity that were soon to come pouring from the fields of France and Flanders, from the beaches of Gallipoli and from other theatres of war, would have overwhelmed Britain's system of government. The pressure would have wasted the very fabric of British society.

Eventually it was a very similar set of pressures which helped destroy the Russian, German and Austro-Hungarian monarchies. That was in the near-future but almost from the beginning of the conflict it became clear to far-thinking British statesmen that defeat for a country still regrouping after the disastrous Anglo-Boer War might well spell the end of Britain as a world power.

Defeat would have meant that the pose of a decent and democratic nation fighting against totalitarianism would have been exposed as the fallacy it really was. There had to be some way to prevent such a potential disaster. There was – propaganda!

Unlike any previous war in history, the conflict that consumed the world between 1914 and 1918 was one of total war. Whole nations were involved, civilians and soldiers alike. For the first time many civilian populations found themselves under direct attack by bombs and shells and as a consequence propaganda machinery was needed not just to maintain morale but, equally as important, to garner hatred of the enemy. The two elements went hand in hand; it was much easier to keep morale high if people, the soldiers and civilians, the generals and politicians, did not want just to defeat the enemy but to grind him into the dust.

It was not only Britain. Convincing populations of each and every combatant nation that God was on their side, that their cause was righteous and that the enemy was evil, were equally as vital. The propaganda war was, quite simply, the one element that nobody could afford to lose.

Given that premise, it is clear that Britain's effective and highly efficient use of propaganda during the First World War was not a happy accident but quite deliberate. The government and the war machine that it controlled were only too well aware of the dangers of the situation they were facing. Within weeks of the outbreak of war they became surprisingly adept in the use of propaganda machinery to hold the country together.

The use of propaganda, its effect and success, was always a double-edged sword, created not only by government but by the people themselves. If the families at home needed to know that their sons were safe and well at the front, the men in the trenches also needed to know that their wives and mothers back home in Bradford or Bolton or Glasgow were equally as well and fit. It was an emotion that composers like Ivor Novello and his lyricist Lena Guilford Ford understood and caught perfectly in one of the most popular songs of the war:

> *Keep the Home Fires burning*
> *While your hearts are yearning,*
> *Though your lads are far away*
> *They dream of home.*
> *There's a silver lining*
> *Through the dark clouds shining.*
> *Turn the dark cloud inside out*
> *Till the boys come home.*[1]

The thought of keeping the fires of home lit, ready to welcome back the returning soldiers might, now, seem somewhat fey and even false but it was a much-needed emotion during the war years.

The British public undoubtedly took something of a lead, a cue or a start, from renowned figures like Ivor Novello and from government officials like Charles Masterman and John Buchan. They and all the other individuals who happily helped control public emotion and responses during the war years did so knowing that they were carrying out their duty for the country.

With the gentle prodding of government, the British public was hugely instrumental in creating a whole network of morale-boosting techniques that were employed throughout the war. These included things like the creation and distribution of patriotic postcards along with writing sentimental and patriotic poems – and publishing them in newspapers across the country. On the face of it such activities were little more than a 'knee-jerk' reaction by the British public to the situation in which they found themselves. Or were they?

The cynical and probably somewhat accurate response would be that none of that vast outpouring of patriotic emotion was accidental. Fuelling the continuing success of people's poetry, idealizing the heroes of the conflict and maintaining the countrywide love of Music Hall performers with their shallow but immediate art was all part of what Private Baldrick might call 'a cunning plan' on the part of the government.

That may well have been the case. Behind the worship of much revered heroes of the war like Leefe Robinson, Edith Cavell and Boy Cornwall, not to mention a million others whose names would never be known outside their families, the shadowy hands of Charles Masterman and others from the Ministry of Information were probably hard at work. Even so, it still required the swell of public opinion to maintain that enthusiasm and keep morale high.

A joint effort, then, between officialdom and the honest enterprise of the general public, was the secret to the success of British propaganda in the First World War. Government-led and government-induced, without public acclaim and public support, all the propaganda in the world would have been useless.

As Hitler and Goebbels realized once British and American bombs began to drop with monotonous regularity onto Germany in 1943 and 1944, propaganda to an empty room was strident and echoing but it was ultimately a waste of effort. The British government and the British people instinctively understood this in 1914 and held firmly to that belief and understanding as the war went on and casualties continued to mount. At times that was hard to do.

The first day of the Battle of the Somme saw 40,000 wounded and 20,000 British fatalities, the most deaths ever recorded in a single day by the British Army. A year later Haig, after the first day's action at Passchendaele where casualties, dead and wounded, amounted to over 30,000, genuinely believed that he had done well. He complimented his troops and, in particular, himself on gaining a few hundred yards of ground at the cost of such a small number of lives lost and bodies mutilated.

Any propaganda unit attempting to get past horror stories like that undoubtedly had its work cut out for it. And yet that is exactly what Britain's media men and propagandists managed to do.

Unlike the French armies, who, following the disasters of Verdun, mutinied and refused to return to the front lines, British troops accepted the party line and kept plodding forward. British propaganda in the First World War was hugely successful. In many respects it was the fourth arm of the fighting forces, along with the army, the navy and the Royal Flying Corps/Royal Naval Air Service (amalgamated into the RAF on 1 April 1918). It had few heroes, few medal winners or martyrs: that was neither its aim nor intention, but its success was instrumental in the Allied victory of 1918.

PART I

Keep Safe,
Keep Believing

'Patriotism (in peace-time an attitude best left to politicians, publicists and fools, but in the dark days of war an emotion that can wring the heart strings) patriotism made one do odd things.'

W. Somerset Maugham, *Ashenden*

Chapter 1

To Have and Have Not

Use your imagination; let your mind drift back over a hundred years to the early years of the twentieth century. Whatever your station in life, whatever political or social views you hold, there is much to enjoy about British society at this time – but only if you have the money and the leisure to exploit it to the full. Without those two resources, money and time, you must fulminate, sweat and hope for a different future.

The early twentieth century is an age, metaphorically at least, of immense self-indulgence and hearty pats on the back for huge swathes of the British population. Let us imagine that you, the reader, are included in the privileged classes. So, for you, it is an age of having it all, having everything you ever wished or hoped for.

And yet, the situation in the summer of 1914 is deceptive as far as Britain and the British Empire are concerned. Many people, looking back from the present day, see it as a golden, idyllic age before the holocaust of 1914–18 ends for ever the pastoral visions of a perfect world – a perfect British world, of course. They are visions that are destined never to be anything more than pure pipe dreams, imagined glories contrasting with the terrors of death and a war such as no one has ever imagined, let alone witnessed.

By August 1914 Britain is in possession and control of, on the surface at least, the greatest empire the world has ever known. In a tide of jingoistic and gloating self-praise the British people wallow in self-righteous glory. The physical manifestations of owning and exploiting foreign territories are clear to see. There are plentiful supplies of tea and coffee in the shops, drinks that are now truly the opiate of the masses; there is an excess of crops and exotic fruits on the market stalls; in upmarket shops delicate silks and fragrant spices are readily available; in the less salubrious quarters of every city there are other, darker goods available like opium for which Britain has already engineered and fought several wars. It is all there and all taken very much for granted as the fruits of the British Empire.

In order to defend the Empire that is so essential to its well-being, Britain has created a magnificent fleet of Dreadnought battleships. In theory at least, it is the largest, most powerful naval force in the world, capable of crushing any enemy craft reckless enough to challenge its might.

On the domestic or home front all appears well. Since the days of the Stuarts the monarchy has been a constitutional body, deserving of respect but with little or no actual control over the destiny of the people. Over the previous two centuries, the country has developed a democratic system of government that is the envy of the civilized world.

Appearances, however, can be deceptive and below the surface danger lurks. By the end of the Victorian era an undertow of immense proportions has been gathering strength beneath the seemingly invincible prowess and power of the nation. Poverty lurks in the overcrowded cities and their festering tenement blocks. Nobody has yet worked out how best to solve the problem of poverty and overcrowding, let alone the delinquency and crime that goes with them. Trouble, when it arises, comes largely from industrial workers demanding better working conditions. It comes from Suffragettes screaming for the vote and from the faint beginnings of nationalism in the overseas colonies.

Most of the upper and middle classes hardly notice the danger; they are content to bask in Britain's glory. The squalor of London's East End, the slums of Birmingham and Manchester, the tenements of Glasgow's Gorbals, they are almost another world. Summer picnics, bicycle rides out into the country, evenings at the theatre – that is what occupies the minds of most privileged people.

But in those seemingly idyllic pastoral surroundings destabilization, even violence, is building, preparing to explode. And the largely unsuspecting British people hurtle directly into its claws. Britain, what Shakespeare called 'this precious stone set in a silver sea', has such engrained self-belief that it borders on the reckless and deluded world of the sleepwalker.

The cornerstones of society, elements like the church which has for years provided structure and control, are beginning to creak – even if the vast majority of the population does not yet realize what is starting to happen. The questioning of creed and culture, the fall of long-established bastions, will take years to fully develop but *will* happen. It is just a case of waiting.

July and August 1914 are dangerous months in a dangerous year. Britain does not have anything similar to the standing armies of Germany, France and Russia, each with massive forces capable of marauding like the warriors of Attila the Hun or Genghis Khan across mainland Europe. The German army alone numbers nearly a million men with many more trained and experienced reservists who can be called on at a moment's notice to answer the Kaiser's call. Russia's military might, on paper at least, is even greater and the French hide their strength behind a mask of Gallic imperturbability.

The relatively weak and diminutive British Army is a result of the pragmatic approach taken by successive British governments over many years. Since the Trafalgar days of Lord Nelson, Britain's proudest boast has been that her navy rules the waves. And on the face of it, dominant power and control at sea does seem to be the most appropriate way to defend vital trade and supply routes.

The British Army, at best 250,000 strong, remains a policing force more than a military weapon and is spread across the globe protecting British interests. Policing the Empire is a vital task from which barely a single man can be spared but it is hardly a prime example of military prowess. The lessons of the recent Anglo-Boer War in southern Africa have not been learned; indeed, the disasters and the defeats have been hastily shovelled aside in the face of an eventual hard-earned victory which has been achieved as much by economic as military prowess.

That is not all. There are still more weaknesses, social rather than military, undermining the creaking edifice of British democracy. Very few of the privileged class realize how close to disaster they now sit; most of them do not seem to care, assuming that things will go on as they have always done and failing to see the brittle vulnerability of their positions.

Britain does not yet have universal suffrage or a health service for all and even its compulsory educational system is barely fifty years old. The class system remains in place, the fox-hunting few – the nobility, the gentry and the merchant bankers – clinging by their fingertips to the final vestiges of power and control.

Apart from the press, which has always prided itself on an independent stance, Britain has no propaganda machine or mechanism capable of enshrining the country's core values while denigrating the strengths and weaknesses of opponents. A seemingly minor matter, in the weeks and months ahead, this will prove an increasingly dangerous situation for the British.

On 4 August 1914, war is declared against Germany. The action is hugely popular with the people who sing and scream their belief in King, Country and Empire. Before this point Britain has not needed any sort of propaganda service. The presence and the effect of the Empire have been enough to 'puff up' the country for an unwitting public who firmly believe that to be born British is to be born great.

But now it is early summer in the most fateful year of the century, the inevitable war against Germany has begun and the smug, self-satisfied world of the British people is about to change. That change will be permanent.

*

The war of 1914–18 was initially called the Great War. We know it now as the First World War but whatever you call it the war was different from any other conflict the British Empire had ever experienced. Up to and including the Second Anglo-Boer War, fought between 1899 and 1902, Britain's overseas contests had always been undertaken by professional soldiers, 'soldiers of the King' as Kipling called them. The Boer War was the last and least successful military enterprise of the Victorian army but that was not how it was presented to the public.

In the aftermath of the war, parades of khaki-clad soldiers through London brought glory to the East and West Ends. The public thrilled to the sound of bugles and drums, little caring about the defeats and the creation of concentration camps that had finally worn down the Boers. The ultimate result was a British victory; that was all that mattered.

The soldiers who fought to create an empire were largely illiterate men who spent their lives in communal barracks or tented cities. They were men who fought and died in their hundreds in places whose names they could barely pronounce and almost certainly could never locate on a map. They had little or nothing in common with the 'ordinary' – middle and upper class – members of the British public.

Most of Britain's defenders during the Napoleonic, Crimean and other wars of the nineteenth century had enlisted in the army for a variety of reasons which might now seem unfathomable, even alien, to us. Many of those reasons were more than a little dubious. Apart from the officers – who paid huge sums for their commissions – they certainly did not join up to make a career out of the military and often came to the colours in an attempt to escape starvation or avoid imprisonment and transportation. Conditions in both the army and navy were harsh, flogging being a common punishment for wrongdoing. If such beatings led to death or permanent disability, well there were always plenty more recruits waiting to fill the ranks.

Promotion was rare, leave almost non-existent and wages were inevitably late, delayed for reasons that were rarely explained to the grumbling soldiery. But, despite all that, there was still a degree of certainty and security in the ranks. The men were at least fed regularly and, depending on their posting, issued with suitably warm or cool clothing. In the navy, until very late in the day, there was always the possibility of prize money. The British Army, proud of its position and status, prohibited looting but everyone knew it went on.

In 1815, on the eve of Waterloo, the Duke of Wellington had called his troops 'the scum of the earth'. Watching them retreat in the rain after Quatre Bras, he declared that while he did not know what they would do to the French when it came to battle on the following day, they certainly managed to scare the living daylights out of him.

The novelist Jane Austen is often criticized for writing in a bubble, for taking little or no notice of Napoleon and the conflict that was occurring on the Continent for almost the duration of her admittedly short adult life. The reason for that neglect is simple. Austen, like the rest of middle-class Britain, did not know anything about the soldiers or the sailors who were doing the fighting, apart from occasionally dancing with wealthier, well-groomed militia officers at country balls. She might partake in refined dinner parties when, following the meal, carpets would be rolled up and music played. Then more dancing would begin. Austen and the rest of her social class had nothing in common with the rough and ready defenders of the British Empire.

Life for Jane Austen and her people continued unabated at a leisurely pace and while unknown warriors might be dying agonizing deaths on the distant battlefields of Spain, Austria and Italy, such violence had no effect on Austen's life. No effect that is apart from artificially elevating the price of silk or ribbons by a few pennies every season!

For many years soldiers and sailors were necessary evils, there to do a job but not really the sort of people you would invite home for tea. They existed purely to fight, one of the reasons that there are still so few war memorials to the ordinary rank and file from the period. The men who fought and died had done their jobs as soldiers of the Queen. They really did not need commemoration – admire their achievements, my dear, but best forget them now.

The First World War was different. Until 1916 – and arguably even after – it was largely a volunteer war, thousands of eager young men flocking to the recruiting stations to sign up and 'do their bit' in defeating the Kaiser's Germany. It was, as the government hinted on its recruiting posters and in the newspapers, a game, a great game, a game you would regret should you happen to miss it.

It began, of course, in late June 1914 with an assassination. Nobody had expected the murder of the Archduke Franz Ferdinand of Austria to lead to a war that would impact the entire known world. Franz Ferdinand? Most people in Britain did not even know who this obscure foreign dignitary was or have the faintest idea about his significance as heir to the throne of Austria–Hungary. Franz Ferdinand was shot by Serbian Gavrilo Princip, a determined assassin whose life was fuelled by fervent nationalistic pride and anger. In many ways his murderous passions reflected the chaos and confusion of the Balkans where the decrepit Austro-Hungarian Empire was desperately attempting to hold onto its few dominions. The shooting took place in Sarajevo as the visiting Archduke was being driven with Sophie, his wife, through the city streets. To the western world it was simply an unfortunate occurrence, a murder that was deserving of a few paragraphs at the bottom of page 2 in the morning paper. That was all.

The affairs of the Balkans and the Archduke's part in the politics of the region were as unknown to people in Britain as his personality and way of life. The toy town operatic world of Anthony Hope's *Prisoner of Zenda* with its quaint costumes and brocaded uniforms was about as close as most people came to knowing what went on in those farthest regions of Europe. From the outset the murder was a somewhat ludicrous affair. Earlier in the day a bomb thrown by one of Princip's accomplices had hit the bonnet of the Archduke's car and rolled away before exploding in the gutter. Franz Ferdinand was angry but did not call off his visit. Gavrilo Princip, like the other members of his group, was despairing of a second opportunity. Bored with standing about waiting, he was ready to abandon his efforts and head home. Franz Ferdinand came within range of Gavrilo Princip's gun by accident. By the middle of the afternoon the formal visit was completed and after making his farewells, the Archduke set about returning to his accommodation. On the way out of Sarajevo his driver took the wrong route and was reversing the car to get back on the right road when they were spotted by the one remaining assassin. Princip, a member of the wonderfully named Black Hand, did not need a second opportunity. He seized his chance, fired and more by luck than judgement hit both the Archduke and his wife Sophie as they sat in pomp in the back of the car.

No one in Britain or Germany, Russia or France could ever have imagined Princip's two shots would have led to such an opportunity – and there is no doubt that the young men of Britain did come to see the subsequent outbreak of war as an opportunity. To begin with the assassination was simply a remote event in a faraway country. The county cricket scores, the prognosis for the coming football season and the results of the Henley Regatta were far more interesting. People were always being murdered, blown up or knifed to death in the Balkans. It was to be expected, an occupational hazard in that part of the world and it certainly did not concern the British.

However, with his two shots, two shots that reverberated around the world, Gavrilo Princip altered the course of history. Like toppling stacks of dominoes, the nations of Europe shivered, hesitated and fell into the chasm that had been yawning in front of them for years. Desperate for revenge Austria seized the opportunity to flex her muscles and duly invaded Serbia. Russia, friend and patron of the Serbs, retaliated by declaring war on Austria. Germany, always eager for a chance to stretch her mighty limbs, decided to throw in her lot with her ally Austria. Before they knew it the whole of Europe was preparing for war. Meanwhile Princip escaped execution but died in prison, apparently from tuberculosis, in 1918.

For the young men of Britain, the situation soon became simple. Britain was not directly involved with the convoluted dealings of the Continent but anything that in any way threatened to promote German strength, German industry and German dominance in Europe was a concern for the British government – and, by default, the British people.

It was too good an opportunity to miss. Forget Franz Ferdinand and the Balkan problems, Kaiser Wilhelm II of Germany had been posing and threatening for too long. It was time now to award him a well-deserved kick in the pants. The German breach of Belgian neutrality was the perfect excuse. It was time to fight and enjoy the great adventure that was waiting for those bold enough to seize it.

To begin with it was a volunteer conflict, an adventure or a jaunt, not unlike taking a charabanc ride to a summer picnic. But after 1916 things changed. It became a conscript war, men being called to serve King and Country and deployed according to the needs of the government and the military.

The initial burst of enthusiasm that had filled the ranks in 1914 and 1915 waned and the government was reluctantly forced to balance the needs of the military with the requirements of industry that kept soldiers and sailors equipped with bullets and shells. The patriotic men of Britain had already joined up and were serving in various theatres. Men still chose to enlist as volunteers but the war was an insistent beast that demanded ever more recruits to fill the spaces left by battle, brutality and disease. The armed forces were faced by a manpower shortage that threatened to cripple the war effort.

Undoubtedly the First World War changed both the nature and, in particular, the class of conflict. Within a few months of its outbreak, it was no longer simply a case of working-class men obeying the orders of middle- or upper-class officers, it was a matter of everyone being in it together. It was, in many respects, the army's first subconscious attempt at meritocracy. Before long university graduates could as easily be discovered in the rank and file of the army as among the members of the officer corps. By the end of the war miners, mechanics, engineers, salesmen and tradesmen were to be found serving as junior officers at the front.

Casualties during the war – on both sides of the wire – were enormous. It was perhaps something that might have been expected when half-trained volunteers were flung over the parapets into the face of artillery and machine-gun fire. Walk towards the guns was a standard order and men did it, shoulder to shoulder, a human equivalent of the volley fire that had been so effective against the spear-carrying tribesmen of India and Africa.

The generals on the Western Front, British, French and German alike, were a fairly unimaginative and consistent group of individuals. Most of them had gained their military experience as cavalry officers during the Franco-Prussian War of 1870 or on the hot and hard South African veld at the turn of the century. They saw no reason to change their attitudes or, as a consequence, their tactics.

They believed, almost to a man, that weight of numbers would surely batter the enemy into submission. Bullets and shells were valuable commodities; men were expendable. There were always more infantrymen to fill the gaps.

That was a theory, a concept or an idea, which was clearly seen in 1916 during the British disaster on the Somme and at the brutal slogging match of Verdun, where the German commander, General Erich von Falkenhayn, went on record saying that he had no tactic other than to outlast his opponents and incur fewer casualties than the opposing French. Douglas Haig and the other British generals silently agreed with him.

Now, with hindsight, it is all too easy to see the murderous fallacy of such an approach. Unfortunately for the troops, the mindless slaughter of the Somme, Verdun and nearly all the battles thereafter were seen and fully appreciated only as the conflict entered its final phase. All of this meant that for the entire length of four bloodthirsty years the situation on the front lines remained as consistent as the attitudes and behaviour of the generals who organized the slaughter – nineteenth-century tactics against twentieth-century weapons. It was, inevitably, a recipe for disaster and it was only in the final months that those in charge finally realized the error of their ways. By then, of course, it was too late to do more than vow never to allow such things to happen again – another profound and significant error of judgement.

In the face of such slaughter the need to keep morale high was an obvious problem, not just among the soldiers in the trenches but also in the hearts and minds of those back home. The primary purpose of boosting morale was obviously to keep the soldiers happy and content, ready to fight to the death if needs be. But it did not take the greatest intellect in the world to work out that the best way of doing this was to ensure that their families, their loved ones back home, were secure and safe and not worrying unduly about their husbands and fathers at the front. Only high morale within the military and the need for each man to do his duty could account for the seemingly endless supply of recruits. For the Allies and Axis alike, new cannon fodder continued to appear on a regular basis. Only good morale at home could possibly create a system where wives, mothers, schools, colleges and employers would permit and encourage continual enlistment and the inevitable route to death and disaster.

When Germany finally slumped to defeat in the autumn of 1918, her armies were still largely intact on the field of battle, retreating yes, but still able and willing to fight. The morale of the people at home, however, in Berlin, Munich and the other German cities had been utterly shattered. And that, arguably, was one of the major causes of the German defeat. It had surprisingly little to do with direct force of arms.

The causes of that destruction of morale in the German homeland were many and varied. On the one hand there was the British naval blockade that led to food shortages and starvation. On the other there were dozens, even hundreds of newspaper stories and subliminal works of literature that impinged on the subconscious of the German people.

British propaganda was designed to prevent a similar fate befalling Britain. Almost from the beginning of the conflict insightful members of Prime Minister Herbert Asquith's War Cabinet knew that eventual victory would require the efforts of men and women who were experienced and capable in the art of puffing up the successes of the British armed forces and demeaning those of Germany. In other words, propagandists. In their own way and over the course of four years of conflict such individuals would become as important to Britain as any member of the armed forces.

*

Soon after the declaration of war on 4 August 1914 the British government came to realize that Germany's efficient and highly effective propaganda department was already active in circulating rumours and stories about British and French inadequacies and mistakes. Many of the stories contained more than a little false, or fake, news. It hardly mattered; the stories were out there in the public domain where they could be believed or disregarded as people chose.

The British and French had known for some time that such an organization existed in Germany but like so many of the laissez-faire policies in operation at the time neither government had chosen to do anything about it. The declaration of war changed matters entirely.

If Germany had a propaganda ministry then Britain wanted one too! That was a given, a necessity. Consequently, before the month of August 1914 was out, David Lloyd George, who was at that time occupying the post of Chancellor of the Exchequer, was singled out by Herbert Asquith and presented with the task of establishing a British equivalent to the German Propaganda Ministry.

Like everything he did the ambitious little Welshman approached his new task with verve, vigour and not a little self-interest. Within a matter of days, the British War Propaganda Bureau had been formed. It was not a formal propaganda ministry in the manner of Germany's long-established organization but it was a clear beginning and, despite the different nomenclature, the aims of the two opposing departments were basically the same.

Knowing that he had neither the time nor the freedom to run the War Propaganda Bureau himself, Lloyd George looked around for a friendly face to do the job for him. He found his man in the shape of a writer and Liberal MP who also happened to be the Chancellor of the Duchy of Lancaster. That man was Charles Frederick Gurney Masterman. Masterman had already worked closely with Lloyd George and the rising political star Winston Churchill in designing government-led social welfare projects, notably helping to form and develop the National Insurance Act of 1911. Lloyd George knew his man and Masterman accepted the post with alacrity.

To begin with Masterman was presented with two basic tenets. One, British propaganda should be geared towards the concept of bringing the United States into the war on the side of the Allies. Two, the existence of the War Propaganda Bureau was to remain totally secret. Both aims were in keeping with Masterman's own beliefs.

He was given a budget of £10,000 per annum, hardly a great amount for any government intent on fighting a propaganda war. However, that budget began to increase significantly as the success of the War Propaganda Bureau became clear and by 1917 the figure had increased to £145,000.

Located in Wellington House at Buckingham Gate, the London headquarters of the National Insurance Company – of which Masterman was also the chairman – the Bureau soon side-lined its official title and became known simply as Wellington House. Masterman did not care what his new organization was called; it had a job to do.

Masterman quickly began assembling a team of capable men to help him in his work. These included people like the novelist Arnold Toynbee, Eric Maclagan (future Director of the Victoria and Albert Museum), the book illustrator Thomas Derrick and Campbell Dodgson, Keeper of Prints and Drawings at the British Museum. The novelist John Buchan who not only worked for Masterman but also, in a bizarre switch of duties and responsibilities later became his boss, referred to the first Director of the War Propaganda Bureau in glowing terms: 'I found his judgement shrewd and bold and his mastery of detail impeccable. But I would stress above all things his loyalty.'[1]

In early September Masterman began by organizing two conferences to thrash out the exact duties of Wellington House – what to do and who to perform it. He knew where he wanted to go but needed to bring others along with him if the enterprise was going to succeed.

At the first of these meetings, called for 2 September 1914, he made sure that many of the leading authors of the day were in attendance. They were going to be pivotal in his strategy. Among others John Buchan, John Masefield, Arnold Bennet, Arthur Conan Doyle, Thomas Hardy and Henry Newbolt were present, all of them agreeing to do what they could to assist. Rudyard Kipling had been invited but was unable to attend. He did, however, send a message of support and an offer to help in whatever way he could.

The immediate task, it was decided, was to produce a series of booklets explaining British war aims and resources. These were the first of 1,160 such pamphlets produced during the war years, only the severe paper shortage of 1917–18 and a change in the direction of British propaganda finally managing to curtail production. Among the early leaflets were *To Arms* by Conan Doyle and *The New Army* by Kipling.

By June 1915 thousands of copies of these and other pamphlets had been printed and distributed. Translated into seventeen different languages which included German, Chinese and Greek, they were widely distributed through a variety of different sources. Distribution was deliberately wide-ranging and widespread in an attempt to keep the activities of Wellington House secret.

Several voluntary organizations undertook to deliver the pamphlets in much the same way as charity information is distributed nowadays. Many were dropped at convenient locations like barbers' shops, embassies and in the hallways of town libraries where they would be picked up by the casual browser and read. Hundreds of leaflets and pamphlets went to the Continent, to the USA and to enemy-held territory.

Charles Masterman had great belief in the value of photographs. He had seen the effect and popularity of German visual newspapers and was determined to achieve a similar product in Britain. The key, of course, was to use good-quality images. He was hindered by the fact that to begin with the military had decreed that only two nominated photographers would be allowed to work anywhere on the Western Front. As it happened both were army officers. Anyone else caught taking illicit images might well find themselves in gaol or even, horror of horrors, in front of a firing squad. Under government pressure things soon changed and it was not long before Masterman's department at Wellington House was collating and then sending out over 4,000 photographic images each week. With the ban on individual soldiers taking photographs still in place, nearly all of the images were the product of official war photographers like Ernest Brooks.

The indefatigable Ernest Brooks, ever present on the Dardanelles beaches during the Gallipoli Campaign, returned to Europe just in time for the Battle of the Somme in the summer of 1916. And there his haunting still images augmented the cinematic work of Britain's early movie industry – more of that adventure later.

The photographs taken by Ernest Brooks and his colleagues went to a variety of locations and venues including British and foreign newspapers. Many of these were, as Masterman had always intended, of the 'illustrated' variety like *The Illustrated London News* and *The Graphic*.

The Wellington House photographs might have been 'official' but it was not just Masterman who marketed images of the war. Already there were other forces attempting to seize their slice of the pie, a process that did little to help but served mainly to confuse things for Masterman.

In August 1916, Lord Northcliffe of the *Daily Mail* paid £2,500 into the coffers of British Army charities in return for the right to publish forty postcard views of the Battle of the Somme. Northcliffe went on to negotiate further deals with the army and soon dramatic images of British soldiers, marketed under the strap line of *Daily Mail Official War Pictures*, were available from every book and newspaper vendor in Britain. They were sold as postcard views of the conflict.

Northcliffe, it was said, was determined to make the *Daily Mail* the *official* newspaper of the British Army. As a consequence, 10,000 copies of the paper were dispatched every day to the front in France and Belgium. They were taken in specially converted military cars and arrived with almost monotonous regularity. Apart from reading the papers, usually full of cheerful and unrealistic advice on how to win the war, soldiers invariably found several other, more practical uses for them, using copies for purposes that Northcliffe would never have thought possible!

Accepting the newspaper was one thing but there were few takers for Northcliffe's offer of payment for any soldier who wanted to write about his experiences. Most of the old sweats who made up the bulk of the

British Army, at least until the volunteers began to arrive in force, would not have had the education to write such articles. And then, even before the days of rigid censorship which came in after the Somme disaster, such activities were discouraged.

Despite Northcliffe's seeming philanthropy, the *Daily Mail* photographs and postcards were a money-making concern and were soon being collected by the families of the troops. Many of them were hoping to catch a glimpse of their loved ones on the cards. The photographs were accurate enough but the captions were often totally misleading. Lines such as 'The Glorious First of July – Our First Prisoners', 'The Smile of Victory – King George V at the Front' and 'Tommy at Home in German Dug-outs' gave a decidedly positive feel to what had been a totally disastrous battle which ultimately produced nearly half a million British casualties. Coined by Northcliffe's copy writers, the wording on the cards certainly failed, in many cases, to match up to the reality of the photographic images.

Perhaps the greatest blunder was a card showing a party of soldiers going up to repair damaged barbed wire. Much to the amusement of men at the front, the caption labelled the image as a telegraph and telephone wiring party about to commence work. One of the intentions, of course, was to encourage the people back home and the captions were part of that morale-boosting exercise. But in reality, with casualty lists growing by the day, the words fooled no one.

Lord Northcliffe was not a member of the government although Lloyd George did briefly consider bringing him 'into the fold' before deciding that the newspaper giant would be more trouble than he was worth. Lloyd George was undoubtedly correct in his judgement.

Northcliffe, real name Alfred Harmsworth, had founded the *Daily Mail* in 1896. Since then, it had become one of the most popular newspapers in Britain. Basing its style and content on American journals of the time – along with *Comic Cuts*, Northcliffe's first venture into the publication business was to provide the working man with a newspaper that was instantly accessible. The use of dramatic photographic images was in keeping with the aim of making the paper easily understood by all sections of society. With its famous strap line of 'A penny newspaper for one half penny', the *Daily Mail* was an instant success. Within a few months it had a daily circulation of 550,000 copies, a figure that leapt to over a million during the Boer War.

Northcliffe was a prickly, self-opinionated man who saw it as his duty to hold those in charge of the country to task. Even before the war he was a distinct thorn in the government side and now, with the safety of the country at stake, he was in his element. It was his right as a public servant, he believed, to criticize and to question the decisions of his political masters even though this did not always work in his favour and his efforts sometimes backfired on him.

He was highly critical of Lord Kitchener, the minister for war. Herbert Kitchener had provided the army with the wrong type of shells, Northcliffe wrote, hoping for an outburst of fury from the public.

Unfortunately for him, Northcliffe had miscalculated. His articles did indeed provoke fury from the British public but it was not aimed at Lord Kitchener. Northcliffe's criticism of Britain's 'favourite son' saw the paper ceremoniously burned by Kitchener devotees and circulation drop, temporarily, to fewer than 250,000.

Undaunted, Northcliffe continued to berate Lord Kitchener, even after his death. The minister for war was drowned when the cruiser *Hampshire*, which was carrying him to a meeting in Russia, struck a mine and sank. Kitchener might be dead but Northcliffe could not resist a final crow over the man's metaphorical grave: 'The British Empire has just had the greatest stroke of luck in its history.'[2]

Kitchener might not have been the most successful or best organized government minister but since his campaign to avenge Gordon of Khartoum in the Sudan, he had held a special place in the hearts of British citizens, civilian and military alike. Northcliffe's continued criticism did him and his paper little good. Even so the newspaper magnate sailed on regardless.

Meanwhile, the work of Wellington House continued. Initial efforts were geared at ensuring the credibility of Britain's actions in the eyes of the world. Specialist telegraph agencies were established in various European cities such as Bucharest and Amsterdam, while Masterman worked like fury in order to develop links with other propaganda agencies. These included the Neutral Press Committee and the Foreign Office News Department which had been created with specific tasks in mind. The Neutral Press Committee, headed up by former *Daily Chronicle* editor G. H. Mair, was intended to supply journalists in neutral countries with information. The Foreign Office News Department did exactly what its name suggested, supplying official statements from the government to officials and reporters of foreign countries.

It was difficult because every agency had its own agenda and lack of coordination between them soon became apparent. Masterman resisted any form of centralization which he felt would destroy the independence he had been enjoying. Wellington House was, after all, his baby. But it soon became clear that the wide variety of agencies involved too often led to confusion and duplication of workloads.

At the behest of David Lloyd George, first while he was still chancellor and then when he became prime minister, there were a number of formal government-funded inquiries into the work of Wellington House. Propaganda had always interested Lloyd George. He had built his political career on a good public image and he was not going to allow the Bureau too much freedom of action.

The first of these reviews highlighted the lack of cooperation between the various agencies involved in the propaganda war. Delivered to Lloyd George in 1916, the report resulted in an inevitable reorganization. Wellington House was brought under Foreign Office control and the Neutral Press Committee was absorbed into the news department of the Foreign Office.

Despite this degree of reorganization, things did not improve overly much from there. Lloyd George succeeded Asquith as prime minister at the end of 1916 and immediately ordered another inquiry into the state of affairs at Wellington House. Written by Robert Donald, editor of the *Daily Chronicle,* and presented to the new prime minister in January 1917 this second report was again highly critical. The hidden or underground activities of Wellington House in the United States was the only aspect of the work to be praised.

Yet another reorganization was put in place. A department of information was created under the control of the adventure writer John Buchan, an ad hoc arrangement whilst awaiting the result of another report to be delivered later in the year. Buchan was to be answerable to Sir Edward Carson, the noted lawyer and now an MP in the War Cabinet.

This temporary department of information was formally located in the Foreign Office, albeit with independent status, where it could be more easily controlled. Wellington House continued to function, now restricted to literary and art activities and with Masterman still in the chair.

However, the third report, when it came, was still critical of the organization. The criticism came mainly because of the lack of unity between the various parts of the whole. It was hardly surprising considering how many different elements were involved. Even Lord Northcliffe had managed to inveigle himself into affairs, leading the War Aims Committee which dealt with propaganda in neutral countries. Just to confuse matters further, Northcliffe had been able to wangle a situation where he was answerable only to the War Cabinet.

Unhappy with the situation, Edward Carson resigned from the War Cabinet in 1918 and Lloyd George, having decided that a senior government figure must be involved in the propaganda business, took the opportunity to revamp the country's propaganda system. This time it was to be a total reorganization.

As a result, on 4 March 1918 the Ministry of Information was finally created, headed up by Max Aitken, Lord Beaverbrook of the *Daily Express.* He was perhaps the ideal man to be in charge but in October 1918 he became very ill and was consigned to his sick bed. His deputy, Arnold Bennett, took over the running of the Ministry of Information until the end of the war.

There were three departments or sections in the new organization: domestic, foreign and military, each of them headed by a significantly experienced official.

John Buchan, now with the honorary rank of lieutenant-colonel, remained as head of the foreign section with an annual salary of £1,000 – considerably more than what he had as yet earned from his writing. The War Office Department MI7 took control of the military section while domestic propaganda came under the remit of the War Aims Committee.

Charles Masterman was effectively elbowed aside in the re-organization but, retaining responsibility for war art, photographs, pamphlets and books, he was now subservient to Buchan. It was an abrupt about face but both men seemed able to live with the change in power and position.

It is hard to see why or how but, in some way, Masterman must have annoyed Lloyd George. The prime minister, mercurial and dynamic as he might have been, made an enemy with a long memory. Even the end of the war did not curb Lloyd George's malicious intent. Never a great politician, Masterman had lost his seat in the House of Commons in 1916 and was desperate to get back into parliament. He might have expected support but was hindered by the very man he expected to afford him that assistance.

In the first post-war general election, Lloyd George actively supported not Masterman but his opponent for the new parliamentary seat of Stratford West Ham. Masterman duly failed to gain the seat, being thoroughly beaten by the Unionist opposition. Buchan, in his autobiography, *Memory Hold the Door*, recorded that in his opinion Masterman had been particularly hard done by but stopped short of levelling blame at Lloyd George: 'He was one of the most brilliant, misunderstood and tragically fated men of his time … Masterman began by being overestimated, or estimated on the wrong lines, and he ended by being most unjustly derided.'[3]

Charles Masterman received no formal honours after the war. He was given no knighthood or any form of official recognition, reward that might have been expected for someone who had played such a vital part in Britain's victory. Many men who had performed less ably were happy to accept medals and decorations from the government. It was hardly Lloyd George's finest moment and Masterman, who had laboured long and hard to carry out the wishes of his master, lost out.

Again, the cynical response – in light of Lloyd George's known propensity for taking payments for honours – was that Masterman was probably not prepared to pay for his MBE or for whatever award he might have been considered. There is no proof for this assumption but John Buchan was another of the propaganda chiefs who received no recognition.

Despite all the critical reports and what had clearly developed into a case of bad blood between Charles Masterman and David Lloyd George, it was not all doom and gloom. Wellington House and the various organizations that followed it or worked in conjunction with it, actually managed many remarkable achievements during the war.

The big success for Britain's War Propaganda Bureau came in the shape of the USA. America did finally enter the war on the side of the Allies although this owed as much to Admiral Reginald 'Blinker' Hall and his codebreakers of Room 40 as it did to Wellington House. The story of Room 40 is now well known, deeply rooted in the annals of the various British secret service organizations, but at the time its existence was a closely guarded secret. In that respect it was like so much of the dark and deadly game of espionage that was crucially important to the survival of the British Empire.

Blinker Hall's men from Room 40 at the Admiralty, part of the new Secret Service, intercepted and decoded the now infamous Zimmerman telegram sent by the German government to their Mexican counterparts on the other side of the Atlantic.

Despite its contents, which shocked Hall and his men to their core, the telegram appeared to be a genuine document. It was a simple enough communication. It asked for Mexican help in waging war against the Western Allies and in return offered the Mexicans the gift of large parts of the southern USA which would be reclaimed once the war was won. This was land that had belonged to Mexico, land the Mexicans had lost to the USA during the Texas war of independence and the American–Mexican War of the 1840s. There was just enough bitterness in the Mexican ranks to make the offer interesting. 'Remember the Alamo' had been the cry of the Texans during their fight for liberty and independence from Mexico in the 1830s. The Mexicans also remembered that famous engagement, a central point of the independence struggle, albeit from the opposite end of the spectrum. The telegram and the offer were a direct challenge to the independence of the United States. It was a direct attempt to influence the status and the policy of what were then two neutral countries.

The rationale was simple enough: if America ever got around to joining the war on the Allied side then Germany would be in desperate need of assistance from allies like Mexico. For the USA it would be a case of fighting a war on two fronts, one of them frighteningly close to the American homeland. The telegram was a bizarre document, one that made many people question its origin. To say that it was indiscreet would be stating the obvious but the propaganda men of Wellington House naturally seized the news. And the rest is history.

The existence of Wellington House as a base for British propaganda had always been meant to be kept a secret. Masterman had been told that in the early days of the War Propaganda Bureau and despite everyone's expectations and the undoubted dread of senior government officers, it stayed as exactly that right to the end of the war. Many members of parliament and several press magnates did not even know it existed.

And yet, in the four short years of its existence, Wellington House managed to influence people and governments the world over. Whatever else it managed to achieve, that was probably its greatest success.

Chapter 2

Daddy, What Did You Do in the War?

Before taking things further, we need to pause in order to take a look at individuals and at some of the specific events in the propaganda war that was waged by the British between 1914 and 1918. Even before that, however, it is worth considering exactly how such propaganda was used by the government and by private individuals during those four years. The short and easy answer is that it was used in many different ways and styles. That explanation or response is rather glib but it can be broken down into following groups or bands.

Leaflets and Pamphlets

The use of leaflets and pamphlets has already been mentioned. They were the immediate response of Charles Masterman and Wellington House, reacting to Kitchener's request and the need to find volunteers to augment the already stretched British Army.

The volunteers came more quickly than anyone had ever imagined, Kitchener's New Army as they became known, and Masterman's leaflets were the first salvo in what was to become a long and draining conflict. It is easy to see why these simple pieces of paper were so successful. Leaflets were cheap to produce, easy to manufacture and quick to print off. Pamphlets, slightly fuller and slightly larger, were not that much more expensive and, being written by some of the top authors of the day, were not long-winded or obtuse. That made them easily understood by all sections of society and by people from a whole range of nationalities.

By mid-1916 millions upon millions of words, in leaflet form, had been published and circulated by Wellington House. The recipients of the leaflets were varied. Most of the leaflets were never intended for the general public or for a mass audience but were geared to influential targets, people such as civil servants, members of the press, and politicians, of all warring sides. There were inevitable leakages, something which nobody really minded, but, importantly, Wellington House was never implicated in their production or recognized as playing any part in the operation.

By the summer of 1915, Gilbert Parker, head of the American Section at Wellington House, had put together a mailing list of 13,000 potential recipients in the leafleting campaign. By the end of 1917 that list had increased to a staggering 170,000. In addition, Parker had compiled an equally impressive list of 512 newspapers that would regularly receive leaflets, pamphlets and other propaganda material.

The contents of the leaflets included official publications or statements, royal messages and the standard propaganda fare about British strengths and victories. Pamphlets, being longer, went into rather more detail.

The *Bryce Report*, one of the earliest and most influential of the pamphlets was circulated in 1915 and was entitled *Report on the Alleged German Outrages*. The Dutch artist Louis Raemaekers provided a series of highly emotive illustrations showing the brutality of German soldiers in Belgium. There will be more about Raemaekers and his work later.

Books, Stories and Poems

If, thanks to compulsory education, the First World War was the world's first truly literate conflict, it was also the first literary one. This was an age of books and magazines, before television and radio made mass communication easier and more immediate. When Paul Fussell declared, 'The efficiency of the postal service made books as common at the Front as parcels from Fortnum and Masons,' he was not talking only about the officers and upper classes.[1]

With post taking just two or three days to reach the firing lines, parcels containing books and magazines as well as food and the ubiquitous woollen gloves and socks, were continually arriving at the front. Everyone from the lowliest private to John French, the commander-in-chief of the BEF, read for personal pleasure.

Contrary to public opinion, war in the trenches consisted mainly of long stretches of boredom interspaced by periods of manic engagement with the enemy. It meant that during those draining periods of inactivity, the minds of soldiers were open to wild and unpleasant swings of fancy when fear, regret and hopelessness were all capable of rising to the surface. Boredom, punctuated by extreme violence, was a potential recipe for disaster, a psychological minefield, and it was important to find ways of filling the tedium.

Books for the masses were the obvious answer. But such volumes also had the decided advantage of being enjoyed by families back home. Classics like *The Pilgrim's Progress*, arguably the most popular book of the war, were always available – Masterman saw to that – but there was a need for more modern, up-to-date offerings.

Masterman had always intended that the authors 'on his payroll' should write books that would be of a patriotic and yet informative nature. It had not been so long before that Erskine Childers had produced *The Riddle of the Sands*, a novel which had been hugely influential in raising awareness of clandestine enemy action and in the creation of the British Secret Service. So Masterman well understood the value of good-quality literature and what it could achieve if used in the right way.

What he particularly wanted was a well-written, informative but easily understood history of the war. Barely fifty years before, the Victorian storytellers Charles Dickens and William Thackeray had been writing monthly serials that were eagerly awaited and snapped up by the public when they appeared. Admittedly Dickens and Thackeray had been writing fiction but why should the history of the war, something that surely fascinated everyone, not be dealt with in the same manner?

John Buchan agreed to write a monthly record of the conflict, produced and printed by his own publisher Thomas Nelson under the title *Nelson's History of the War*. Each one was, effectively, a freestanding book on its own. The first instalment appeared in February 1915 and was followed by twenty-three issues. Each instalment consisted of around 30,000 words, the production of which was a mammoth task for the writer. None of them contained any criticism of the conduct of the war, at least not by the British, but they were unashamedly patriotic in both style and content. Even so, Buchan's histories were hugely popular at the time. Written within the strictures of national security, they were also reasonably informative. Buchan, awarded the honorary rank of lieutenant, was given all the intelligence and facts he needed in order to write the books/articles and even made several visits to the front in France in order to see and experience action.

In the early 1920s all twenty-four monthly parts were pulled together, just like the novels of Dickens and Thackeray, and published in book form. They are still in print. What is remarkable is the fact that Buchan continued to write his well-known thrillers and undertake work for Wellington House while producing his 30,000 words a month for the *History*. His best-known book, *The Thirty-Nine Steps*, was written and published, first as a short serial in *Blackwood's Magazine* and then as a book in October 1915. *Greenmantle*, the second of his Richard Hannay novels and possibly the greatest spy story of all time, was published in 1916, while *Mr Standfast*, although not published until 1919, was written in the final year of the war.

Adventure thrillers by other writers were published during the war, often for children, but in the main they were not quite of the first rank and written independently from the Propaganda Bureau. As long as they met the requirements of Wellington House, that was fine. Even John Buchan's three great war novels, whilst conforming to propaganda expectations, were not written at the behest of Wellington House.

The government did have a hand in procuring stories. They used writers such as Ford Maddox Hueffer (better known as Ford Maddox Ford – he changed his name in 1919) and J. M. Barrie, much to the disgust of many of their colleagues. D. H. Lawrence and Virginia Woolf in particular were appalled at the stories, remaining adamantly opposed to the whole conflict.

Some of the commissioned stories, *The Scaremonger* by Hueffer/ Ford for one, are total propaganda and scarcely believable. They are interesting now for their adherence to the popular support for the war rather than for any literary excellence. Ford's story centres on a local squire from South East England and the capture of a German U-boat and its crew by the men of the Mid Kent Cycle Corps. The message, really, is one of patriotic defence of the country, regardless of the cost: 'Every bush, every barn, every bridge, concealed for him an armed spy; behind every cloud there was a dirigible bearing two tons of great, explosive and poisonous projectiles. The two words "national regeneration" were continually on his lips.'[2] *The Scaremonger* is hardly one of the best pieces of writing produced by Ford Maddox Ford, a man who went on to write *Parade's End*, which really is one of the great novels of the war, but, published in *The Bystander* in November 1914, it was exactly what the men of Wellington House were looking for from the country's writers.

One of the most successful short stories of the early war years was Arthur Machen's *The Bowmen*. Originally published in September 1914, it is a piece of speculative fiction describing how St George and the bowmen of Agincourt come to the rescue of beleaguered British soldiers at the Battle of Mons. Much to Machen's dismay the story came to be accepted, not as a piece of fiction but as a true account of the battle. It was rescripted as the legend of the Angel of Mons and used as a major propaganda tool by the government for the rest of the war.

Practically all of the great novels, plays and memoirs of the war – Siegfried Sassoon's Sherston trilogy, Edmund Blunden's *Undertones of War*, R. C. Sherriff's *Journey's End* and the German Erich Maria Remarque's *All Quiet on the Western Front*, to name just a few – were not written, performed or published until the late 1920s or early 1930s. By then the War Propaganda Bureau was long dissolved and, beyond the standard censorship laws, government had little involvement in what writers published.

Poetry was rarely commissioned by Wellington House and as the war went on the genre increasingly became the medium through which writers, who had initially been patriotic in the extreme, expressed their abhorrence of the way things were being handled. Wilfred Owen, Isaac Rosenberg, Ivor Gurney and most other anti-war poets did not receive wide recognition until after the conflict ended. There was the exception of Siegfried Sassoon whose two wartime collections, *The Old Huntsman and Other Poems* and his later, more virulent *Counter-Attack*, met with some success and acclaim. Both books were published towards the end of the war when criticism of the generals and the government was considered acceptable and the immediacy of his words, combined with bitter savagery and sarcasm, made his verses easy to remember.

That was not so in 1914 when the overriding aim was to fight – and die – for one's country. There was considerable encouragement for patriotic poetry, particularly in those first few months when the newspapers were full of delusional offerings about how good and right it was to offer your body on the altar of self-sacrifice.

The one name that was on everyone's lips was, of course, Rupert Brooke. The darling child of the age and certainly a lot more hard-nosed than most modern readers allow, by early 1915 Brooke had made the leap from soft-edged socialism to full-on, patriotic support for the war. It was an inevitable journey considering the company in which he moved. In August 1914, while the war crisis was looming, a sick and ailing Brooke spent three weeks lodged in, of all places, 10 Downing Street, a guest of Prime Minister Herbert Asquith and his daughter. Lunches with Winston Churchill, then First Lord of the Admiralty, and his personal private secretary, Edward, or 'Eddie', Marsh, a renowned protector and advocate of poets and handsome young men, were regular events.

Between them, Churchill and Marsh arranged for Brooke to receive a commission in the Royal Naval Division, a far more decorative unit than any of the army regiments. Brooke was exactly the type of man for whom Churchill was looking. Handsome, popular, highly educated and with a talent for words, he fitted the bill in every respect.

To begin with, however, Brooke was uncertain about the justness of the conflict and was torn between the twin choices open to him – joining up or remaining a civilian. Naturally something of a pacifist, he did eventually come down for war but quite how much he was influenced by Churchill and the others remains unknown. Whether it was at their behest or from somewhere deep in his subconscious, Rupert Brooke's poetic output changed. For the brief final months of his life, he was the perfect patriot for whom the thought of England, her standards and her values were paramount.

1914 and Other Poems, the only book published by Rupert Brooke during his lifetime, quickly became the epitome of public feeling.

And yet the five poems for which he is most famous – included in the book – remain untypical of his writing, being wordy and full of empty rhetoric. They did, however, manage to catch the mood of the moment and the attitude of the people. The lines that particularly resonated with the British public at the time came from his sonnet *The Soldier*:

> *If I should die think only this of me*
> *That there's some corner of a foreign field*
> *That is forever England.*[3]

These days, many years after the sonnets were first published, the poems ring particularly hollow and written for a purpose – to encourage enlistment. It is doubtful that had he lived beyond the Gallipoli Campaign, he would have written anything so ethereal or even remotely similar again. The realistic side to Brooke's nature, which once drove him to write about being seasick on a cross-Channel ferry, would have resisted anything in a like-minded vein. The deed was done, however, and he could not take back the words. Modern poets have since vilified him for his lines: 'If there was one poet my generation really hated – really spat when his name was mentioned – it was Rupert Brooke. He stood for all the attitudes to the war which we detested.'[4]

Wellington House may not have commissioned such verses but there is no doubt that they used poems like *The Soldier* and the Canadian doctor John McCrae's *In Flanders Fields*, arguably the most popular poem of the war, to advance their avowed aim of keeping up public morale.

Newspapers

In the early twentieth century, newspapers were by far the best way of receiving up-to-date information. That was particularly the case in the First World War. There was no radio or television, letters took time to arrive, word of mouth even longer and the early crude examples of newsreels were usually weeks behind the times.

As a result, people trusted the papers to tell them the truth about what was happening at the front, one of the reasons that nearly all newspapers increased their circulation during the war years.

Charles Masterman realized, early on, that his propaganda machinery would have to rely heavily on the papers and he made sure that the Defence of the Realm Act of 1914 took this into consideration. A highly significant part of the Act listed what journalists and correspondents could and could not write about and what the papers could or could not print. It meant that from the outset the press, at both national and local level were, by default, supportive of the government.

Criticism had to be moderated and facts accurate. The idea of what has been called 'yellow journalism' – exaggeration and crude sensationalism, best shown in the wildly inaccurate and inflammatory US newspaper coverage of the sinking of the battleship *Maine* in Havana harbour in 1898 – was to be limited. Limited, that is, unless Wellington House approved, as in the stories of the Belgian atrocities.

Charles Masterman went out of his way to develop strong links with the press. There had to be some degree of consultation and, as a consequence, concessions had to be made. So, in the spring of 1915 the ban on journalists going to the front was lifted and if Masterman did not have the press in his pocket before then he certainly did afterwards.

The four main daily papers at that time were the *Daily Express*, the *Daily Mail*, *The Times* and the *Daily Mirror.* They, along with Sunday newspapers like the *News of the World* and *The People*, were the main instruments for getting news to the public. All of them published morning and evening issues while local and provincial papers, mostly weeklies, also printed national news. It was an enormous web of information, one that needed careful handling but which, in the right circumstances, would be invaluable to the Propaganda Bureau and the government.

Getting news into the papers was only a quick telephone call away or, at worst, a short memo. Wellington House could be quite confident that the papers would print the news and the messages they wanted.

Posters

Simple, eye catching and direct, the use of posters to help recruitment was one of the most successful of the Wellington House tactics in 1914 and 1915. The most famous, of course, was the artist Alfred Leeke's startling depiction of Herbert Kitchener, the newly appointed minister for war. All moustache and glaring eyes, the message was simple – 'I need you – you there, staring at me – I need you in particular – yes, you! not the man standing next to you – to join the forces and fight for your King and Country'. The appeal was personal and the young men of Britain fell for it hook, line and sinker. The success of the Kitchener poster cannot be underplayed. He and Masterman had expected it to provide 100,000 volunteers by Christmas 1914. As it turned out they got nearly a million, far more than the army could ever hope to deal with.

As a result, large numbers of the 'Kitchener men' simply sat and twiddled their thumbs for months on end, waiting until there were sufficient weapons and uniforms for them all. The majority of them did not go into action until the Battle of the Somme in the summer of 1916. Many of them did not return from that particular bloodbath but that did not stop the call to arms.

Clearly then, the use of posters was both successful and immediate, the images playing a major role in recruitment and in sustaining morale. Most of the posters had twin thrusts, aims which might have been oblivious to the men who answered the call but only too obvious to the propaganda experts at Wellington House. To begin with there was the basic aim of dragging men out of their safe, cosy environment and putting them into the fighting forces. The second message was simple: the army is exciting and it is every man's duty to join up, but it is also fun so come and enjoy a new way of life.

Posters that declared 'Women of Britain Say Go' (May 1915) and 'Remember Scarborough' (following the German bombardment of Scarborough in December 1914 when 137 civilians were killed) were unashamedly aimed at men's consciences. A train full of happy new recruits in their flat bus conductor's hats with waving arms screamed out the message, 'There's room for you! Enlist today!' It was a direct appeal to the comradeship that joining the army would bring.

As the war went on the use of sporting images grew. Following the Battle of Loos where British soldiers kicked a football in front of them as they charged – an action that was to be repeated at the Somme a year later – Wellington House saw another opportunity. War was suddenly part of a game which men played together with their mates. It was as friendly and as character forming as the activities of a village football or cricket team. One of the lasting poster images is of a soldier bowling something like a cross between a cricket ball and a hand grenade under a simple but powerful message: 'That Arm – Your Country Needs It'.

Catching the emotion of the nation was only one aspect of the recruiting posters. They were also meant to be informative. Here, however, they were not so successful. The strength of the really effective posters was their immediacy, a simple message together with a dramatic or heart-wrenching image. Posters such as 'The Scrap of Paper', a commemoration of the 1839 treaty with Belgium, the treaty that brought Britain into the war, supposedly to protect Belgian neutrality, were just too wordy to have any real effect. Theobald von Bethmann, the German chancellor, had sneered at Britain's willingness to go to war over a simple 'scrap of paper' and this poster attempted to explain the situation, showing the treaty with its six signatories and the terms of the agreement. The result was a cluttered and ineffective single-page poster when, really, a whole leaflet would have been required to explain the intricacies of the situation.

The use of posters continued even after conscription was introduced at the beginning of 1916. 'Attest now' was an attempt to inform the men of Britain that they would soon be called up to fight but if they wanted to attest an unwillingness to take part – through physical infirmity or religious beliefs – they should attest immediately.

Painting and Artists

The use of art as a propaganda tool effectively began with James Clarke's rendering of *The Great Sacrifice*, painted in 1914. It was issued as a print by *The Graphic* in its Christmas issue and was immediately seized on by churches and schools whose officers pinned it to the walls of their buildings where the reproduction could be seen and appreciated. Teachers used the painting/print as a visual aid and, in the chapels and churches the vicars and ministers even gave sermons on the subject and its imagery. Everyone scrambled to get hold of a copy, one reviewer going so far as to claim that the painting had turned railway bookstalls 'into wayside shrines'.

The original painting was later bought by George V and at his request a stained-glass version was placed in one of the windows in the church of St Mary Magdalene at Enfield. With its idealized image of a youthful, unmarked soldier lying dead at the feet of Christ, Clarke's painting was the visual equivalent of Rupert Brooke's *The Soldier*.

James Clarke went on to paint other patriotic works of art, notably *The Bombardment of Hartlepool* commemorating the German naval attack on the seaside resort in 1914. He was never to quite gain the fame and the accolades of painters like C. R.W. Nevinson, William Orpen and the Nash brothers but his work certainly caught the mood of the people. His real claim to fame belongs in what his painting went on to kick-start. Charles Masterman noted the effect on the general public of Clarke's painting and in early 1916 he recruited the artist Muirhead Bone to travel to the front where he could capture by sketches and if the opportunity arose in paint, images of the conflict. By October of the year Bone had completed over 150 drawings of the war. Exhausted and more than a little shocked by what he had witnessed, he was then replaced by his brother-in-law Francis Dodd.

Soon other painters were being added to the stable of war artists. Some of them like Augustus John actually produced very little, something that might have been expected, given his somewhat bohemian personality. Others like Orpen, Nevinson, John Singer Sergeant and Paul and John Nash turned out dozens of powerful images in a variety of different styles. Between 1916 and the end of the war, over ninety war artists were working in the combat zones, each of them commissioned by Masterman and the men of Wellington House.

John Singer Sergeant produced perhaps the most lasting image of the war: a line of blinded, gassed men outlined against the skyline. He had been asked by Lloyd George to produce something showing the cooperation between British and American soldiers. He refused and instead painted the iconic image of the later war years. Most of the war artists managed to make similarly effective statements about the conflict.

Several women artists were approached to join Masterman's band of war artists. None accepted, fearing tokenism and lack of acceptance from their male counterparts. However, the War Museum did commission ten women painters to produce a wide variety of work. These included Olive Maudie-Cook who went out to France as an ambulance driver, Victoria Monkhouse and Anna Airey whose magnificent paintings of munitions factories at work perfectly caught the atmosphere of these gigantic industrial concerns.

Whether they had been appointed war artists or not, painters of all styles and abilities continued to produce images of the war, some realistic, the majority sentimental. Many artists, minor figures in the art world, produced works which, because of the local rather than national celebrity of their names, were destined never to receive wider acclaim. Due to their inability to visit the front their product was invariably either romantic or cartoon-like in nature. In either case the accuracy of the portrait did not matter.

Almost to the end of the war painters were forbidden to show dead British soldiers, something that greatly annoyed Paul Nash. He claimed that the ban destroyed the reality of his paintings, so that what you were getting was a watered-down version of the battlefield. Showing German dead was another matter altogether, as both Orpen and Nevinson were to prove in their creations.

Painters like the hugely popular Richard Caton Woodville – considered far too old to become a war artist, despite his unofficial position as the most recognized battlefield painter of the age – were commissioned to produce paintings for charities such as the National Institute for the Blind.

Caton Woodville's work *When Night Sets In, the Sun is Down*, depicting a blinded soldier being led from the battlefield, raised huge sums of money for the charity when produced as a postcard. The painting, and the cards that followed it, remain a sentimental and hugely idealized version of comradeship but for the British public it was exactly what was needed at the time.

When Lord Beaverbrook took over the reins of propaganda in 1918, he relaxed the ban on showing bodies, believing that the purpose of propaganda was not just to encourage enlistment but to tell the story of the war. It was now a case of total war and the entire population had to be involved.

Photography and the Cinema

The power of the visual image was apparent from the start. Two devastating nineteenth-century conflicts, the Crimean War and the American Civil War, had provided the public with heart-rending examples of death and destruction. This new conflict promised more of the same. From the mid-nineteenth century photography had become a practical process, available to anyone with the money and the aptitude to make use of the new technology. By the early years of the twentieth century, it had developed into a major hobby and also into a profession so that Charles Masterman and the men of Wellington House could see its value.

Many, if not most, of the newly enlisted soldiers going off to war posed stiff and unsmiling before the photographer's camera. The images that resulted were posted home and stood for many years in china cabinets, on mantelpieces or on sideboards. The conflict itself, however, was different.

Realizing the importance of the medium, Masterman created a specific department within Wellington House to handle wartime photography. Although some of the images were staged, many were not. It meant that the general public was given a view of the war but by adhering to the same rules that affected artists – no dead bodies, no shots of troops suffering defeat – the photographers kept the people from the horrors of death and destruction on the battlefield.

Just as there were official war artists, Charles Masterman quickly arranged for official war photographers to take up the reins. By the end of 1915, men such as Thomas Keith Aitken, Ernest Brooks and David McLellan were active on all fronts, happily providing Masterman with the 4,000 images he needed every week.

It would be wrong to say that there were no amateur photographers at work. Lots of young officers were interested in the photographic art and took their cameras with them into the front lines. Although not officially allowed to use their cameras, they did take photographs of what they saw and experienced. It all depended on the attitude of their senior officers. Many commanding officers turned a blind eye; others forbade any form of recording whatsoever.

The shots of British and German troops fraternizing on Christmas Day 1914 were certainly not taken by official photographers. Invariably they came from the cameras of those involved. For that we need to be grateful to the COs of the men of both Allied and German forces.

And then the advent of the cinema brought a new dimension to the whole process of capturing images of the war. Cinematography had been around for some time, mostly available to the public in bioscopes at the annual travelling fairs. London might boast an increasing number of permanent cinema houses but for most people the bioscope shows with their combination of provocative dancers, barkers and, once inside the tent, ten-minute slots when out-of-focus, hazy silent movies were shown, offered the first and perhaps only experience of cinema in a would-be viewer's life.

As far as the public was concerned, in 1914 moving pictures were still a novelty but Masterman quickly realized that the art of cinema and its possibilities as a propaganda tool went far beyond the antics of Charlie Chaplin and other Hollywood comedians. There was, as yet, no sound to accompany the images on the screen but pianists and organists at the front of the cinema halls were always available to add atmosphere as required.

The earliest film of the war was *Britain Prepared* which came out in December 1915 and showed the country's strength and determination. Being concerned largely with matters behind the lines, it was not a huge success but Charles Masterman was undaunted. He knew the potential of the new medium and was determined to exploit it.

In order to achieve the maximum effect, Masterman decided to direct his next effort at the heart of the coming British military offensive. He would send out people to film what was soon christened the Battle of the Somme. He had no desire to film a losing cause so it was a risky business but Masterman, like so many others, was convinced that the Big Push, when Kitchener's volunteers would be thrown into action for the first time, could only result in a British victory.

Using cinematographers from leading agencies, he laid plans to film the run-up to the battle and the action itself. At his urging, Geoffrey Malins of the Gaumont-British Picture Corporation and his assistant Edward Tong moved to France in the early summer of 1916. Unfortunately, Tong fell ill and had to be sent home to recuperate. He was replaced by John McDowell of the British and Colonial Films company.

The film was a unique production which, unheard of at the time, showed British and German dead and genuine action shots. There was some 'staging' but by and large the film was as realistic as Malins and McDowell could make it. The film – known simply as *The Battle of the Somme: Kitchener's Great Army in the Battle of the Somme* when it was released in America – was five reels long and lasted seventy-seven minutes.

David Lloyd George was given a private showing on 2 August, one month after the first attack had gone over the top. He gave his approval and the film was premiered eight days later. It duly opened to the public on 21 August. An amazing twenty million people watched the film in the first six weeks after its release and despite what was clearly a British defeat – or, at best, a stalemate – they appeared to enjoy the experience. The critical response was also positive:

> Crowded audiences … were interested and thrilled to have the realities of war brought so vividly before them, and if women had sometimes to shut their eyes to escape for a moment from the tragedy of the toll of battle which the film presents, opinion seems to be general that it was wise that the people at home should have a glimpse of what our soldiers are doing and suffering in Picardy.[5]

It had been a hectic and dangerous operation for Malins and McDowell. With their cameras camouflaged and covered in sackcloth, they came under fire many times and some of their equipment was damaged. It had been worth it, Masterman decided, and he went on to organize other films.

A second 'war' film which showed the second stage of the Somme battle was released in 1917 under the title *The Battle of the Ancre and the Advance of the Tanks*. Like the first release it was a realistic production, particularly in the views of transport companies conveying munitions and equipment up to the lines. The enormity of the task was staggering.

Further productions included *The King Visits his Armies in the Great Advance* and, finally, *The German Retreat and the Battle of Arras*. They were all popular with audiences and undoubtedly achieved what Masterman had hoped for but they somehow lacked the sheer novelty and exuberance of that original, ground-breaking depiction of the Somme.

Black Propaganda

The issue of 'black propaganda' might not be particularly palatable, even now, but by the beginning of 1915 it had become clear that this was going to be an important element of the war. Put simply, black propaganda was, and is, information that purports to come from the side it is intended to vilify. In other words, it is a series of lies that supposedly emanates from one side in the conflict, in this case the German, when in reality it comes from the other, the British. In the First World War and in later conflicts, what that came down to was false information purporting to come from one side when really it originated from the other.

There are numerous examples from the war of British black propaganda. Perhaps the most notorious remains the *Bryce Report* which was commissioned by Charles Masterman in 1914 and was published in May of the following year. Headed up by the Viscount James Bryce, former ambassador to the USA and a friend of Woodrow Wilson, the commission consisted of six influential citizens. Their number included the renowned judge Sir Frederick Pollock, historian H. A. L. (Hal) Fisher and newspaper editor Harold Cox. The report, supposedly an unbiased appraisal and analysis of German atrocities in Belgium, turned out to be an unashamed hotch-potch of lies and falsehoods, condemning the barbaric behaviour of German soldiers. It was, arguably, one of the first examples of outright psychological warfare and, of course, it was perfect black propaganda. The report now reads like the worst type of cheap fiction – and fiction is what it mostly was. The members of the commission were not allowed to interview witnesses but a team of barristers was appointed to collect statements from over 1,200 Belgian refugees. In the main the tales of horror and violence were accepted at face value: 'At Boort Meerbeck a German soldier was seen to fire three times at a little girl of five years old. Having failed to hit her he subsequently bayoneted her. He was killed with the butt end of a rifle by a Belgian soldier who had seen him commit the murder.'[6]

Stories of rape, murder, looting and destruction, all perpetrated by German soldiers, became accepted fact and vilified the German troops. So popular was the view that the derogatory term 'Hun' was used for the first time in the war, drawing an unsavoury parallel with Attila the Hun, the fifth-century Roman nemesis. Masterman ensured that 40,000 copies of the report were sent to the USA where, by chance, it was made available a few days after the sinking of the *Lusitania*. The German government retaliated with *The White Book*, giving examples of Belgian atrocities against the German Army but it had little effect. The opinion of most people who bothered to read it was that the volume simply reflected Shakespeare's words: 'Methinks the lady doth protest too much.'

Another example of black propaganda from Wellington House included the vilification of the Turks for their part in the Armenian Genocide. The exact number of Armenians killed by the Turks in 1915 – desperate to vent their anger after a humiliating defeat by Russia in the Caucasus – remains unknown but Masterman and his team were happy to push the total up over one million, probably not too inaccurately. By 1916 concern about the Middle East had risen to such a level of paranoia that Masterman was forced to open a Department of Muslim Affairs within Wellington House.

There was also the gleefully accepted story of a Canadian soldier being crucified by German troops in full view of his comrades. The story had several versions, location differing each time but always involving a Canadian soldier as the victim. It caught the imagination of the troops, whatever their rank or position, tapping into their subconscious fears while reinforcing the image of the barbarous German foe. The story was not aimed only at the soldiers. The folks back home shuddered in horror at the thought that such a fate might befall their loved ones. And that made the propaganda message so much easier to impart: work harder at the factory bench, send more of your sons out to France, and defeat the German monster before he can commit more atrocities. The story had no validity but clearly originated from the haunting image of soldiers caught hanging on enemy barbed wire. That fear, lingering and real, gave the tale of the crucified Canadian all the credibility Masterman could have wished for.

One of the more bizarre pieces of black propaganda seen during the war was the curious case of the German corpse conversion factory. An article printed in *The Times* in April 1917 alleged that the Germans were operating a corpse factory near Coblenz. The British naval blockade, the article went on, was so effective that fats and oils, necessary for the German war machine, were just not available any longer either in Germany or in Austria–Hungary. Consequently, the article said, the bodies of dead German soldiers were being collected, boiled down and converted into various products. These essential products included lubricating oils, candles, pig food and even dubbin for soldiers' boots.

The article included eyewitness reports of the process but, inevitably, there were no reference points regarding the sources or confirmation of any type. Despite this, the story was soon being reprinted in the *Daily Mail* and even in some American newspapers.

Various people have claimed to be the originators of the story, notably Jon Charteris, head of army intelligence who later went on record as saying that it was all part of an attempt to bring China into the war on the side of the Allies. The claim, widely believed at the time, was later repudiated.

The Northcliffe Press, owners of both *The Times* and the *Daily Mail*, was also said to be involved in what was, depending on your stance, the most popular or the most appalling atrocity story of the war. The one person who did not claim any involvement was Charles Masterman – and you can read what you like into that. Masterman was asked by Lloyd George to prepare a leaflet on the subject of the corpse factory. He wrote the piece as requested but it was never used. Cartoons by Louis Raemaekers and Bruce Bairnsfather did appear in the press, however, with Raemaekers' work showing German bodies being stacked neatly onto the back of a wagon. Bairnsfather's more direct effort showed a German munitions worker gazing at a can of glycerine and saying, 'Alas, my poor brother.'

The truth of the matter is that the corpse factory was nothing more than an urban myth. It had been circulating for years and while Wellington House might not have been active in its origins, it certainly did nothing to suppress the story once it became semi-official.

Like nearly all of the more effective black propaganda stories, the odd grain or two of truth was important. That was something that Charles Masterman appreciated from the beginning of the War Propaganda Bureau – the alternative was pure fantasy, easily discerned and ignored by those it was attempting to influence.

The legend of German troops filing serrated edges into their bayonets so as to better rip apart British bodies is one piece of black propaganda that had at least some elements of reality. Such implements *were* actually used by the German Army but not as weapons. They were tools issued to pioneer battalions and used to saw down the branches of trees. They were rarely, if ever, used in battle.[7] Arthur Ponsonby, an independent analyst, along with several others, later showed that the majority of the atrocity stories were at best exaggerated, at worst total fabrications. Nothing unexpected there, then, but the news did have ramifications that were entirely unexpected.

Ponsonby's revelations led to many surmises, notably regarding the Nazi atrocities of the Second World War. They could not possibly be true, people thought, and promptly consigned them to the realms of black propaganda. How wrong can you possibly be?

Miscellaneous

Wellington House was involved in so many varied activities during the war that it is sometimes difficult to identify the hands of Masterman, Buchan and the rest among some very murky and decidedly unpleasant business. The very nature of the work and the motivation behind the War Propaganda Bureau was secret and has remained that way. Much has, even now, still to be identified and assimilated.

Although Wellington House was not always at the forefront of affairs, its influence was still there. That was how the department had been conceived, working behind the scenes and maintaining its covert nature. Importantly, even when operating in the background, pulling strings and easing the way for various operations, it somehow always managed to maintain control.

Masterman was clear that for propaganda to be effective it should not look like propaganda at all; effective propaganda should remain hidden and covert, which was one of the reasons why none of the books produced by the writers in Masterman's stable was ever attributed to Wellington House but came from the regular publishing houses of the time – Random House, Nelson and the rest. Relationships between Wellington House and the publishers of Britain were, to say the least, cosy and cordial.

One of the publications that Masterman and Wellington House did have a clear hand in developing, however, came in the form of the now famous *The War Illustrated*. The magazine/newspaper began life just eighteen days after war was declared and ran, without a break, until 8 February 1919 before coming back into existence during the Second World War. Consisting mainly of photographic and artistic images, the magazine was aimed directly at the home market, the photographs transporting people – in their minds at least – across the Channel to the fields of Flanders. If good photographs are worth a thousand words, Masterman certainly got value for his money out *The War Illustrated.*

There were also a number of articles, notably Stanley Wood's commentary on the German atrocities in Belgium. Winston Churchill and H. G. Wells also contributed to the journal which soon achieved a massive circulation figure of 750,000 copies per issue, rivalling even the *Daily Mail* in its sales figures.

There were many more projects from Wellington House, perhaps not as obvious as *The War Illustrated* but all equally as important. Tottering, perhaps, along the edge or on the rim of black propaganda was the matter of the Kaiser's supposed criticism and description of the British Expeditionary Force as 'a contemptible little army'. Even now those four words remain one of the most memorable quotations of the whole war. The comment briefly infuriated the British soldiers. Then it began to appeal to the Tommies' self-deprecating sense of humour. It actually originated not from the Kaiser at all but from Wellington House and from the Foreign Office. British propagandists felt that the martial nature of the British regulars – soon to be virtually wiped out during the engagement outside Mons and in the first Battle of Ypres – needed honing and what better way to get them on their metal than to invent a little insult from the man everyone hated, Kaiser Wilhelm II of Germany. They got that wrong, of course and the phrase became positive propaganda rather than negative.

The Princess Mary Christmas Gift Box was designed and created to be given, as a Christmas present, to every soldier and sailor serving in the British Army or Royal Navy at Christmas 1914. The gesture was a cross between magnanimity and pure morale-boosting propaganda. Princess Mary was the 17-year-old daughter of George V, a pretty, vivacious member of the royal family. She, like other representatives of the monarchy, had been placed on a pedestal by the British public and was admired in much the same way as film stars and singers of later times.

However, all was not totally well. The Germanic nature and background of the royal family was already beginning to raise a few eyebrows, particularly with the threat of Zeppelin raids looming in people's imaginations. In 1917, that concern eventually caused George V to change the family name from the Germanic Saxe-Coburg to the altogether more English Windsor.

At Christmas 1914, however, such an eventuality was far from people's minds. Yet it was felt that some gesture by the royal family needed to be made. Using Princess Mary as a morale-booster might well, it was decided, do something to alleviate the stigma. With Masterman's backing, an appeal for donations was made in the daily newspapers in the weeks leading up to December 1914. Over £152,000 was raised with the result that 2.5 million tin boxes, silver for officers, brass for other ranks, were distributed to the troops. The boxes contained tobacco, cigarettes, a lighter or pen, a Christmas card from the Princess along with a suitably iconic picture of the young girl. Princes Mary's image appeared again, in relief, on the front of the tin along with suitable martial images on the sides. Where possible, non-smokers were given tin boxes full of sweets and lemon drops. This was not always possible or even desirable as cigarettes and tobacco were more easily bartered than sticky, inedible sweets. The Christmas boxes were a great idea, certainly one that kept up morale both in the trenches and at home. Even before they were opened, though, many of the tins were immediately sent back to families in Britain where they were put into storage or displayed.

Sadly, however, only a few thousand of the tins were delivered by Christmas Day. Some of the gifts did not arrive in the recipients' hands until 1920 which may well account for the fact that so many of the boxes keep appearing for sale at present-day antique fairs.

Approval of activities like the establishment of Selfridges War Window was little more than the wielding of a rubber stamp for the propaganda experts. Such approval was something that was almost standard practice for Wellington House. Selfridges department store in London had always prided itself on its window displays, employing a team of specialists in an age long before window dressing became commonplace, in order to make the windows of their Oxford Street store attractive and appealing. During the Balkan War of 1912, Selfridges dedicated one of its shop windows to displaying news of the conflict. The Balkan crisis was a distant war but it was still one that interested British Empire builders and the public in general.

Often the news in the shop window pre-empted the stories that the public would read about in the papers the following morning and the window display always managed to attract good crowds. Finding a good spot at the front of the crowd was usually more difficult than finding a seat on the new underground trains. The store decided to operate the same news window in 1914, once again providing news and pictures of the conflict in France and Flanders. The subliminal aim was that the people of London should gather together in front of the window, read and view the latest news and, most importantly, discuss the events and matters on display. The War Window was a serious attempt – and a hugely successful one – to bring people together to express their opinions. It is not difficult to identify the source for the information and material on display. Encouraging journalists to travel to France for their stories was commonplace, even though there was an initial government ban on reporters at the front, unlike the rebel uprising in Cuba and the Boer War where even serving soldiers like Winston Churchill were granted detachment from their units and employed as war correspondents. Churchill, in particular, regularly appeared at the thickest point of the fighting And yet journalists were not welcome at the fighting front in 1914. Nobody in official circles had quite cottoned on to the fact that preventing reporters telling things as they saw them merely gave rise to suspicion and doubt. It was typical of the cloistered thinking of the time, something that would soon have to change.

Change it certainly would but in the final months of 1914 few government ministers grasped the fact that pontification abhors a vacuum. If journalists could not go and see for themselves, they would probably invent it. The ban on journalists appearing at the front was lifted in April 1915 but not before the enterprising writer Basil Clarke had hidden himself on a train full of French soldiers bound for the trenches. He made it to the front but was soon turned around and sent back to what was regarded as safety.

Clarke later went to Dublin during the Easter Rising of 1916 and sent out dispatches from the rebel HQ. Very few British journalists were able to gain the confidence of the Irish rebels but Basil Clarke managed it because of the honesty of his reporting. Put simply, the Irish patriots trusted him to be accurate. He went on to gain fame as the United Kingdom's first public relations expert but not before he had spent three months as a fugitive in Dunkirk because of the ban on journalists at the front. He also became the first reporter into Ypres after the German shelling and virtual destruction of the city.

Basil Clarke was an enterprising and adroit reporter who would not allow little things like a government ban from getting his story. Intrepid, in the best traditions of all investigative journalists, his activities were approved by Masterman. If Clarke was determined and dedicated then Charles Masterman in his office at Wellington House was equally as committed. Both men had their roles to play, different as they might be, but both were effective elements of the propaganda war.

It is hard not to allow imagination to take over and allow yourself to conjure images of Masterman sitting like a giant spider at the centre of his web, pulling strings and casting his influence. That, after all, was his role. Lloyd George had set him to the task and in fulfilling that task Masterman had turned himself into something of a monster. In the months and years ahead, that would become a spark in the relationship between Wellington House and the government that may well have contributed to Masterman's demise, both as propaganda maestro and politician.

PART II

No Thin-spread Lines of Bloodied Heroes

'If you can, look into the seeds of time and say which grain will grow and which will not.'

Shakespeare, *Macbeth*

Chapter 3

Music Halls and Home Entertainment

Two of the greatest influences on Victorian and Edwardian Britain were diametrically opposed in their nature but uniquely uniform in their effect. They were the Church (or Non-Conformist Chapels) and Music Hall. Both provided structure, both gave purpose to people's lives and both offered participants the opportunity to sing, loudly and in chorus, reverently or bawdily. Singing was an essential component of British society in those days, a vital element regardless of its roots or reason. More of the influence of the Church later but for now we focus on that essentially British form of entertainment and art, the Music Hall.

By the end of the nineteenth century, Music Hall had essentially become a working-class form of entertainment. Thousands upon thousands of labourers and tradesmen flocked to the halls every night, leaving theatre for the better-off, upper-class toffs. Nevertheless, music halls had their origins in the large assembly rooms attached to the famous Georgian coffee houses of British cities, and in their early days such establishments were nothing if not cosmopolitan. To begin with, coffee houses catered for both working and upper classes – there being no such thing as a middle class in those days. Even so, the two sections of society kept to themselves within the assembly rooms and there was no attempt at integration. Apart from the occasional brawl, ribald and often drunken singing by the participants was the one and only real way of passing the time. It was informal and totally ad hoc.

The assembly-room gatherings were popular but at the beginning of the nineteenth century, catch and glee clubs began to offer a more formal style of entertainment. These clubs sprang up in the saloon bars of public houses and were places where men – and it was definitely 'men only' – could gather to drink and sing in what was felt to be good company. The clubs existed in most cities but, as with the assembly rooms, London soon became the centre for such activity. When the bohemian, well-to-do element began to abandon the saloons in favour of more refined gentlemen's clubs, the catch and glee clubs found themselves left with just the working classes, the labourers and tradesmen.

In order to cater for what was now a more limited clientele, they began to change the format of their offerings, evolving and turning themselves into what soon became known as song and supper rooms.

These song and supper rooms were exactly what the name suggested, places where customers could enjoy a hot meal and sing – or listen to others singing. The price of the meal was invariably included in the entrance ticket. The chairman, usually the owner of the public house, sat at the front of the room and called up anyone who might like to contribute. Amateur singers who could perform to a reasonable standard soon found themselves in great demand.

As the popularity and renown of the supper rooms grew, amateur performers were augmented – and eventually supplanted – by professional entertainers who would call in for a meal and a few drinks after their own shows had finished. It was, you might say, the best of both worlds for the owners. The first and most famous of the song and supper rooms was Evans's in London's Covent Garden. Here a whole section of London society was kept entertained. While women were not allowed onto the supper room floor, they could listen and watch from behind screens on the balcony.

By the 1850s the owners of the public houses, particularly in London, had realized that they were sitting on a potential goldmine. As a result, specialist halls – music halls – were built alongside existing pubs, even replacing them in some instances. With the welcome addition of a wide range of variety acts – dancers, professional singers and reciters – the Music Hall as we know it was born.

By 1865 there were thirty-two large music halls in London as well as a number of smaller emporiums. By 1878 that number had risen to seventy-eight significant establishments. Large cities across Britain, places like Cardiff, Glasgow and Birmingham also had their music halls, over 300 of them in all, and soon entertainers were travelling the country in what became a Music Hall circuit, performing on a nightly basis.

In the latter part of the nineteenth century, the Grecian Theatre, known to everyone as The Eagle, was probably the most popular music hall in London. It even managed to find its way into one of the songs of the time:

> *Up and down the City Road,*
> *In and out of the Eagle,*
> *That's the way the money goes –*
> *Pop goes the weasel.*[1]

Unlike theatres where the audience sat, more or less sedately, to watch the performance, music halls were filled with men – and, as the century drew to a close, with women – all standing up or squatting on their haunches to watch. There were still amateur performers but entertainment was now provided by professional or semi-professional acts. It was a significant shift in emphasis, an inevitable move away from home-spun, participatory acts to artists who made their living from performing for the public.

With beer and spirits flowing readily, the audience was never averse to letting performers know exactly what they thought of them. With an audience of around 500 drunk or semi-drunk people crowded into a venue, the atmosphere at the nightly show was invariably rowdy.

Singers and comedians like Dan Leno, Marie Lloyd and Little Tich quickly became household names while Corney B. Grain and Bransby Williams proved themselves more than capable of silencing the most antagonistic and unruly of audiences with their dramatic or humorous monologues. It was a rough, tough way to earn a living but this was the stage, the environment where entertainers chose to make an honest pound or two. Significantly, music halls were venues that government recruiters used to further their own ends when war broke out.

*

When war against Germany was declared on 4 August 1914, the summer holiday season was in full swing. People did not have long breaks as they do now but the Bank Holiday Act of 1871, which provided workers with four statutory holidays a year, had come into force. They were the first public holidays in Britain.

That legislation, combined with the weekend that preceded it, meant that the August Bank Holiday did at least make for a three-day break, the height of luxury for most working men and women. Each summer, resorts like Clacton, Southend, Blackpool and Scunthorpe were filled to bursting with eager holidaymakers keen to forget their worries for a day or so and August 1914 was no different from any other year, regardless of what was happening on the Continent.

As an essential part of the holiday, young men and their wives or girlfriends dutifully turned up to watch the nightly show at the end of the pier. It was a 'must do' activity and no summer break would be complete without a trip to the music hall or variety show.

This time, with war so recently declared, the men in the audience were in for a surprise. They found not just pretty ladies urging them to join the army to do their bit but, in some cases, well-lubricated and spectacularly uniformed recruiting sergeants standing on stage, ready and willing to hand them the King's shilling. Many men were induced to sign up there and then.

It was not just in the holiday resorts but was a process that was repeated in music halls all over the country as managers and artists alike saw an opportunity to swell their profits and still help the country in its hour of need. The recruiting that went on through August and September 1914 marked what was later seen by many as the high-water mark of the popularity of music halls. Rallying support for the war effort was something that was suddenly in huge demand and as August melted easily into September and October, there seemed to be no sign of it slacking off.

Significantly, it was women more so than men who sat in awe watching the shows. It was women who sang with gusto the recruiting songs being offered by the performers on stage. It was women who were caught up in the mood of the moment, happy to be a part of the drama, the simple act of giving their sons and sweethearts to the army. And, cynical as it might seem, it was women who sat there secure in the knowledge that they were slightly aloof from being too involved themselves. Grief and tears came later!

The most popular of all the many singers and performers of the age was Gertie Gitana. She was never a Music Hall artist per se although she did use material from the halls when she sang to groups of wounded soldiers and their families. Her medium was the concert hall where she invariably performed to packed galleries. As far as music halls were concerned, that left the way wide open for other female artists.

Vesta Tilley, famous for her cross-dressing and male impersonations, was the undoubted hero of the hour. Appearing as 'Tommy in the Trench' or 'Jack Tar Home from the Sea', she was often referred to as 'Britain's best recruiting sergeant', particularly when she sang her famous *The Army of Today's All Right*. If anything was guaranteed to get the young men out of the audience and onto the stage to join up, it was that particular number.

There were many other recruiting songs that have since become renowned. Perhaps the most famous, sung by dozens of different women performers in so many music halls across the country, was *Your King and Country Want You*.

Better known by its chorus line, 'We don't want to lose you but we think you ought to go', the song was an immediate success in music halls large and small. Its popularity was something of an unexpected phenomenon. The majority of the music hall audience was working class, yet the opening lines were aimed at anything but:

> *We've watched you playing cricket and every kind of game,*
> *At football, golf and polo you men have made your name.*[2]

Football and cricket, fair enough – but golf and polo would have been well beyond the experience of most working-class lads at the time. For most of the audience there was no way they could have identified with such lyrics. Nevertheless, for some strange reason the song hit the right note. It was hugely popular and did what it was supposed to do – encourage young men to enlist.

Other music hall songs from the period included *Belgium Put the Kibosh on the Kaiser* and *Here We Are! Here We Are! Here We Are Again!* This latter piece, as performed by Mark Sheridan, was apparently described as the battle cry of the British Army.[3]

Many of the famous soldier songs of the war, beloved by troops at the front, began their days as Music Hall tunes. These included *Take Me Back to Dear Old Blighty* which was originally sung by Florrie Forde but which came to symbolize the thoughts and wishes of almost every Tommy in the second half of the war. Another Florrie Forde song, the ubiquitous *Pack up Your Troubles in Your Old Kit Bag* became perhaps the most recognizable of all the Music Hall tunes that made the transfer into the trenches. It had competition, however. *It's a Long Way to Tipperary* was actually written before the war but by 1918 the sheet music for the song had sold over eight million copies as families back home quickly picked up on its symbolism and sentimentality.[4]

It is easy to see why such tunes became popular on the home front. Not everyone could get to a music hall or a theatre but in those long-gone days many homes possessed a piano. Sing-songs around the fire on winter nights were hugely popular, particularly when the songs were patriotic, sentimental and able to bring a tear to the eye. And if the family did not own a piano there was always the harmonica. There might, with luck, even be a banjo. Anne Hughes from Bridgend in South Wales has recollections, second hand maybe, but still clear memories of the value of the family evening sing-songs:

> I was too young to experience those evening sing-songs myself. In fact, I wasn't even born then, but years later I can remember my grandmother telling me all about them. Lots of Scottish ballads, she told me – both of my grandparents were from Scotland; Mary Bella Matheson was her name and she came from Elgin in the north of the country. My granddad, Bob as Nanny always called him, was from Castle Douglas but during the war he wasn't there with them very much at all; he was usually away, first in the army at Gallipoli and then as an Engineer Officer in the Navy.
>
> They sang *My Love is Like a Red, Red Rose* and *I Love a Lassie*, all the Harry Lauder pieces. And of course, there was *Tipperary* and the other soldiers' songs, they sang them all. I don't know where they got the tunes and words from, the nearest music hall was seventy or eighty miles away and, of course, there was no radio in those days.
>
> But they got an awful lot of comfort from those get-togethers, all the extended family together, Nanny said. It became a bit of a family tradition, even when her brothers went off to war as well. There's no reason to believe my family was anything unusual or special so those evenings singing all the sentimental songs of home were probably typical of many other families.[5]

Arguably the comfort that the songs brought to the people on the home front or rather the comfort which coming together – ostensibly to sing those maudlin efforts but in reality, for mutual support – was huge, almost immeasurable. The men, like Anne Hughes's grandfather, might be away fighting at the front and many would never return, but by coming together to sing and maybe shed a tear or two, these homely gatherings gave hope and comfort to so many families.

Charles Masterman of the Propaganda Bureau realized early on in the war that coming together as a family group to sing and reminisce was a valuable act, something he actively promoted. T. P. Ratcliff of the *Daily Chronicle* was just one of many who gave their support: 'Singing together is a form of amusement and delight. It is a glorious way in which we can, in large bodies, express something which we could not tell in any other way. But the love of Community Singing should be started and finished in the home.'[6]

And it wasn't just singing. The Victorian and Edwardian ages had also been the time of parlour poetry. It was a simple enough process – those who couldn't hold a tune at the evening gatherings around the piano would recite poetry instead. People wore their hearts on their sleeves and many were moved to tears by poems of noble sacrifice and starving orphans, abandoned by society, sheltering from the elements.

The reciters who performed in the music halls provided great examples to follow and the patriotic poetry of the time – everything from Kipling to Henry Newbolt – meant that there was a huge store of offerings to choose from. By the time war broke out the music hall reciters, Bransby Williams, Corney B. Grain and the rest, were as famous as Marie Lloyd and Vesta Tilley. They excelled in the performance of patriotic ballads like *The Green Eye of the Little Yellow God* and temperance poems such as *Come Home Father*, both guaranteed to quieten the rowdiest of audiences who stood with tears in their eyes as the poetic tragedies were played out on stage.

The reciters were magical, highly acclaimed performers and were well paid for their efforts. The famous actor and poetry reciter Barebone Tree was paid £100 a week to declaim *The Absent-Minded Beggar* at the Palace Theatre in London, an amazing sum of money in the 1890s.

Of course, men and women weren't paid to recite poetry in the amateur evening get-togethers during the war, but everyone had their speciality piece and the poems made a welcome change from the sentimental dirges that took up most of the evening.

Harry Lauder and Will Fyffe, both Scotsmen, were two of the most popular entertainers in the Music Hall system. They were singers and comedians who broke up their acts with patter, sometimes stopping in the middle of a song to offer a comedic word or two. And that was something that the amateur performers around the fire or the piano realized that they could copy.

Welsh historian and geologist Roger MacCallum remembers his mother telling him about such entertainments in the village of Llanreath just outside the dockyard town of Pembroke Dock:

> I think it might be something to do with being Welsh or having Celtic origins at least but everyone in those days seemed to like a good story. They loved telling them, as well, holding the audience – even if it was only the people from the street – spellbound by the power of their words. They called it 'yarning,' just people from the village coming together to tell stories – yarns – about characters they had known. One person would start; another would add a bit more – 'Do you remember the day when old Tommy Jones' etc. It was almost an art form and according to my old Mum, everyone had something to say about days gone by. I suppose it made a change from singing.[7]

The popularity of the music halls continued throughout the war. There was hardly a soldier who, when back from France or Flanders on leave, did not find time to visit at least one show. Many music halls, at least in the earlier days of the war, gave free admission to men in uniform but their generosity died as the casualty figures mounted.

By 1916 the content of the entertainers' acts had begun to change. Gone were the overtly patriotic offerings like *Soldiers of the Queen*, which suddenly seemed hollow and insubstantial now that the reality of the Western Front and other theatres had exposed the basic immorality of the songs and what they promised. In their place were tunes that showed a clear desire for home. *Goodbyee* from 1917 is a classic example of the restrained but heartfelt yearning to be out of it all:

> *Goodbyee, goodbyee,*
> *Wipe the tear, baby dear, from your eye*
> *Tho' it's hard to part I know*
> *I'll be tickled to death to go.*[8]

It was not easy to laugh or be noble in the face of such casualties as the war produced and when conscription was introduced in 1916 there was anyway no need to urge the young men of Britain to enlist. But the dropping of the recruitment songs went deeper than that. The subtle change that had begun to affect the upper echelons of British society, the coming of meritocracy rather than obtaining position by rank and accident of birth, were reflected in the offerings of the music hall. It was effectively a microcosm of British society.

Forget 'Your King and Country Need You', forget Kitchener's pointing finger, now it was time for men and women to make their own choices. And that might well involve laughing at things that had previously been sacrosanct. In place of patriotic appeals to honour and duty, sarcasm and irony began to make themselves felt, as in the 1917 hit *Oh! It's a Lovely War,* sung by male impersonator Ella Shields. Ella was probably more famous for her *Burlington Bertie from Bow* but her anti-war satire proved almost equally as successful. Despite the appeals to answer duty's call, three years earlier the very idea of a 'lovely war' would have been unthinkable

By 1917 Siegfried Sassoon was writing about music halls themselves with more than a degree of scepticism and anger:

> *I'd like to see a tank come down the stalls,*
> *Lurching to ragtime tunes or Home Sweet Home,*
> *And there'd be no more jokes in Music Halls*
> *To mock the riddled corpses round Bapaume.*[9]

The end of the war saw a decline in the popularity of the music halls. There were many reasons but to some extent music halls had become respectable, shedding the layers of decadence and immorality that had always cloaked them.

Vesta Tilley's husband, theatre owner and entrepreneur Walter de Frece, even received a knighthood in 1919, a gift from Prime Minister David Lloyd George in recognition for his help in sustaining morale. Harry Lauder was similarly honoured.

Nobody then – and arguably nobody now – would begrudge de Frece and Lauder their honours. In their own way they had fought for the country, just as the Tommies in the trenches at Ypres and on the Somme had fought their fight for the same piece of home turf.

However, public or official recognition was the start of a slow slide into respectability that undermined everything the music halls stood for or represented. It did not happen overnight but slowly and surely other forms of entertainment began to replace the halls.

The advent of cinema, the coming of the jazz age, the appeal of radio – or wireless as it was known – the sudden popularity of swing all had their part to play. Licensing laws changed as well and that had a more significant effect on music halls than anybody had imagined.

Lloyd George had manoeuvred new licensing laws through parliament in 1915 in an attempt to stop munitions workers spending long hours in public houses. Too much alcohol invariably meant absences from work the following day and Lloyd George would do almost anything to keep his workforce at their benches. The new licensing laws included fixed times for the sale of alcohol and places where it could or could not be sold. Most people regarded the laws as a temporary arrangement, something just to help with the war effort; however, when peace returned, there was no return to the freer practices of pre-war Britain.

In the new post-war world of entertainment alcohol was no longer available in the auditoriums of the music halls but was now, as in the theatres, available only in separate bars and lounges. That was almost a revolutionary practice. Standing, joining in the singing, weaving your way to the bar to refill your glass, it had all been part of the evening's entertainment. And now it was being denied them. To the men and women who had thoroughly enjoyed standing with a pint glass in their hands as they watched and shouted at the acts, this new regime was the end of an era.

The new laws eliminated much of the rowdiness of music halls where 'audience participation', to give the drunken antics of the crowd a name, was all part of the evening's entertainment. Once that was removed, much of the appeal went as well. In its place came variety and theatre, altogether more refined and cultured experiences. That was all fine, quite acceptable in its way but it was just not Music Hall.

Chapter 4

The Church Has One Foundation

Britain in the late nineteenth and early twentieth centuries was populated by large numbers of men and women who were committed to a life of church going. The words 'church going' have been chosen specifically and are used deliberately rather than the all-encompassing but less accurate term of a commitment to Christian worship.

At the end of the nineteenth century church (or chapel) attendance was at an all-time high. True, in the fourteen years leading up to the outbreak of the First World War, there was some dropping away as attendance at Sunday worship began to see a reduction but, even so, before 1914 this was a relatively minor concern.

More worrying was the quality of men entering the clergy. So many other professions, new and well-paying professions like the civil service, law and journalism, were beginning to offer an alternative to men who had previously, perhaps without thinking, become clergymen. The manifestations and effects of that change would take some time to occur but it would undoubtedly come in the years ahead.

Meanwhile, on the surface at least, things appeared to be the same as they had been for the past hundred years or so. It took a perceptive mind to look carefully beneath the coverings. Each Sunday, all over the land, the places of worship – Anglican, Non-conformist, Catholic – were as full as the public houses had been and would continue to be on the other six days of the week. Even during wartime, Sunday evening offered the amused onlooker an imposing sight: men, women and children all in their Sunday best, streaming to their chosen location where they could see and be seen, washed and scrubbed, all upright, even a little pompous in their sanctity.

It was a recognized fact that industrial communities were more than well equipped with three strategically important institutions – pubs, public urinals and places of worship. These were the three staples of community life, one for pouring in physical relief after a hard day of manual labour, one for getting rid of excess fluid from the body and the last one for spiritual solace – maybe!

Attendance at services on a Sunday was backed up by church-led activities in the week: youth clubs, bible classes and Band of Hope, to name just three. There were so many more of these clubs or groups within the larger remit of the church or chapel, particularly in the rural areas. In small towns and villages across the nation, the church or chapel was the community; the community was the local church or chapel.

And yet, then as now, church going and belief in God were two very different matters. From this distance it is impossible to say how many of those who attended divine service each Sunday actually were Christians in the true meaning of the word. It might be a generalization but for many men and women going to church each Sunday was simply the thing to do. It was a routine that had been imposed on them when they were very young by parents who had suffered the same stringencies when they were children.

Sunday schools, choir practice and other routine events when added to morning and evening services, were ways of filling the otherwise empty day and if nothing else giving the adults a few hours to themselves. The inevitable risqué stories and jokes about what the adults got up to while their offspring were otherwise engaged at Sunday school in particular lasted for many years into the twentieth century.

As youngsters grew into adulthood there was little choice, at least for most of them, about whether or not to continue with church. The strictures of society imposed regular attendance and was something that was rarely questioned by the participants:

> We all went to church each Sunday, St Catherine's in Pontypridd. All the family went; every single one of us. We weren't great church goers or Bible thumpers but I suppose we went because it was the 'done' thing. My mother was quite keen on church but I can't honestly say it rubbed off on the rest of us when we had grown up.[1]

There was a pragmatic side to it, of course. For many young men the weekly attendance at church or chapel was a chance to ogle the girls – followed by the inevitable evening promenade along the streets – and the opportunity to open their lungs for some of the most stirring tunes they could find outside the music halls and theatres.

The great hymns of the time are still well known – *Onward Christian Soldiers, Fight the Good Fight, Guide Me O Thy Great Redeemer* and *Abide with Me*. Most of them had hugely powerful and obvious trochaic rhythms with the stress on the first syllable of each poetic foot; they were obvious talismans or anthems when war broke out.

They were soon replaced by the bawdy soldiers' songs that we now know so well but some were adapted with more risqué purposes than the original writers could ever have believed possible. *What a Friend We Have in Jesus*, for example, soon became *When This Bloody War is Over*:

> *When this bloody war is over, no more church parades for me.*
> *When I get my civvy clothes on, oh how happy I will be.*[2]

With the declaration of war in August 1914, the Church of England immediately adopted a pro-war stance even though, along with many of the non-conformist sects, it had previously supported both pacifism and disarmament. This was different, however; this was not mere rhetoric. Britain was now under attack and the Kaiser and the Germany were demonized. At least, that was the stance adopted by so many churchmen. As Arthur Winnington-Ingram, the Lord Bishop of London, was soon to declare: 'We are on the side of Christianity against the anti-Christ.'[3]

Perhaps such a statement might have been expected from the bishop who was regularly seen about in military uniform. Randall Davidson, Archbishop of Canterbury, took a more circumspect approach but even so the support of the Church for the war brought many thousands of young men to the colours. After some hesitation the leaders of the Catholic, Non-Conformist and Jewish faiths all eventually added their support.

The churches and chapels of Britain became something of the people's mouthpiece and conscience – without their permission, of course. The message they preached was that Britain was in the right, God was on her side and that the enemy was, naturally, evil.

The German and Austro-Hungarian churches, Lutheran and Catholic alike, propounded the same message albeit from the other side of the spectrum. Britain was the aggressor, her people spewing out lies and deceit. God was on Germany's side.

It was inevitable that the churches of all the belligerents took a nationalistic stance and adopted what could only be called a patriotic perspective. That applied to whichever country you cared to look at, even in Tsar Nicholas's Russia where the state-supporting religions, Orthodox in particular, were already beginning to be side-lined by the Bolshevik and Menshevik factions.

Masterman and the secret men of Wellington House would not have tolerated anything but the full backing of the established Church. *What a Friend We Have in Jesus* was not just an abstract concept limited to Sunday morning gatherings but a guiding principle to which the government could retreat whenever questions grew too close for comfort.

There were also practical matters to consider. They were of a wider consideration than mere belief but, obviously, hugely important for a state-run religious body like the Church of England.

The Church was an integral part of the State and had been since Henry VIII broke with Rome in the sixteenth century. If the power of Lloyd George and parliament could silence the Suffragettes – temporarily and, admittedly, with all sorts of promises for future discussions and agreements – they would certainly never have allowed the Archbishop of Canterbury and his minions to get away with anything but full backing of the war effort.

Quakers and other pacifist religions maintained their anti-war stance until the end. That was not unexpected but initially there had also been some opposition to the war from other religious quarters, particularly from the Baptist Chapels of Wales. A great many non-conformist congregations refused to accept the seemingly headlong rush into war, viewing it as nothing more than government-sponsored militarism. Together with the anti-war stance of the labour movement in Wales – strong both in the mining valleys of the south and in the industrial areas of the north-east – the non-conformist objection to militarism soon came to be seen as a matter of principle, one that was almost exclusively confined to the working class. It is easy to see why.

The workers, for whom the non-conformist sects had always had an appeal, held a deeply rooted and long-ingrained sense of injustice. It was a belief which centred on the view that they were constantly being exploited by the capitalist owners and bosses. And they were not far wrong. Greed and the desire for more money than they could ever spend had set the mine owners, the factory bosses, the monied classes and the newly rich so far apart from the ordinary men and women of Britain that there could never be any real type of rapprochement without a revolutionary degree of social and political change. That would take many years to achieve.

And when it came to the war, many of the workers felt that it was nothing more than a case of yet more exploitation by the privileged classes. To them, the war was a conflict that was being fought by the ordinary working men of the country on behalf of the rich and privileged.

Not only that. If it was an English war, as so many of their religious leaders claimed, let the English fight the damned thing themselves:

> On Sunday evening last, at Stanwell Road Baptist Chapel, the pastor, the Rev Gwilym O. Griffiths, made a special reference to the war and in no uncertain manner protested against England being implicated in the present hostilities between Russia, France and Germany. A resolution was passed deploring the European crisis.[4]

Arguably the combination of the workers' attitudes and the deeply held beliefs of the non-conformists provided the only significant pacifist opposition for the whole four years of war. At this distance and with our view of the war coloured by the paintings, photographs and writings that Charles Masterman so cleverly produced, it is sometimes hard to believe that support for the conflict was not a universal emotion. Far from it:

> I was just fourteen when the war broke out, working on the family farm. Lots of my mates from school joined up almost immediately. I thought I might do the same. But my family were staunch Baptists – Gilgal Chapel three times every Sunday for me.
>
> And our vicar was strongly anti-war; he'd be up there in the pulpit every service telling us how wrong the war really was. I don't suppose I thought much about it. I knew I was doing a valuable job on the farm and later, when conscription came in, farming was a reserved occupation so I never had to make that ultimate choice.
>
> I remember one sermon when the *hwyl* was really on him, Mr Williams, the vicar, went stamping around the chapel with a pitchfork in his hand. Talk about visual aids! I wouldn't have minded but he'd got the thing from my granddad's farm!
>
> 'Would you use something like this on your fellow man?' he kept shouting. We'd just heard the news about the

Battle of Jutland where the fleets of Britain and Germany met for the first and, as it happened, only time. Three of my relatives had gone down on the *Defence* during the battle and I remember thinking that if Mr Bloody Williams didn't shut up, I might be inclined to use that pitchfork on him.[5]

The anti-war stance of the non-conformists was a viewpoint which, in some cases, lasted throughout the conflict. Others were soon to change their views, particularly in the wake of the atrocity stories so adroitly spread by Charles Masterman and his staff at Wellington House.

Regardless of their initial stance, many anti-war supporters soon changed their minds, particularly when the stories of German brutality in Belgium were spread about. The Reverend Griffiths from Penarth, quoted above, made such an about turn that by 1915 he was serving as a padre in France and extolling the righteousness of the British soldiers' work in 'combating the Hun'.[6]

On the home front religion undoubtedly brought succour to a great number of families and the dependents of those who were away in the forces. For such people the church was a focal point, not just an emotional or spiritual crutch but an actual physical location where hope, belief and a comforting shoulder to cry on could come together to help anyone filled with anxiety and dread.

In the army, with the threat of death immeasurably closer, things were different. Church attendance was compulsory and it was not something that most troops enjoyed. The necessity of the Sunday morning church parade was lost on tired, frightened men and did little other than annoy the majority who would have preferred to remain at rest in their billets. Above all, the self-indulgent hypocrisy of so many senior churchmen – who would come to deliver a sermon before battle and then, when the guns began firing and the whistles started blowing, retire to safety behind the front lines – held little appeal for the ordinary soldiers:

> He went on to recall the reputation of the division and the high position it held in the eyes of the army commander, and reminded us of the German treatment of the occupied countries, of the violation and of the rape and the bestiality until it appeared to be our sacred duty to die fighting in such a cause as we had. … As I began to walk off after the others,

> I saw Blackett turn to Appleby and make a rude noise with his mouth. 'They told us all that eyewash at Loos,' he said.[7]

Of course, there were genuine, hard-working men of God who took their roles as padres seriously. They were brave men, content to spend their time in the trenches, giving comfort and help with not even a rifle and bayonet to protect them. Many of the ministers and vicars back home were, in their own way, equally as courageous. But even though they provided an invaluable service, they had little hope of overcoming the increasing cynicism of the men in the trenches.

With the exception of people like the Anglican chaplain Woodbine Willy – more of him later – belief in a divine being was far from a communal and community activity. It was more of a personal thing, a momentary contemplation at times of solitude or grief. There is no doubt that the services of the Church were well used by those waiting and worrying at home, particularly if there had been a fatality in the family, but for the men at the front religion seemed very distant when the shells were dropping and machine guns spitting out death.

It was not all as prescribed, however, not nearly as black and white as that. For all those thousands who questioned what religion was all about or perhaps doubted the existence of God, even the most cynical of critics would have had to admit that there were still many who accepted belief in a divine being at face value. For them it was a matter of faith, an acceptance of values and beliefs without there being clear concrete evidence to back them up.

For those who did believe, church attendance was a process of unthinking and unquestioning acceptance. There was, admittedly, a degree of superstition involved: if I stop going to church now, if I refuse to believe any longer, will that bring down the wrath of a cruel and unforgiving God down onto my head? 'As God wills it', a popular refrain from those who blindly accepted his presence, gave some sort of solace even though there seemed little sense in the slaughter. It was certainly easier to say that there had to be a purpose which was beyond the comprehension of ordinary men than it was to go over the top believing in nothing.

The million-dollar question of course, one that can never be answered: how many of those soldiers prayed as they waited at the foot of the trench ladders? And for those who did, was it genuine belief or simply a return to basic fears that had been hammered into them all their lives.

Believers, then, genuine believers, along with those who might doubt but would never admit it, were commonplace, both at the front and at home. Christian values were taken for granted by the believers. They had little time for the words of Charles Darwin and his *Origin of the Species.* For them it was a case of trust in God and hope against all hope that things would eventually work out.

Unquestioning belief was comforting but whether or not it would survive the hard knocks that lay ahead was, in the autumn and winter of 1914, unknown. The existence of an outside agency was important for many:

> We were all christened in church but then Mam had a disagreement with the vicar. He set up a huge cross outside the front door of the church and expected all of us to bow to it every time we passed. I could see where he was coming from, with all the casualties and so on, but Mam totally refused to have anything to do with it.
>
> Bowing to crosses, well that was far too close to Catholicism for her liking. My brother had joined the Salvation Army some time before so we started going to the Salvation Army services instead.
>
> It was a heavy commitment, children's services early in the morning, then up for the senior church service until midday. Back home for lunch and then off for Sunday School at 2.00PM.
>
> In the evening we'd be in a junior service while the adult service was going on. I only stopped going to the Salvation Army when I reached sixteen, not because I was old enough to make choices but because I had started working and it was all too much.[8]

For the men at the front there was no such thing as choice. You declared your affiliation when you joined up and if you had no religion of choice, the army would choose one for you. After that, church parades – just like the pre-battle visits by bishops and the like – were organized for you. The Tommies had no choice but to grin and bear it.

Belief, tokenism, wherever they stood, one thing the soldiers did enjoy was the respite offered by the church drop-in centres. The most famous of these was Toc H at Poperinghe in Belgium. Toc H is an abbreviation of Talbot House (Toc represented the letter T in the army signals alphabet) which from December 1915 operated as a rest and recuperation centre. Situated not far behind the front lines at Ypres, in the battered and often-shelled town of Poperinghe, it was self-styled as an 'everyman's club' where all ranks and nationalities were welcome. Toc H provided soldiers with an alternative to the bars and brothels of the town.

The slaughter on the Western Front caused many to question the old ways and beliefs. How could God be on the side of the British when the French and the Germans believed in the same divine being? How could He differentiate? Whose side was He really on? And how could He justify such terrible casualties? Those were questions that no one could answer. In his heartfelt but emotionally shocking poem entitled simply *They*, Siegfried Sassoon brought everyone up short. He has the bishop declare in answer to all the questions and examples of suffering with which he is assailed, 'The ways of God are strange.'[9]

The ways of God are strange, a magnificent final line to the poem but one which provided little comfort to the troops. As for the people back home, they preferred to bury their heads and keep believing:

> And so, he had died the death of a hero and his name will ever shine on England's Roll of Honour.
> He has left us with the good example of self-sacrifice – 'For what greater love hath any man than this; that he laid down his life for his friends.' So now we leave him in God's keeping, trusting we shall meet him in the great 'Beyond' where war shall be no more and everything shall be at peace.[10]

That heartfelt epilogue was written by Gwennie Thomas, the young sister of Private T. H. Thomas, three times wounded and finally killed in the attack on Pilkem Ridge during the Third Battle of Ypres. Her attitude and values were typical of the time. Whatever our modern preconceptions about such belief, there is no doubt that it brought comfort and relief to many in the summer of 1917.

PART III

Moving Mountains

'He was a man; take him for all in all, we shall not look upon his like again.'

Shakespeare, *Hamlet*

Chapter 5

Is There Really a Price on His Head?

By the spring and early summer of 1915, an obvious lack of military success for the Allies – rebuttal at Loos on the Western Front, failure to get off the beaches at Gallipoli and a shapeless muddle of a campaign in Mesopotamia – was causing members of the British government many sleepless nights. For a brief moment there was a distinct and very real possibility that the Liberal government of Herbert Asquith might even fall in the face of mounting criticism.

However, Charles Masterman knew that one sure way of ensuring continued support for the war was to arouse in the collective bosom of the civilian population a hot-headed and indignant fury. He would take their minds away from the military disasters by bringing them to the edge of reason.

The rumours of German atrocities in Belgium had been circulating since the previous year. They did not start with Masterman but he was astute enough to see what a rare chance fate had given him. True or false, exaggerated or accurate, the stories were like manna from heaven and day after day they were constantly falling into Masterman's outstretched palms. Between them he and his staff soon saw the rumours as a potentially major propaganda tool.

Support for the underdog had long been a national trait for the British and now, in the early days of what would become the greatest conflict ever known, it could be traced back to the summer of 1914. British indignation sprang screaming and kicking into life as soon as it was realized that mighty Germany was intending to attack France by launching a strong right hook through neutral Belgium.

The so-called Schlieffen Plan had been devised by a long-dead German general many years before but nobody had considered it a serious option until German troops began massing on the Belgian frontier. By the time everyone had woken up and started to demand action, it was too late: Belgian neutrality had been breached.

The moment the German artillery opened up and their armies began to march, reality replaced any lingering shreds of indecision and scepticism. Now the refrain on everyone's lips was noble little Belgium, poor helpless little Belgium whose neutrality had been guaranteed by the British at the Treaty of London in 1839.

Nobody in Britain, least of all government ministers, even remembered or had considered the treaty before. But now in the autumn of 1914 it suddenly became a matter of honour and a solemn promise that was written on the hearts of almost every British man and woman.

The invasion itself, when it occurred, was not as clear cut as the German military had assumed it would be. The Belgians fought heroically, infuriating the German commanders and delaying their advance. Belgian defiance also caused many German casualties which may or may not have had an adverse effect on the behaviour of the invaders.

Despite the heroics of the outnumbered Belgians, German artillery bombardments eventually ground down the defenders. The massive frontier forts were destroyed and whole villages laid to waste. Thousands of Belgian civilians were evicted. Most of them fled the country heading either for Holland or, preferably, for the more obvious safety of Great Britain which was at least separated from the continent by water. By the end of the war in 1918, nearly 200,000 Belgian refugees had sought sanctuary across the North Sea in Britain.

Caring for the influx of Belgian refugees became almost a national occupation. Tea and concert parties to raise money on their behalf, finding homes and jobs for the displaced thousands, the British public did whatever it could. It was a significant effort, starting a tradition of aiding and assisting refugees that has lasted almost until the present day.

What the Belgians gave back was equally momentous. In the main it consisted of stories of rape and pillage, murder and mayhem carried out by the victorious German troops in the course of their advance through Belgium. Many refused to believe the stories, certainly the more lurid ones of babies being roasted on open fires and nuns being bayoneted to death for trying to protect the innocent. The British and French press loved it all, hardly caring what was truth and what was mere fantasy.

There was, however, at least a degree of truth in some of the rumours. Like all good legends a little fact went a long way and tales of Germans shooting and executing civilian snipers who had fired at them from behind cover were later proved accurate. Masterman heard the stories, fanciful and real, and knew he could use them to increase the anti-German feelings in the country. But to do that effectively he needed help. He found it in the shape of Dutch artist Louis Raemaekers.

*

Raemaekers was born on 6 April 1869 in the town of Roermond in the Netherlands. It was a time of huge political and social discord in Holland, traditional Catholic values increasingly at odds with liberal or left-wing thinking. Louis's father, Josephus Raemaekers, was publisher and editor of the liberal, anti-Catholic weekly *De Volksvnorid* (*The Friend of the People*) and his open dislike of the establishment set the tone for many of his son's later attitudes and views.

When he had finished school, Louis Raemaekers studied art in Amsterdam and at the Brussels Academy. After graduating he settled in Haarlem and began work as a drawing teacher. In his spare time, he illustrated children's books and, for his own amusement, drew cartoons on contemporary issues. His skill with pencil and paper, rather than as a painter, was soon realized, however, and his reputation quickly grew. In 1906, he accepted an offer to produce political cartoons, firstly for the Dutch paper *Algemeen Handelsblad* and from 1909 for *De Telegraaf*, one of the most prestigious papers in Holland. He had found his metier.

And so Raemaekers would have gone on, teaching, publishing his cartoons and selling the odd drawing or painting, had it not been for the German invasion of Belgium in the summer of 1914. That invasion and what it brought with it changed his life for ever.

Despite his mother's Germanic background, Raemaekers was violently opposed to German imperialism and when he began hearing stories about the atrocities perpetrated by the invading army he was horrified. If only part of what he heard was true then something needed to be done.

He had already drawn his first anti-war cartoon, *Christendom after Twenty Centuries*, which was published two days before the Germans marched into Belgium. It was more abstract than his later work, depicting a woman bent low below sabres and lashes, but was striking in its complexity and yet simple in its message: 'It is an idea he attacks and not a nation, and although he is bitter against the idea for which Germany stands you can find no personal bitterness against Germans in his cartoons.'[1]

With German forces pouring into Belgium and the stories of rape and pillage refusing to die away, Raemaekers became increasingly disconcerted. He might dislike the threat of Germanic despotism but these were his mother's people and his own experiences of the country as a child and adolescent made the stories hardly credible.

As a consequence, he travelled to the Dutch–Belgium border to discover the truth for himself. Despite the danger he managed to cross into Belgium which was then under occupation and martial law. He never told anyone what he witnessed but in light of his future drawings, it must have been horrific. He returned home filled with righteous indignation.

Only once, a year or so later, did Raemaekers feel comfortable enough to speak about the horrors he had encountered. It was at a dinner held at the prestigious Savage Club, given in his honour by the literary men of London: 'Pointing to the portraits and trophies of Peary, Scott, Nansen, Shackleton and other explorers which hang on the walls he said, "I too have been an explorer, gentlemen. I have explored a hell and it was terror unutterable."'[2]

Everyone knew that he was referring to his experiences in 1914 but he refused to be drawn and would say no more. It was clear, however, that he had talked with Belgian citizens and, with his own eyes, seen enough to confirm his suspicions. On his return from Belgium and safely back in his studio, Raemaekers immediately began to produce cartoons depicting the violence and brutality of the German troops on their march to Brussels. His anger knew no limits.

Kaiser Wilhelm was, in Raemaekers' opinion, an ally of Satan's and he made no secret of the fact that the only way to proceed – the only noble way, at least – was for Holland to abandon its neutrality and enter the war on the side of the Allies. The Dutch government, anxious about the safety of its people, was unhappy with his viewpoint but to the general public in the Netherlands and Belgium, the depictions of German barbarity were humorous, heart wrenching and real, all at the same time. Raemaekers' popularity soared.

He made several more trips into Belgium, a highly dangerous series of adventures given that war was still raging and that the Germans were not best pleased with Louis Raemaekers. That is probably an understatement. They were not just unhappy, they were furious. They complained to the Dutch government and John Loudon, the Dutch Minister for Foreign Affairs and owner of *De Telegraaf*, was warned that he should keep a firm grip on the imagination of his famed cartoonist. German tolerance went only so far and Dutch neutrality was nothing if not tenuous.

Loudon got the message. In his political capacity he even confiscated several of Raemaekers' drawings, along with a slap on the wrist for endangering Dutch neutrality. As might be expected, Raemaekers ignored the warnings and his cartoons continued to appear in the papers.

The German government continued to fume and fulminate but it was powerless to do more. Then in the summer of 1915 a rumour began to circulate that Germany had placed a reward of 12,000 guilders on Raemaekers' head, dead or alive! No proof has ever been found but the story was widely believed in the Low Countries. Even Raemaekers took it seriously and in November 1915 he left Holland to settle in London.

He had regularly received threatening letters from anonymous German sources but one of the more worrying missives was sent to his wife just as he was about to leave for England. It said simply that any ship on which her husband might sail would be tracked by U-boats and torpedoed. Before he left his native country there was one more trial for Raemaekers to endure – literally. The German government coerced their Dutch equivalents, persuading them to arrest him and put him on trial for endangering Holland's neutrality. It was a difficult time but, in the end, Raemaekers was acquitted, the jury believing that he had the right to express his personal opinions in whatever way he chose.

Charles Masterman was waiting for Raemaekers in London and arranged, as soon as he arrived, for his work to be exhibited by the Fine Art Society in Bond Street. Christmas was only a few days away and the exhibition had a slow start. Then a review in *The Times* which proclaimed that 'this neutral is the only genius produced by the war' turned what could have been a flop or a non-event into a raging success.

News about the exhibition grew swiftly and as a result hundreds flocked each day to view the drawings. The exhibition ran for twenty weeks and was crowded on every single day. Raemaekers was immediately acclaimed by the British public and almost all the work on display was sold. From a situation where his life had been under threat Louis Raemaekers suddenly found himself not just a celebrity but a fairly well-off one at that: 'In Holland Mr Raemaekers always carries a pistol and is always receiving threatening letters – from Germans, not from his own countrymen. They are proud of him; for what he says with his pencil nearly all of them feel.'[3]

By now he had realized that, no matter how popular or successful his artwork might be, he had no hope of persuading Holland to abandon its neutrality. His homeland was a dangerous place and, in the spring of 1916, he was joined in London by his wife and family. He had married Johanna van Mansvelt, soon after graduating from Art College in 1902. Now they would make England their home, at least for a short while. The arrangement suited the Dutch government very nicely as they were finally able to wash their hands of the errant artist and distance themselves from Raemaekers' more critical and damaging work. He was now Britain's problem.

Masterman had already used several of Raemaekers' drawings to illustrate the public version of the 360-page *Bryce Report* on German atrocities. The *Report*, which appeared in May 1915, had had a huge effect on the British public even though most of it was a collection of lies, fantasy and fables, denigrating the German Army for the sake of propaganda. The truth did not emerge until many years later.

Masterman had noted the effect of the drawings and could hardly believe his luck when fate suddenly and a little unexpectedly thrust the artist into his waiting hands. In a series of discussions with Raemaekers, various proposals by the British propaganda chief were laid before the artist. With Raemaekers' agreement, Masterman immediately arranged for mass distribution of his work.

Forty of the more dramatic cartoons were published by the Caxton Publishing Company, appearing on the bookstalls as *Raemaekers' Cartoons*, the accompanying text being translated into eighteen different languages. The book was given worldwide distribution and received rave reviews – everywhere, obviously, except in Germany.

At Masterman's urging, early in 1916 Raemaekers signed a contract with the *Daily Mail* and went on to produce weekly war cartoons for the paper for the next two years. It was an arrangement that suited everyone – Masterman and Wellington House, Raemaekers himself, the paper and, of course, its readers. But that was only the start of the major propaganda campaign that Masterman and Wellington House had in mind.

*

Over the next few months Raemaekers was sent on a series of lecture tours, public discussions and art exhibitions across the country, even occasionally venturing over the Channel into France. At Liverpool it was estimated that in the space of a single afternoon at least 5,000 spectators turned up to view his drawings. They left full of admiration for the work on show and, most important of all as far as Charles Masterman was concerned, with heightened detestation of the German war machine.

Masterman and his staff worked frantically in the background and soon postcards, albums and cigarette cards showing Raemaekers' work were being produced in their thousands. They were avidly collected by the British public who not only appreciated the art but also unquestioningly accepted Raemaekers' views and the way that the Kaiser's desire for world domination was being depicted in his work.

This had now become a major propaganda effort with, it was later believed, over a million copies of Raemaekers' drawings being distributed for show and purchase. But that was only the beginning: there was soon to be an even bigger target to aim for. Masterman wanted to see Raemaekers' work distributed in the USA and in 1917, at the request of Wellington House, the Dutch artist sailed for America to begin what soon became a triumphal tour. Lectures, interviews, regular exhibitions, Raemaekers did it all. The USA had only recently entered the war and wherever he appeared he was feted by the American public, hailed as someone who had experienced and understood the conflict.

He met President Woodrow Wilson and former president Teddy Roosevelt but the most significant contact he made was with newspaper magnate William Randolph Hearst. He had soon signed a contract with Hearst, promising to supply the outspoken, dogmatic newspaper owner with cartoons and artwork for his various publications.

Hearst was distinctly pro-German in his views and many questioned what Raemaekers thought he was doing. The answer was simple. Hearst and his readers were his ideal audience – if he could convince them of German barbarity his work was done.

By the end of 1917 over 2,000 US papers had published cartoons by Raemaekers. In addition, there were hundreds, even thousands of postcards and booklets available in the shops. Soon it was estimated that millions of his drawings were in circulation in the USA alone, in various styles or guises. It was the largest propaganda effort of the war, orchestrated by Charles Masterman and executed by Louis Raemaekers.

Raemaekers' celebrity was assured and the man who in 1915 had nearly been imprisoned by the Dutch government for endangering their neutrality had become the most famous artist in the world.

It was inevitable that his work would go out of fashion once the war ended. In 1919 he published *Raemaekers' Cartoon History of the War* in two volumes and returned to the continent, settling in Brussels where he became an advocate of the League of Nations. He continued to draw, producing a regular newspaper cartoon called *Flippie Flick*. Compared with his output during the war, the new cartoons were rather trite and shallow but they became very popular with the public, particularly in the Low Countries. Based on rhymes by the poet Clinge Doorenbos, the popularity of the cartoons even led to a musical for children, the props and clothing bearing a distinct similarity to the drawings of Louis Raemaekers. In all, nearly 1,500 Flippie Flick cartoons were produced although from October 1934 much of the artwork was done by Raemaekers' son, Robert.

Raemaekers remained suspicious of Germany, particularly once Adolf Hitler came to power in the early 1930s and began producing anti-Nazi drawings for *De Telegraaf*. Once again, he had put himself in a difficult, not to say dangerous position. He fled to the USA just before the start of the Second World War, knowing that he was a targeted man. He remained in America until 1946, continuing, as he had done in the first great conflict of the century, to produce anti-German cartoons. Perhaps inevitably the simplistic clear-lined drawings that had marked down his First World War productions as being very different from ordinary, run-of-the-mill cartoons began to fade and much of his work from this period lacked the clarity of his earlier efforts. It did not stop him working.

He died in 1956, having been awarded the French Legion of Honour and being made an honorary citizen of the city of Roermond.

There is little doubt that Raemaekers' fame slowly declined in the interwar years. Between 1914 and 1919 he had been a necessary focus, providing a visual accompaniment to the sentimental songs of the music halls and the poetry of men like Rupert Brooke. By the early years of post-war Europe, he was no longer necessary and a proposed collection of his work was even turned down by a Dutch publisher because, it was felt, the world had seen enough of bloodshed and war.

With the decline in his reputation much of his skill also diminished. It was inevitable, given his previous productivity and the sheer immediacy of his subject matter. Even so his obituary in *The Times*, 27 July 1956, admirably summed up the man's significance between 1914 and 1918. Attempting to put his position and value during the war into some sort of perspective, the bituary writer took a rather portentous but nevertheless quite accurate:

> There were a dozen or so people – emperors, Kings, statesmen and commanders in chief – who obviously and notoriously shaped policies and guided events. Outside that circle of the great Louis Raemaekers stands conspicuous as the one man who, without any assistance or title or office, indubitably swayed the destinies of people.[4]

Like all creative artists Raemaekers would have enjoyed the compliment. He was a modest man who believed in letting his work speak for itself and, arguably, for him as well. But the artistic ego, the force that had driven him to create such a significant body of work – nearly 2,000 cartoons during the war years – could never be ignored.

Charles Masterman had seen the potential in Raemaekers' work early on, long before he came to Britain and was, literally, known only by his local fame in Holland. Alerted to this talented and capable artist by journalists and British dignitaries who had seen its effect at first hand, Masterman gathered the Dutchman into his stable of propagandists, and the rest is history.

The cartoons were, Masterman realized, poignant and heartfelt but above all they were powerful. In particular they were powerful in a way that ordinary men and women who might otherwise never have looked at a work of art could appreciate and understand. This was art for the common man, appealing to their emotions and their intellects, striking at the very core of their beliefs.

Together with the early work of James Clarke, it was undoubtedly Raemaekers' dramatic cartoons and their effect on the public that led Masterman to instigate the war artists scheme. In 1915, the two artists were at different ends of the spectrum, Clarke appealing to the sentimental and romantic side of human nature, Raemaekers to the more realistic and one-dimensional aspect of life.

Regardless of where they sat in the pantheon of artists, no matter how you defined their appeal, Masterman knew that if this reaction and acclaim could come from two artists, what price a whole battalion of them? By the end of the war that was almost exactly what Masterman had created.

The exploitation of Raemaekers' work during the war years remains one of the most significant of all the propaganda exercises carried out by Wellington House. The soldiers at the front had their own views of the war but for the families and friends back home the art of Louis Raemaekers was one sure way of keeping the passions burning and the drive for victory alive.

Chapter 6

Gathering Lilacs, Keeping the Fires of Home Burning

The most popular song of the First World War came about almost by accident and contrary to its elegant, easy-flowing melody, the lyrics were devilishly difficult to write. As a consequence, the piece almost never saw the light of day.

The song is, of course, *We'll Keep the Home Fires Burning* – or, as it was first known, *Till the Boys Come Home* – and was written by Welsh musician, actor and impresario Ivor Novello. He was then relatively unknown but the song transported him from small-time music teacher and would-be composer to the heights of fame. After *Home Fires* he could do nothing wrong.

The song was then, and remains now, a wonderful piece of music, catching perfectly the sentiment and mood of the time. It had immediate appeal both for the soldiers in the trenches and for their families who were anxiously awaiting their return. It was a lyrical alternative to the robust soldiers' songs that the men roared out as they marched to the trenches or crouched in their dugouts. This was gentle, heart-warming, and even melancholic in a peculiarly uplifting sort of way. So popular was the song that it could be heard everywhere, wherever you went in France or Belgium, in Britain and even America. It was not, however, to everyone's liking.

The poet Siegfried Sassoon, waiting for the next burst of action in the trenches before Mametz Wood on the Somme, was sickened by the constant whistling and singing of the refrain by soldiers up and down the line. So much so that he threatened, when the war was over, to find the man who wrote it and shoot him! The soldiers grinned, put it down to just another of 'Mad Jack's outbursts' and went on singing.[1]

Mad Jack Sassoon did indeed seek out Novello but he didn't shoot him. Instead, he and the Welsh songbird had a brief love affair. It was indeed brief, mainly because of Novello who was nothing if not a committed philanderer. As John Stuart Roberts has written: 'He was a consummate flirt who collected lovers as he gathered lilacs. In contrast to his lyrics, he was devoid of sentiment when bored with a relationship or romance; Sassoon would not have lasted long.'[2]

Sassoon apart, the song's popularity transcended the war and the horrors that men experienced, transporting them, metaphorically at least, to what quickly became the most longed-for journey of their lives – back to their homes, to their loved ones and everything they held dear. The tune was haunting and powerfully evocative: once heard, never forgotten. For those who waited back home the lyrics seemed to sum up all their emotions. The simple words gave them strength and hope at a time when belief was under incredible strain.

Along with the lyrics, words that cut right to the heart of parting, the tune remained a firm romantic favourite once the war was over and in the immediate post-war years. Throughout the thirties and even during the course of the Second World War, *We'll Keep the Home Fires Burning* was never far from the lips of men and women kept apart by fate and by circumstances they could not control.

In the summer of 1914 Ivor Novello – David Ivor Davies to award him the name he was given by his parents at birth – was just beginning to make his name in the field of popular music and musical composition. His life so far had been interesting but unspectacular. One song, arguably his greatest ever composition, would change that forever.

*

Ivor Novello was born on 15 January 1893 at the family home in Cowbridge Road, Cardiff. His father, David Davies, was a rather insignificant man who worked as a rent collector for Cardiff City Council. He was overshadowed by his wife and the mother of Ivor, Madam Clara Novello Davies. She was, from the beginning, a major influence on the life and career of young Ivor. Clara – or Mam as she was invariably known – was a renowned singing teacher and choral conductor with a reputation that reached far beyond the confines of Offa's Dyke. A grandee of the grandest sort Madam Clara Novello Davies was certainly a force to be reckoned with.

Today, changes in taste and musical appreciation have rendered Clara something of a Welsh joke at the hands of entertainers like Ryan and

Ronnie, Max Boyce and others. But at the end of the nineteenth century, she was famous throughout the principality and beyond. In her home, in the concert halls and in the salons of the city Madam Clara Novello Davies ruled like minor nobility.

Well-known singers such as Clara Butt and Adelina Patti were regular visitors to the family home in Cardiff and, later, when Madam Clara moved to London, to the flat above the Strand Theatre where she took up residence. From his adolescence onwards that flat was to become Ivor's home and base for the rest of his life.

From an early age Ivor enjoyed dressing up and parading around the house in his mother's jewellery and costumes. He loved to drape himself in her gowns, something which might, perhaps, have shown an early propensity for what was then still an illegal sexual proclivity. He also loved to perform. Clara Butt taught him to sing *Abide with Me* when he was just seven years old and it was not long before he was competing with great success at the Eisteddfodau that were so popular in Wales.

On one well-recorded occasion the young Ivor entered an Eisteddfod competition which was intended solely for girls. Dressed in female attire he duly won the competition. One of the judges called his performance that of an 'angel' but it was then discovered that he was a boy. Disqualified from the event, he was awarded a special prize by the judges but whether it was for his skill and talent as a singer or for his effrontery is not known.

Mam was determined to push her son's career, entering him in competitions and having nothing but praise for her young maestro. Even when he was a baby she was enchanted by his ability: 'She detected in him the signs of an infant prodigy, even in his wailing. "I can remember the funny way in which he used to cry, in perfect thirds, which were not at all inharmonious to listen to."'[3]

Initially Ivor was educated in Cardiff but Mam had bigger and considerably grander ideas for him. He had to be educated in line with his talents and therefore he was duly put forward for a choral scholarship at Magdalen College, Oxford. Supremely happy in his little world, Ivor did not want to leave Cardiff and when his father David, who was also opposed to the idea of his son living away from home, hid the entry form in a chest of drawers Ivor was not greatly upset. It was possibly the only sign of rebellion against his domineering wife that David Davies ever showed and he must have revelled in his success. Mam, however, fretted and fumed, wondering why the college had not been in touch to offer an audition.

By the time she found the dreaded document the entry date had passed. Undismayed, Mam shot off to Oxford, dragging her still somewhat-reluctant son in her wake. The college must waive its rules, she declared, for a boy of such obvious talent. Such was the power of her reputation and her rather formidable personality that the audition was rearranged and Ivor, of course, won his way into Magdalen. He was just 10 years old.

Contrary to his fears, Ivor loved Oxford. The architecture, the carefree students, the sheer elegance of the city all imprinted themselves onto his precocious, willing mind. From 1903 until the end of the decade, he led a very privileged lifestyle, singing in the choir most Sunday nights and often in the week as well. He enthralled the audiences that flocked from all over Oxford and beyond simply to hear him. And then his voice broke!

His time at Oxford, along with his potential career as a chorister, was over. He rarely sang in public again but those six or seven years at Oxford had been an important period for him. More than anything it was a time when he learned the glorious pleasure of standing before an audience and holding them spellbound with his skill and personality.

Where to go and what to do was now a real problem for Ivor. Mam had not finished, however, and almost before he knew it Ivor found himself enrolled as a student of Dr Herbert Brewer, the renowned organist at Gloucester Cathedral. He was to study harmony and counterpoint but from the beginning there were problems. If Oxford had been magical, Gloucester was a real anti-climax. The trouble lay with Brewer and the music he required Ivor to play, solemn religious pieces which to the young man were little more than dirges. Ivor Novello wanted and needed something lighter and more appealing to his ear.

The young Ivor was one of just three pupils studying with Brewer – himself, the future war poet Ivor Gurney and the composer F. W. Harvey. Ivor got on well with Harvey but he and Gurney detested each other from the start. Each was too mercurial and too highly strung for the other's taste. Finally, Ivor could stand it no longer and walked away from Gloucester with Brewer's infamous words of condemnation hanging over his head: 'You will never make a career out of music, boy.' The comparison with the recording manager from Decca who turned down the Beatles at their audition in 1962 is hard to ignore.[4]

Ivor retuned to Cardiff where he began composing and, even at such a young age, taking a series of pupils. By the time war broke out he had moved to London to be with his mother and to widen the possibilities for his work. Slowly but surely, he was beginning to establish a reputation.

On the strength of his early compositions, Ivor was soon asked to write the score of a pageant that was to be part of the Festival of Empire, held in Canada. In the event the pageant never materialized but the project did at least provide him with an all-expenses paid trip to Canada and New York.

He had a lucky escape on the return voyage. The original vessel on which his passage had been booked, the luxurious *Empress of India*, was rammed by another liner in dense fog. She sank, taking 900 passengers with her to the bottom. Ivor had missed sailing on the doomed ship because he was searching for a pet dog. The dog was found after he had left New York on a second, replacement ship. The dog disappeared into the pages of history but Ivor Novello did not.

Perhaps the most seminal moment of his life came when Mam, with war now raging, suggested he should write a piece of music 'to encourage the boys at the Front'. He refused. There were already far too many patriotic renditions doing the rounds, he declared. Never one to miss an opportunity, Mam decided she would write the tune herself.

Ivor took one look at the finished article and knew, instantly, that her composition, given the title *Keep the Flags A-Flying*, was nothing short of dreadful. It could only damage her reputation – and his as well. He had no option, he felt, but to take over from her.

The piece he produced was the sensational and sentimental *We'll Keep the Home Fires Burning*. The comparison between the two titles was obvious but lyrics to suit Ivor's composition proved difficult to find. He was a composer, not a poet or lyricist; his job was to create the music.

He rarely wrote the lyrics to any of his songs, using people like Christopher Hassel, future biographer of Rupert Brooke, to produce them for him. This time he turned to the American poet Lena Guilbert Ford who was now living in London and trying to make her name as a lyricist.

Frustrated and increasingly desperate, Ivor and Lena sat for hours in Mam's flat above the Strand Theatre. The words just would not come and the harder they tried the more mundane were the offerings with which they came up.

The story is probably apocryphal but legend has it that, when they had nearly given up hope, the maid then came in to bank up the fire.

'Got to keep the fires of home burning brightly,' Ivor quipped – and that was it. They had it. The idea was noted down and work on the crucial set of words began. Ivor wrote the chorus, Lena the verses. Lena Ford was nothing if not a perfectionist. She went home and continued to work on the song. Then she telephoned the finished lyrics through to Novello. From the first few lines it was clear that the work was a masterpiece of sentiment and romance:

> *They were summoned from the hillside,*
> *They were called in from the glen*
> *And the country found them ready*
> *At the stirring call for men.*[5]

A few days after it was finished, *We'll Keep the Home Fires Burning* was given its first public airing. That first performance was part of a Sunday League concert held at the Alhambra Theatre on Leicester Square. The singer, a young pupil of Mam's, was the up-and-coming Welsh soprano Sybil Vane. She included it in the second half of her performance and Ivor Novello accompanied her on the piano. The Band of the Grenadier Guards, also in the programme, watched the performance from the back of the stage.

Sybil sang the first verse and the refrain and when she began to repeat the refrain, to her utter amazement she found that the audience was joining in. Already they had picked up on the tune and the lyrics and were singing as if they had known the piece for years. The song had to be repeated nine times before, reluctantly, the audience allowed the performers, including Ivor, to leave the stage. The song and its composer were an instant success.

Sadly, the same could not be said for Lena Ford. On the night of 7/8 March 1918 she was killed in a bombing raid on London, the first American civilian to perish in such a fashion. Her young son Walter died with her. Lena died without the acclaim which came pouring down on Ivor Novello, a terrible tragedy as the words of *We'll Keep the Home Fires Burning* were as important and as crucial to its success as the melody.

What made *We'll Keep the Home Fires Burning* so special was the simple fact that although it was clearly of its time, it was also suitable for all time and all seasons. It painted an idyllic image to which every man in the trenches or every woman at the kitchen hob could relate. It offered the picture of a perfect world, a perfect relationship and a perfect end to the conflict. The words and music gelled, not only with each other but also with the things that were happening across the globe.

Home and home fires might, in reality, be in a tenement or a single room in the most rundown part of the city but in the Novello–Ford-fuelled imagination it would invariably be a rose-covered cottage by a stream or a farmstead nestled peacefully in the lee of a hill. It was the image, the picture in the mind that was important. And that was exactly what the song exuded.

The song had begun life as an up-tempo piece but that soon changed to the melodic, poignant style that we know today. It worked in either tempo, particularly the slower, more reflective one, and was played so often by military bands that many Frenchmen later mistook it for the English national anthem.

Overall, the song was as important to the maintenance of British morale as any of the Music Hall tunes of the day. It was also far more immediate than the poetry of the ilk of Rupert Brooke and therefore able to appeal to men and women of all classes and educational levels.

*

After *We'll Keep the Home Fires Burning*, Ivor Novello was in constant demand. He did not have to go looking for work; it came rolling up to his door in ever-increasing quantity. He contributed music and songs to shows like *The Bing Boys* and in 1916 wrote much of the score, along with Jerome Kern, for the smash hit *Theodore & Co*.

This last production saw another near-disaster, to which Ivor Novello seems to have been prone all his childhood and adult life. Near but 'not quite' disasters such as the sinking of the *Empress of India* without him on board, accompanied him throughout his career. Ivor took them all in his stride.

This time, with the first performance of *Theodore & Co* looming, Novello left the music he had written for the show in a taxi and was forced to rewrite it from memory once he reached his dressing room. The fact that he could achieve such a miracle of memory speaks volumes about his talent.

In 1916 Ivor Novello was called up for military service. He chose to serve in the Royal Naval Air Service, mainly it was later said because he could augment his uniform with silk scarves and velvet gloves! Appearances were one thing but Ivor was a truly awful pilot. Whilst still training to fly, on his first solo flight, he crashed his aircraft – and continued crashing. It was near-disaster again and this time he was saved by the Royal Naval Air Service which declared that he was causing more damage to their aeroplanes than the whole of the German air force. They grounded him. He would, in due course, have been returned to flying duties and almost certain death but was saved again, this time by Winston Churchill's private secretary Eddie Marsh.

A devotee of art and literature, the poet Rupert Brooke, the first wartime protégé of Eddie Marsh, had recently died during the Gallipoli Campaign. Marsh now took Ivor under his wing. He used his influence as Churchill's secretary to arrange for him to be transferred to a non-flying job at the newly created Air Ministry in London.

The new posting was hardly taxing and it gave Ivor as much time as he needed to write and yet still pose and parade around London in his elegant RNAS uniform. He was supremely happy, with both of his skills – composing and gathering attention – being exploited to the full.

After the war Ivor Novello solidified his reputation and began to move in circles much, much further from home than London's West End. Despite his renowned homosexuality – known but never referred to – he became a matinee idol, appearing in a wide range of silent films. The most notable of these was probably *The Lodger*; this was a story based on the Jack the Ripper killings of the previous century, a film which terrorized all of those who paid their money to sit in the darkness, breathless and sweating as Ivor 'did his stuff'. He later remade the film as a talkie, one of the early films directed by Alfred Hitchcock. It was again hugely popular although it seemed to lack the dramatic terror of the earlier, silent version.

Ivor next tried Hollywood where he was successful as both an actor and as a scriptwriter. With self-deprecating humour, he later said that his greatest success as a writer was the first Tarzan film where his contribution was to write the immortal lines, 'Me Tarzan, you Jane.'

Stage shows, personal performances, films, there seemed to be no end to Novello's talents. He fluttered between England and Hollywood until the Second World War broke out. During the war, established now mainly in England, his hit revue *The Dancing Years* and songs such as *We'll Gather Lilacs* – another tune, like *We'll Keep the Home*

Fires Burning, that tapped into the latent sentimentality of the time – confirmed his popularity.

Near-disaster loomed again in 1944 and this time no amount of good fortune could help him when he was arrested and charged with illegally procuring petrol at a time of severe petrol rationing. Such niceties as petty regulations rarely bothered Ivor but, on this occasion, they resulted in a month spent at His Majesty's Pleasure in Wormwood Scrubs.

Despite being put in charge of the prison choir – rather than endure the normal prison work of making mailbags and such like – Ivor was forced to spend much of his sentence alone, locked up in his cell. It undoubtedly had a major effect on his health and arguably may have contributed to his premature death.

Things could have been a great deal worse given his propensity for same-sex relationships. In the 1940s same-gender sex was punishable by a lot more than the four weeks he was given for flouting petrol regulations. Everyone knew of his sexual propensities but it was not something that was ever held against him. Nothing, it seemed, could hurt or damage his popularity.

Ivor had always worked under his mother's name. That was how everyone knew him but it was still not a legal acknowledgement. In 1936 he decided it was time to change that and formally adopted the name. Thereafter he officially became Ivor Novello.

He died of a coronary thrombosis on 6 March 1951, his ashes being scattered under a lilac bush at Golders Green Cemetery. Ivor would have undoubtedly appreciated the symbolic, theatrical nature of the act.

Despite his acclamation as a Welsh entertainer, an acclamation that resulted in a rather fey-looking statue in Cardiff Bay and a blue plaque on his first home in Cathedral Road, he had more or less severed his connections to Wales by the end of the First World War. London was always more important to him. And yet something of his Welshness remained. He had long left his Welsh roots behind but not his Welsh accent which he took with him to the grave.

Ivor Novello might have wanted to be a pilot – then again, he might have wanted just to pose. But he undoubtedly did his best work for his country by composing *We'll Keep the Home Fires Burning*. He achieved what amounted to almost monumental status, as a composer and as a performer. It is perhaps only when you read what the great Noel Coward, on meeting Novello for the first time, had to say about him that you even

Above left: Charles Masterman, propaganda genius. A cartoon depiction of the man who controlled much of Britain's morale during the war.

Above right: Charles Masterman as he really was.

Gavrilo Princip arrested by police after the assassination of Archduke Franz Ferdinand.

Left: The most famous recruiting poster of the war: Lord Kitchener's eyes, finger and moustache say it all.

Below: Recruits for Kitchener's New Army in training.

Above left: A Raemaekers cartoon depicting German atrocities.

Above right: Remember Belgium, a recruiting poster from 1914.

Emblem here of rage—amaze—
Poor deluded caddie says:
   " Hello, Bill, we're bunkered."

A satirical postcard showing Kaiser Wilhelm as a bunkered golfer with Austria-Hungary as his hapless caddy.

RUPERT BROOKE WRITING IN GARDEN
OF THE OLD VICARAGE, GRANTCHESTER.

Don't be Alarmed,
the Cardiff Pals are on guard

Above: Poet Rupert Brooke in the garden of the Old Vicarage, Grantchester.

Left: A postcard from 1915 supporting the Cardiff Pals, one of many Pals regiments across the country.

SELFRIDGE'S "War Window"   In this window were displayed maps, bulletins, etc., of the Balkan War. It is now being used for the same purpose during the present great War.

Selfridges war window, and the crowd in front of it.

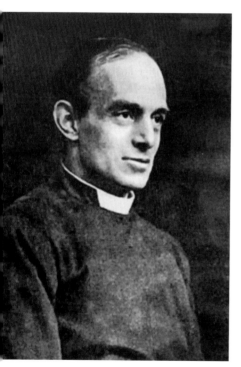

Above left: Woodbine Willie, army chaplain and philanthropist.

Above right: Welsh composer Ivor Novello, writer of the most popular song of the war.

OUT FOR VICTORY.

THE MERCHANT SEAMAN.
Going home to sign on again.

Miss Edith CAVELL

Above left: Determined to win: British strength and courage shown on this morale-boosting postcard.

Above right: Nurse Edith Cavell, martyr and patriot, executed in 1915.

Sinking of the Lusitania

The last plunge.

6.

The *Lusitania* sinks beneath the waves.

" BYSTANDER " COPYRIGHT.

" There goes our blinkin' parapet again."

Above left: One of the most famous of Bruce Bairnsfather's Old Bill cartoons.

Above right: Bairnsfather's drawing of the Christmas Truce, 1914. The caption reads, 'Look at this bloke's buttons, 'arry, I should reckon 'e 'as a man to dress 'im'.

An unofficial photograph of German soldiers during the Christmas Truce.

Left: Bruce Bairnsfather, the most famous artist of the war.

Below: Fergus McKain captures the most important part of the soldier's day: the rum issue.

Sketches
of Tommy's life
Up the line — Nº 7

One of the bright spots in our life.

Visé Paris 763

Recruitment, as seen by McKain.

A *Daily Mail* card, the caption reading, 'Tommy at Home in German Dug-Outs'.

Above left: A Raemaekers card showing German soldiers killed on their way to Calais.

Above right: A homemade postcard produced by an unknown soldier. The Kaiser is depressed and crying for comfort.

A Christmas card from the trenches.

A prisoner-of-war card from Duisburg, 1916.

Above: The Princess Mary Christmas Box, issued to troops in December 1914.

Right: The most renowned poet of the war, Siegfried Sassoon.

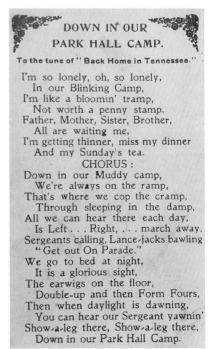

Above left: A humorous card showing the Kaiser in a bit of trouble.

Above right: People's poetry and a morale booster: a poem from soldiers at Park Hall Camp.

Above left: Caton Woodville's romanticized painting, *When Night Sets In*.

Above right: Food rationing and, as a consequence, having to queue for meat and vegetables – trials and tribulations for the people of Britain.

Right: Bairnsfather's self-portrait (of a sort) with him painting or drawing one of his early Old Bill sketches on the wall of his billet.

Below: A roll of honour, showing the community dead.

Post Card.

ONLY THE ADDRESS TO BE
WRITTEN HERE.

Stamp

An advertising postcard for some of the Music Hall acts appearing in the Pavilion on Penarth Pier.

GERMAN
PRISONERS
BY THE
ROADSIDE
IN FRANCE
From a
drawing by
Major Sir
William Orpen
A.R.A.
(Ministry of
Information)

William Orpen's classic picture of German prisoners standing at the roadside – issued and sold as a postcard by the Ministry of Information.

Above left: The end of the war, time to celebrate.

Above right: A memorial card for a dead soldier.

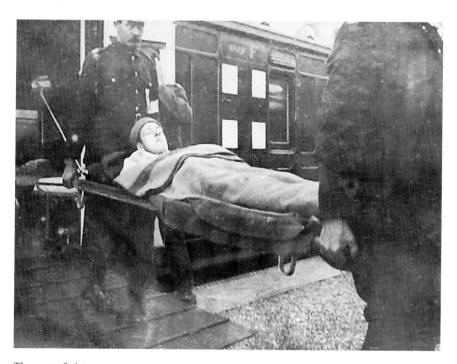

The cost of victory.

The Armistice is signed in the famous railway carriage.

Lutyens' memorial, The Cenotaph.

A French postcard from early in the war captures the poignant nature of the conflict.

begin to realize the extent of his status and fame: 'I just felt suddenly conscious of the long way I had to go before I could break into the magic atmosphere in which he breathed and moved with such nonchalance.'[6]

It is impossible to quantify the effect of the song on public morale. The Great War had no individual Vera Lynn figure, a forces' sweetheart, as there was during the Second World War. Perhaps the closest was Gertie Gitana who had been making gramophone recordings long before the war began. She spent the war years singing to wounded troops and people on the home front but she was never asked, officially, to undertake these tasks.

No Vera Lynn, perhaps, but there was an equivalent of her famous *We'll Meet Again*. It was, of course, Novello's *We'll Keep the Home Fires Burning*. Novello's song was a tune on almost everybody's lips for the four years of conflict and for that, if nothing else, it is only fair to say that it has to be regarded as one of the great songs of the war. And therefore, its effect on people's morale has to have been enormous.

Chapter 7

Woodbine Willie

The Reverend Geoffrey Studdert Kennedy is now something of a forgotten figure but from 1916 until the end of the war he was hailed as a national hero. He was revered not only by the troops in the front lines but also by their families back home. He won the Military Cross for his bravery but, more significantly, he won the affection and respect of the soldiers in the trenches. He had little in common with the officers, rarely socializing with them and maintaining a respectful distance, but for the ordinary working-class men who made up the rank and file of the British Army there was mutual respect, even love.

The soldiers awarded him the sobriquet of Woodbine Willie, a name which came to mean a great deal to Studdert Kennedy. To him it was far more important than any little piece of tin and its accompanying strip of coloured ribbon. The nickname meant acceptance and, importantly, showed that his message of Christian compassion and faith was getting through. He was, arguably, the perfect example of a morale-boosting man of belief and faith.

Amazingly, many of the troops at the front had no idea whatsoever who the Reverend Studdert Kennedy actually was. For that matter many of them could not even place or identify their own regimental chaplain. But they all knew and respected Woodbine Willie. He was one of them. It was hardly surprising when he spoke to them in their own language.

One famous story about Woodbine Willie tells of two soldiers wandering down a stretch of trench and coming across a homemade sign declaring that the dugout in the trench wall was The Vicarage. ''Ere, look at that,' remarked one soldier, 'It's a bloody vicarage.'

Woodbine Willie's head suddenly appeared from behind the dugout gas curtain. 'Yes,' he said, 'and here's the bloody vicar!'

A poet and prose writer of some skill, Kennedy was renowned for his ability as a preacher. Holding congregations – audiences, he would have called them – in the palm of his hand quickly became second nature to him. And that was no small skill, to enthral men who had endured hell in the trenches and had little time or truck for false sympathy and pontification.

Studdert Kennedy was not above using jokes and occasionally even swearing to add emphasis to his preaching. He often began a sermon with the line, 'Here comes the bloody vicar again.' After that he could do no wrong as far as the soldiers were concerned. As a result of his love of the vernacular, Kennedy often found himself in trouble with church authorities for the levity of his words. Yet he was clear – he was using the language of the common man and he was damned if he was going to lose the attention of even one soul because his language was thought to be too high and mighty.

Grab them, hold them, and bring them to God – that was Woodbine Willie's technique. These were men who were shortly going to put their lives at risk; there was no way he was going to bore them to death before the battle had even begun. It might have been a risky ploy, a dangerous tactic – after all, the troops needed to see his approach as genuine, not idle words from someone who was talking down to them. But there is no doubt that it worked.

*

Geoffrey Studdert Kennedy was born in the vicarage of St Paul's parish church in Leeds on 27 June 1883. Woodbine Willie was born thirty years later in the trenches of the Western Front. Kennedy was always destined for the church, his father William Studdert Kennedy being vicar of St Mary's in one of the poorest parts of the city of Leeds. The elder Kennedy was the son of an Irishman. He had been born, raised and educated in Ireland and, like Geoffrey and his eight other children, to the end of his life he retained a strong Irish accent.

The young Geoffrey did well at school, excelling in his academic studies and also at contact sports like boxing and rugby football. Otherwise, his calm, reflective character was always to the fore, making him a popular friend and companion. He left school in 1901 and began a course of studies at Trinity College, Dublin, where he obtained a first-class degree in classics and divinity.

A short period as a teacher in West Kirby was followed by entry into his true vocation, the Anglican Church. After a period at Ripon Clergy College, he was ordained at Worcester Cathedral in 1908 and began his clerical career at Rugby Parish Church. It was one of the largest churches in an industrial town which, despite its relative prosperity because of the railway works, also had many slums and rundown areas. There, in the least prosperous parts of the community, Geoffrey Studdert Kennedy was at his best. He gave away much of his own money to help the hungry and the poor and offered assistance, financial and spiritual, to whoever needed it, regardless of whether or not they were practising members of his congregation.

Above all, his preaching, often in the open air, was regarded by everyone, church authorities, his congregation and anyone who just stopped to listen, as remarkable. He had the Irish 'gift of the gab', backed up by strong Christian ideals and beliefs. His interaction with adults and children was equally memorable, with an ability never to talk down to people but to treat them with respect and affection.

A move back to Leeds, to his recently deceased father's church and parish was on the cards but in the event, after marrying Emily Catlow, he took up a post as vicar of St Paul's Church in Worcester. His salary was just £300 a year and his parish – again in the poorest part of the city – was made up of over 4,000 needy souls. He took up the post on 9 June 1914. Within a few weeks, Britain was at war.

To begin with Geoffrey Studdert Kennedy was all in favour of the war. He saw the Germans as a brutal people who needed to be checked in their drive for world domination. Every fit and able man, he said, should be prepared to enlist and serve his King and Country: 'I cannot say too strongly that I believe every able-bodied man ought to volunteer for service anywhere. There ought to be no shirking of that duty. Those who cannot volunteer for military service can pray.'[1]

To that end, after much deliberation, at the beginning of 1915, he applied to become an army chaplain. There would be a waiting period. His bishop would need to find someone to replace him at St Paul's and the army had to approve his application. Despite the delay there was little doubt that he would be accepted. He had all the right qualifications and he was both young and keen.

It was not exactly a test but while he was waiting for acceptance, some senior officers from the army asked him to spend time preaching to thousands of new recruits at a barracks outside Worcester. He accepted willingly and on a number of occasions he held thousands of initially reluctant listeners spellbound with his eloquence.

After a wait of almost a year, during which time he continued as a parish priest, on 21 December 1915, Studdert Kennedy was finally appointed chaplain in the British Army. Thereafter things moved quickly. Within a few days he was in France and on Christmas Day he conducted his first service as an army chaplain. Early in the New Year he was active among the troops at Rouen, distributing bibles – and, for the first time, packets of Woodbine cigarettes. Almost immediately somebody called him Woodbine Willie and the name stuck.

He soon devised a series of talks for the troops, emphasizing the need to be clean in mind, body and spirit – never an easy task in and around the base camps where prostitutes, gambling dens and estaminets were in plentiful supply. Kennedy's message was hardly what the troops wanted to hear but he delivered his lectures with such skill and aplomb that nobody complained and everyone stood fascinated until he finally called an end to the evening's 'entertainment'.

Lectures and sermons were one thing but they were hardly what Woodbine Willie wanted to do. He knew where the real work lay and he fretted about not being up in the trenches with the soldiers. He did not have to wait long to be in the thick of things. With the Somme offensive looming, he was soon serving alongside his beloved working men in the front lines. There he quickly began to understand life at the front, enduring the shelling and the snipers, and the mud and the blood of combat.

He suffered as all the soldiers suffered. He clawed at the earth when the whizz bangs came raining down, he sang their songs and breathed in relief when periods of rest or respite were called and the men marched out of the trenches for a few glorious days. He felt their terror, he helped them write letters home; he was, effectively, one of them.

Over the coming months Geoffrey Studdert Kennedy, Woodbine Willie by any other name, became the human face of the church and the army. The key to his success was simply that he was there, with the men, whenever they needed him – and sometimes when they did not. The one thing they always needed was cigarettes and true to his nickname Kennedy happily handed them out. Apparently, he used to cram his rucksack full of Woodbines, the roughest but most powerful cigarettes available at that time, and take them out into no man's land. There he would tend the wounded, help carry them back to safety and all the while distributing cigarettes. By the time he returned to his billet, his rucksack was always empty.

It is estimated that Kennedy gave away nearly a million cigarettes during his time as an army chaplain, something that cost him around £43,000 in today's money. And that money came out of his own pocket. He never asked the army or the church for a single penny to help out in what was clearly an incredible act of philanthropy.

During his time in the trenches, Woodbine Willie was wrestling with a major matter of conscience and belief. His patriotic, warlike stance of the early days of the war had gradually changed under the influence of what he experienced at the front. To some extent that was inevitable with a thinking man like Kennedy. By 1917 he had become totally opposed to war but that left him with a serious moral dilemma. How could the God he worshipped and believed in allow such carnage to continue? It was a question he was never able to effectively answer, falling back on the old cliché that God did not want automatons but left mankind to make its own judgements.

Woodbine Willie won his Military Cross at Messines Ridge in 1917, going out to help recover wounded men from no man's land, all the while under severe shellfire. There were numerous other examples of his bravery, running the gauntlet of enemy fire to bring morphine to a seriously wounded soldier being just one.

All the while he was writing, mainly poetry, which was often produced in dialect form to reflect the accents and the speech patterns of his listeners. While the poems were later produced in book form, they were initially written to be read aloud. As an orator of world-class proportions, the spoken word was, to him, far more important than seeing his lines on the page.

He knew his limitations, however, calling what he produced rhymes rather than poetry. He was accurate enough in that statement but it did not stop his verse being incredibly effective. He often used the rhymes in his sermons to the troops, little addendums that the men listened for and chortled at whenever he dropped them into his words of Christian compassion and wisdom.

Woodbine Willie certainly knew his audience and with his innate ability to tap into the minds and motivation of the troops, he might arguably be called the most successful poet of the war. There is little doubt that more people knew about him and his verse than they did about men like Edward Thomas, Isaac Rosenberg or Siegfried Sassoon.

When his first book of verse, *Rough Rhymes of a Padre*, appeared in 1918, the first edition sold out within weeks. By 1922, it had been reprinted several times and before the year was out there was also a second book, *More Rough Rhymes of a Padre*, in print. Someone then had the ingenious idea of binding the two volumes together under the title of *The Unutterable Beauty* and within a few years his poems had sold over 400,000 copies. The combined first and second volumes was effectively a 'Collected Poems' and found a more-than-welcome home on the shelves on many ex-servicemen.

Very few, if any, volumes of poetry had ever sold in similar numbers. It could have made Studdert Kennedy a very rich man. It didn't. He gave away almost all the profits.

Thanks to the poetry books, Woodbine Willie soon became as famous around the home fires as he was at the front. Many soldiers copied down his rhymes, long before they came out in book form, and sent them home to their loved ones. They were as effective there as they were when recited in the trenches or at Sunday Service:

> *When there ain't no gal to kiss you*
> *And the postman seems to miss you*
> *And the fags have skipped an issue*
> *Carry on.*
>
> *When you've got an empty belly*
> *And the bully's rotten smelly*
> *And you're shivering like a jelly*
> *Carry on.*[2]

His verse may have been more like the ballads of Canadian outback poet Robert Service – the creator of *The Cremation of Sam McGee* and *The Shooting of Dangerous Dan McGraw* – or any of the Music Hall rhymers than that of Wilfred Own or Isaac Rosenberg. It hardly mattered to those who read and appreciated his words. The poems were straightforward and direct, in language they understood and knew. Woodbine Willie would never have claimed to be a great poet but his poems certainly hit the mark. They were a crucial part in sustaining morale both at home and abroad.

Throughout the war and in the immediate post-war period, Kennedy's verses were read and listened to, laughed at and cried over. They were undoubtedly people's poetry of the highest order – and that remains something very different from the more erudite but less approachable offerings of Owen, Graves and the other renowned war poets. If there has to be a comparison, it can only be to the inimitable Siegfried Sassoon.

*

In the winter of 1916, rather than be returned to a front-line regiment, Woodbine Willie was given a somewhat different appointment. As part of the newly created National Mission for Repentance and Hope he became preacher at large with the main aim of improving morale in the base camps. It was necessary work but it was no longer working directly in the trenches. He was not happy with the change but accepted it as God's will and approached his new task with his usual enthusiasm and skill.

Over his first ten-day period in the job, he preached three times every day to groups of between 500 and 1,500 men. Every time Kennedy gave it everything he had. It was not just a routine hour of preaching but a full-on performance that held his audience transfixed. It was inevitable that his health would suffer. He had always been afflicted by asthma and now the disease came back with a vengeance and laid him low. He spent a number of weeks in hospital before being sent to a rest camp in the South of France for an extended period of convalescence.[3] If the authorities thought that being sent to an army camp in the South of France would keep him quiet and speed up his recovery, they were gravely mistaken. The easy life was never the way for Studdert Kennedy.

By April 1917 he had visited and spoken at almost every army base in the region. The army gave up and by the summer of 1917, he was in the trenches again, this time at Ypres. He was just in time for the Third Battle of Ypres, Passchendaele as it is better known. What Kennedy experienced at Passchendaele finally erased any remaining vestiges that this was a 'just war'. In its own way the battle was as bloody and as brutal as the five-month offensive on the Somme only the year before.

It began to rain on the first morning of the battle and did not stop for several months. The drainage systems of the Flanders fields were soon destroyed by the constant shelling with the result that the land was inundated and men from both sides floundered and sometimes drowned in a sea of mud. It was arguably the deadliest battle of the war. Woodbine Willie spent his time comforting the dying, bandaging wounds and carrying in the wounded. He was never still, never out of the firing line. As ever he continued to offer words of comfort and to dole out his famous cigarettes.

He received ten days' leave that summer, heading home and seizing the opportunity to baptise his new son at St Paul's in Worcester. It was inevitable that he would find the time to stand up and preach several sermons.

Back in France another new job beckoned. He had hoped to be returned to a fighting unit but he was now detailed to work in the infantry training camps, of which there were now many in the areas behind the front. It was a logical, important move but it was not to Kennedy's liking. He was given a horse to help him get around. It was a luxury that Woodbine Willie appreciated and yet deprecated at the same time. There is no record of his ability as a horseman and he never really spoke about it. The task he had been given was considerably more important than his own comfort or discomfort. He never changed his opinion that his was a soft job, one which he disliked intensely. He kept pestering his superiors to allow him back into the front lines. That, he knew, was where the real work was waiting. Time after time his requests were refused.

It was not just him working alone in the training camps. He was part of a team with several others, including the renowned boxer, former world champion Jim Driscoll. This was too good a chance to miss and, on several occasions, Kennedy actually sparred with Driscoll or even wrestled with one of the two professional wrestlers who accompanied him in what he termed as his 'travelling circus troop'. The soldiers loved every minute of what was really an artistic show.

In March 1918 his continual requests to get back to the action were finally successful. He returned to the front, this time just as Germany's last desperate offensive of the war was launched. He remained there, throughout the German assault and the Allied counter-offensive until the Armistice was signed in November.

Later, after the war, Robert Graves and several other writers – bitter and disenchanted by what they perceived as a 'sell out' by those in authority – were critical of the work of many of the Anglican clergymen employed by the army. They were too superior and distant, Graves felt, unable to relate to the men. Not Woodbine Willie, however, or Philip 'Tubby' Clayton, founder of the Toc H movement. Both men were a different breed altogether. And Graves, like so many of the men Kennedy had helped, knew it only too well. In all 172 chaplains were killed during the war, eighty-eight of them being Anglicans. Out of those who survived, Woodbine Willie was easily the best known.

*

Studdert Kennedy stayed on in France for a short period after the war ended. While there were still men to care for, prisoners of war to rehabilitate and damaged soldiers – emotionally and physically – to repatriate, he knew that it was his duty to stay with the army. His superior officers had no complaints and would have kept using him for as long as they could. His commission, however, was only short term and he was finally demobbed and returned home in March 1919.

After the excitement of life in the trenches Kennedy soon discovered that he desperately needed a new challenge and this came in the shape of the Industrial Christian Fellowship for whom he became a travelling speaker and preacher. He left his parish in 1921, although he and his family remained in the Worcester area. His leaving St Paul's was an occasion much lamented by his congregation who had welcomed him back with relief at the end of the war.

Preaching to huge crowds, many of whom he had encountered during the recent war, now became his staple work – and, of course, he did it perfectly. He had lost none of his eloquence or skill as a public speaker. If anything, he had only got better.

He also found time to write a number of books of prose with eye- and ear-catching titles such as *Lies, Food for the Fed-up* and *Democracy and the Dog Collar.* Their contents may not have been as amusing as the titles suggest or, for that matter, as his verses and rhymes, but they were certainly thought provoking.

He was highly critical of the Treaty of Versailles which formally ended the war. To punish Germany too heavily, he declared, was nothing more than an invitation to start the conflict again. Of course, the great statesmen ignored him and twenty years later Woodbine Willie was proved correct.

By the early 1920s Kennedy had become a firm socialist although he refused to join the Labour Party. To him all men were equal, the sons of nobility and the offspring of the local greengrocer alike. They were all the same in the sight of God and he was not sure how his views would fit with those of Britain's new socialist political party.

Geoffrey Studdert Kennedy died on 8 March 1929, one of the many victims of the various flu pandemics that hit Britain in the post-war years. He died in Liverpool while on his way to a speaking engagement. He was just 45 years old. Intending to stay at one of the local vicarages, he was clearly ill when he arrived and was confined to bed. The fact that he allowed himself to be ordered to bed should have told everyone that his condition was serious. His wife was summoned to his bedside but Kennedy was unconscious when she arrived. He lapsed into a coma from which he never emerged and died within a few hours.

King George sent a telegram of condolence to his wife and family and, at the funeral service ex-servicemen – many of whom were now out of work, thanks to the Great Depression – clubbed together to send an enormous wreath with a packet of Woodbine cigarettes at the centre. His death was front-page news, greeted with genuine sorrow by the soldiers he had tried so hard to help. Over 1,700 mourners filed past his coffin as his body lay at rest in a Liverpool church, many of them having made the journey from many miles away.

Woodbine Willie was a remarkable man who, arguably, worked himself to death, not for his own benefit but for the glory of his God and for the men who were battling to survive the Western Front. Selfless and unassuming but with a mischievous wit, he developed a real affection for the soldiers with whom he spent his days. It was an emotion that stayed with him long after the war was over and he was back in Britain. It was also an emotion that was reciprocated by almost everyone he ever met. You would have to look long and hard to find an ill word spoken about Woodbine Willie.

He was not patronizing, as so many Anglican chaplains were during the war, and became more and more convinced that the working man should have a say in the running of the country. It was an in-built and deeply held conviction that the British system of government, based on the rule of the few and the acceptance of the majority, had to change.

Generous almost to the point of madness, his compassion knew no bounds. Once his wife came home to find him dismantling their bed so that he could give it to a woman of his parish who had told him she had no bed to sleep on. Such stories were common where Woodbine Willie was concerned.

Perhaps not a great poet but certainly a memorable one, he had a knack of catching the moment and making a clear, concise statement which would have taken many others whole volumes to express:

> *I can hear the steady tramping of a thousand, thousand feet,*
> *Making music in the city and the crowded village street,*
> *I can see a million mothers with their hands outstretched to greet,*
> *For the Army's marching home.*[4]

But, above all, it was his courage that marked Geoffrey Studdert Kennedy down as different. He rarely considered his own safety and thereby created a reputation that went far beyond the battlefields of France and Belgium. Always in the trenches with the men, handing out compassion and cigarettes, Woodbine Willie was one of that rare type of men – a selfless human being on a mission. To the soldiers and to their families at home Woodbine Willie was someone very special indeed.

PART IV

Keep Smiling Through

'You may find temptations both in wine and women. You must entirely resist both.'

Kitchener, 1914

Chapter 8

Art for the People

By 1914 Queen Victoria had been dead for a dozen or so years yet Britain was still, in the main, a traditional Victorian society. The old hymn with its telling lines 'the rich man in his castle, the poor man at his gate' more than adequately summed up the general attitude of the populace. Know your place was a common aphorism: stay in line and whatever else you might do make sure you never rock the boat. Put simply, the masses did as they were told; the elite of the country guided and directed them in the right direction. That was how it had always been and in the eyes of many that was also how it was always going to be.

In fact, that was decidedly not the case. The future remained unknown but inevitably the situation would alter and, when the time came, it would alter markedly. Indeed, that alteration had already begun, albeit slowly and almost unnoticed by many. It would take the cataclysmic events of what was, then, rightly known as the Great War for the full effects of those changes to be felt. In 1914, however, there were more important matters at hand – like putting the Kaiser in his place!

In the early stages of the war, despite growing industrial unrest which manifested itself in events like the South Wales Miners' Strike of 1910 and the National Railway Strike which almost brought the country to a halt two years later, the general impression was that the upper classes still knew best! With almost two-thirds of the wealth of the country resting in the hands of less than one hundredth of the population – *plus ça change* – it is relatively easy to see how such emotions and such a situation continued to exist.

Charles Masterman and the men of Wellington House were, in the main, traditionalists. Their view of the masses, the ordinary working-class men and women of Britain, was that they had not been given or granted the benefits of a liberal education; they were still like little children who needed guidance and a firm hand.

It was patronizing, it was hierarchical but it was not necessarily a totally inaccurate point of view. In keeping with that attitude, propaganda was something that would be imposed on the people because those in power knew best. When it came to the matter of measuring the effect that visual art had on the senses and imaginations of the working classes, that attitude was something which was particularly noticeable.

The war artists were doing a valuable job. But by 1916, after the one-dimensional sketches of Muirhead Bone and Francis Dodd had been replaced by more complex offerings, what the artists were producing had become increasingly abstract and experimental. It was a development that mirrored the changes in avant-garde art taking place on the Continent but it was largely alien to the majority of British people.

Cut off and isolated by the English Channel most Britishers were intent on retaining their traditional attitudes and values. A plate of jellied eels, a pint of best bitter and paintings or sketches that looked real, that was what the men and women of Britain wanted, wasn't it? That was what Masterman believed and by the middle years of the war, it seemed he was not far wrong.

Impressionism, cubism, post-impressionism and the various forms or styles, call them what you will, had little real impact on the workers of Britain. The people of the working classes, toiling in the armaments factories or ploughing the land, simply did not have the time, the motivation or the education to look deeply at a picture and fathom out what the artist was trying to say.

Direct representation, Wellington House believed, manifesting itself in art that was as much like the subject as it was possible to make it, that was what the people wanted. The proof of their belief lay in the phenomenal success of Louis Raemaekers' cartoons and appreciation of the work of men like the early war artist Muirhead Bone.

It was equally as significant, perhaps more so, that working-class people did not have the money to buy works of art from professional painters like Paul Nash or William Orpen – even if they did manage to summon up the inclination. They could look at the paintings in galleries but it was not the same thing as ownership. For that they turned to the humble postcard.

Postcards had 'arrived' in Britain somewhere around 1894, not necessarily as collectible items but as an early form of social networking. With six or seven postal deliveries a day, more in London and other big cities, it was possible to write a card in the morning, a short request to a friend or relative and have it delivered and maybe even answered the same day.

Brevity was the essential element; there was no room for anything else on a postcard that had a picture or drawing taking up all of one side, and the address of the recipient on the other. There was perhaps a half-inch-wide strip below the image for a very brief message or signature.

Postcards were a cheap method of communication. Cards cost just a few pennies each, postage a ha'penny. In the days before widespread use of the telephone there was no better way of keeping in touch with distant friends and family – or close ones too, come to that.

Picture postcards were also attractive, particularly the ones that featured subjects drawn by talented, well-known artists. All sorts of topics were represented on the cards, everything from pictures of battleships and Music Hall stars to views of the Scottish Highlands and famous works of art. It was inevitable that, rather than throw them away, people began to collect them as mementoes and as beautiful or desirable objects in their own right.

As printing techniques improved so the collecting habit developed. By 1902 when the divided back was introduced on postcards, allowing more room for messages, a card-collecting mania erupted across Europe. Every home had its postcard album, even members of Britain's royal family actively filing away their collections for posterity.

In 1910 Britain's Postmaster-General declared that in the previous eight years, over six billion postcards had been sent through the post. This could be interpreted as showing, statistically at least, that every person in Britain had sent approximately 200 postcards during that period.

What the collecting mania really meant was that every person in the country could, if he or she desired, build up a personal art collection. Keep them in a shoe box or mount them in an album, stick them to a mirror or rest them on the mantelpiece, the aim was to collect and show off the result. The postcard companies quickly realized they had hit on a bonanza. Everyone wanted postcards.

It was ready money for artists and many soon began to specialize in producing work for the postcards. Painters like Louis Wain – the Cat Man as he was known – Aubrey Beardsley, Raphael Kirchner and even Marc Chagall were soon drawing for the great postcard companies like Tuck and Valentine.

It was an interesting phenomenon. No working man could ever dream of owning an original Kirchner painting but he could for just a few pennies purchase a card showing one of the famous Kirchner beauties. Within a few years Kirchner had painted a thousand different postcard images of his women – most of them based on or inspired by his wife. Kirchner, like Alphonse Mucha, strode the line between respectability and soft pornography. His pictures were tantalizing but not so explicit as to upset either the delicacies of the women receiving the cards back home in London or Paris or the morals of the army censors.

If Kirchner wasn't on the sleazy or squalid side of art appreciation, a wide range of pornographic art and photography was always available to men who needed it, invariably found behind the lines and in the side streets in the embarkation ports of France. Many men bought these cards. They were never intended for family members but, if the soldiers survived, were stored in drawers and other out-of-the-way places, to be taken out at rare and highly personal moments. If they were killed or wounded, then mates would make sure the images were destroyed or passed on to another man in the same unit.

Pornography remained something of a niche market and did not feature in any of Masterman's plans. 'Below the counter' it may have been but for many of the young recruits, away from home for the first time, such images were their introduction to the hidden world of sex.

*

Early on in the game Charles Masterman realized that if his Propaganda Bureau did not take advantage of this collecting mania, it would be missing a trick. And that was something Masterman was never going to allow. Patriotic postcards had been used effectively during the Boer War, images of departing troops and lyrics of popular songs like *Goodbye Dolly Grey* being used to whip up enthusiasm for the distant conflict. But never before were they employed by the government or in such an intense and deliberate fashion as Masterman now put into action.

So, how to make best use of the card-collecting craze? It was not really a dilemma or a problem for Wellington House. Masterman had, from the onset, a pretty fair idea of what he would do and how he was going to do it. It was going to be a structured approach. His first step was to ensure that the postcard publishers had the materials they needed to produce good-quality cards. These included enough thin but strong card on which to print. Seemingly a minor issue, this was in fact crucial – too thin and the cards would tear, too thick and they would become unwieldy. To become collectors' items, they would have to look and feel just right.

Then there was access to quality images. Without these no one would buy the cards, no one would dream of collecting them, and so Masterman had to ensure that there was no hindrance to the postcard companies accessing modern images. It was all about the look, the artistic element of the drawings being as important as the photographic images on the official war cards.

Unlike those 'official' photographic cards, the subject matter did not have to be about the war. Many were, of course, but romance and sentimentality – hugely important to homesick soldiers – were part of the subliminal message they wanted to be sent to loved ones. I will be back soon, wait for me, that was the single most important message ever sent by the troops on the Western Front.

Publishers in England, Belgium and France published cards so that wives and girlfriends back home would regularly receive a wide range of new items. They could look forward to the cards arriving and add them one by one to their collections. The message was simple – keep your mind on the cards, not on the death and destruction on the battlefields of Europe.

Masterman's second step was to get the Propaganda Bureau and later the Ministry of Information to print and publish cards themselves. It would augment the official photographic views of the war that had been appearing since 1915, giving a somewhat gentler and more subtle view of what was occurring in France, in the Middle East and at sea.

Artists like William Orpen found that some of his less-surreal drawings were in great demand. One in particular, his pen and ink drawing of German prisoners standing at a roadside somewhere in France was a perfect example of what Charles Masterman was looking for. The drawing showed German soldiers already defeated, looking downcast and exhausted as they waited to be marched off into captivity, and that could only be good for British morale.

Humorous depictions which attempted to dehumanize the enemy were also very popular. So, drawings of the Kaiser shown as the sharp nose of a Zeppelin or up to his neck in snow, complaining of 'cold feet', were soon filling the sales racks of newsagent shops. Anything which would depict the Kaiser and the German people as foolish and already as good as beaten was fair game to the men from Wellington House. Such cards were a classic example of what became known as negative propaganda, as opposed to the positive style which tried to support the war effort by showing scenes such as soldiers and their waiting wives, home fires burning brightly and children dressed in martial uniforms ready to take up arms in defence of the country.

As the war went on, a third strand in Masterman's policy became obvious. The British government, through Wellington House, began to produce postcards that were totally blank. Their purpose was to allow soldiers to express themselves and draw on the cards. In this they were mirroring the German practice of using soldier's sketches on the otherwise blank field postcards which were available to all military personnel.

Such drawings were not meant to be sold and, as a result, depictions of cramped quarters, bored soldiers and unhealthy living conditions were fairly common. Certainly, they were a great deal more honest and accurate than many of the mass-produced cards available from the postcard publishers. Because most of them were never posted but crammed into the soldier's haversack or wedged into a tunic pocket until they got home, a large number of sketches managed to avoid the gaze of the battalion censors. Painting or drawing pictures on blank postcards had been popular long before the war. It was how Adolf Hitler had managed to keep himself alive in the back streets of Vienna and Munich in the decade before 1914. Hitler would sketch famous or traditional views and then sell them to tourists. Very few of the purchasers knew the identity of the artist they were buying from – he was then totally unknown, of course – with the result that only very few of Hitler's drawings now exist.

That was before war broke out. The self-drawn cards of the First World War were different, mainly because they were intended for personal enjoyment and satisfaction, not sale. Even so the basic premise was the same: here are the materials, now use them to get rid of your anger and your fear – pour out your emotions onto the card. It was therapy of the most basic sort.

It was also an interesting development. Soldiers – other ranks at least – were forbidden to keep diaries but here the government was actively encouraging them to express themselves in a visual and fairly dramatic style. A drawing might be more immediate than a few pages of writing but it could be just as critical, just as cutting in its viewpoint.

The one thing soldiers rarely ever produced were scenes of battle. During combat they were usually too busy trying to survive but afterwards, out at rest, they would sometimes sketch what they had recently experienced. These offerings were usually fairly bland and non-committal. As recollections such scenes were useful but as most of these drawings finished up in the hands of family members, the men in the trenches did not want to paint too realistic a picture for their loved ones. Quite apart from the fact that they had no one to analyse or interpret what had been drawn, the restrictions meant, of course, that their therapeutic value was minimized.

The quality of the drawings, obviously, varied according to each man's skill but that was often part of their appeal. Crude, almost primitive depictions of the soldier's life had an immediacy that struck straight at the heart, in much the same way as Lowry's later depictions of working-class life in northern England tapped into a subconscious memory of childhood.

Occasionally these drawings were sold by soldiers home on leave, even though such practices were strictly forbidden. A couple of shillings or a glass of beer in the local pub was enough to ensure the cards changed hands, particularly if the artist was skilled at his craft. However, very few ever found their way onto the desks of the professional postcard producers who might then reproduce them to be sold en masse. Most were just added to postcard collections.

As ever, cards that depicted the Kaiser as a buffoon were very popular. Privately produced Christmas, New Year and Easter cards were also immensely popular. It was a simple enough process – take a blank card, draw something that relates to the season and send it off in the post. The end result, like the efforts of young schoolchildren, were far better and more fully appreciated than the mass-produced variety.

At Christmas men who were holed up in prisoner of war camps were conscious of being deprived of contact with their families for yet another year. Many of the British and French prisoners had been held in incarceration since the first German assaults of 1914 which made their loneliness and home sickness more than understandable. Prisoners of war were allowed to post home a certain number of communications each month. It was undoubtedly a humane practice that was not replicated in the second great war of the twentieth century. They were also able to receive letters and cards, provided they were not overtly political or militaristic. Taking advantage of this, enterprising artists in the camps in Germany began to producing seasonal offerings to send back to Britain. If nothing else it helped to pass the time.

It can be argued that these cards were effectively mass produced, albeit it on a small scale, within each prison camp. Perhaps a hundred or so would be drawn and published each time, often showing characters and events that had a special significance for the POWs. They provided families back home with an immense fillip when they dropped through the door in the weeks leading up to Christmas or New Year's Day. If anything was guaranteed to boost morale on the home front it was that.

Prior to 1914 many of the more attractive postcards had been produced in Germany where the *Gruss Aus* cards (translated as 'Greetings From' – fill in the blanks for yourself!) were particularly popular. But the war obviously put a stop to that particular supply. The German producers had always specialized in artist-drawn cards, beautiful little works of art that had collectors clamouring for more. Their absence was lamented by everyone.

The gap was filled by the now-famous British postcard companies and by the government itself. The craze for collecting postcards continued and made a great impact on Masterman's strategy to boost public morale.

In its own way the publication of these cards, either directly or by the discreet encouragement of postcard companies, was an effective a propaganda tool. It was certainly as effective as the famous poster campaign of 1914–15.

Far more subliminal in their appeal than photographic cards produced by Wellington House and by Northcliffe's *Daily Mail*, these artist-drawn cards offered some small relief from the horrors of trench warfare, regardless of their topic or subject. They provided a sentimental look back to how things had been before the war – and, significantly, how they would be again, as long as everyone did his or her bit to defeat the enemy.

The postcards, along with the work of the war artists, made a significant contribution to the war effort. They were immediate and satisfying for all recipients – after all, who doesn't like to receive cards in the mail? Receive them, keep them, and build up a collection as part of the return to normality that would soon reappear – that was the message.

*

By the mid-1918, however, things had begun to change. The war had been raging for nearly four years, thousands had died, but now, finally, the conflict had reached new dimensions. The war in the Middle East had been concluded, in Europe the Germans were retreating and it was clear to everyone that the High Seas Fleet was never again going to venture out of its home ports. Germany was tottering on the edge of defeat.

The aims of the new and now-thriving Ministry of Information had gone far beyond the simple task of keeping up public morale. People were tired of the war but now they could at least see the end approaching. They would see things through to the finish; that was something that became almost a given fact in propaganda circles.

The coming of Lord Beaverbrook saw the closure Wellington House as a base and the relocation of its staff into a cramped and totally unsuitable London Hotel. After three years in the comparative luxury of Wellington House the men of the Propaganda Bureau were not best pleased.

More importantly, Beaverbrook was insightful enough to realize that with the end of the war not far away a change of direction was needed. Morale-boosting, which had been the most significant part of the work of Wellington House, was no longer a major issue. The war was as good as won. It stood to reason that all it needed was one more push and then it would all be over. The army, as Woodbine Willie later said, would soon be 'marching home', much to the relief of the families who were waiting.

There was almost a fatalistic approach to the people on the home front. They had endured so long, there was now no need to keep watering the crop! It was hardly the most caring of attitudes but Beaverbrook, like his fellow newspaper man Lord Northcliffe, was a businessman with clear visions of what was required of him.

For the soldiers, success on the battlefield and the defeat of Kaiser Wilhelm's much-vaunted armies was morale boosting enough. Britain's 'Contemptible Little Army' had won the day! It was an understandable emotion, one that left Masterman's artists and the amateur sketchers with a somewhat different objective for the final few months of the conflict. The war was almost over and a bright future was beckoning. And yet, what the soldiers had experienced was not something that could be just forgotten or, consigned to memory. It had to be marked or remembered in some way – that was clear to everyone.

Lord Beaverbrook was nothing if not a first-class pragmatist. He did not want to end the production of war pictures, he simply wanted to change the focus: 'Pictures were no longer considered primarily as a contribution to propaganda; they were now to be thought of chiefly as a record.'[1]

By the autumn of 1918 Britain had fought, and as good as won, the costliest war in history. A record of British achievement, showing the success of British and Colonial force of arms was now felt to be essential. It was a complete turnaround but with the war virtually finished – even though men from both sides continued to fight and die for several more months – Beaverbrook obviously felt that morale could look after itself. Clearly, winning the peace was now far more important.

*

There were a number of other artistic elements that became important in keeping morale high. By and large they were independent of Wellington House and either grew or continued their previous existence out of a public need for continuity. Security in what you know! Perhaps because of this, one art form in particular is often overlooked when attempting any form of analysis of British propaganda. What we now refer to as 'classical music' was, in its own way, as important as the Music Hall tunes that beguiled the front-line troops. It was certainly as important as the postcard views of famous artists so avidly collected by the people at home. It may have been a minority interest, at least as far as numbers were concerned, but it was still an art form that was hugely appreciated by certain sections of society.

Classical concerts were held throughout the war, although the popularity of such events did decrease as the conflict went on. In the face of mounting casualties, the patriotic pieces that had dominated the various programmes in 1914 and 1915 gradually died away so that music like Sir Edward Elgar's *Carillon*, written to support Belgian resistance, were replaced *The Spirit of England* which he wrote and produced between 1915 and 1917.

There was something of a resurgence of interest in classical music towards the end of the war when it assumed a central role in the collective mourning of the country. John Foulds's *World Requiem*, hindered because it needed over 1,000 performers to produce, was one such piece but Holst's *Planets* was perhaps the most popular. *Mars, the Bringer of War*, provided exactly the sense of horror that a traumatized British public desired.

One piece of Elgar's that did maintain its popularity was his revised version of *Land of Hope and Glory*, originally written in 1902, which quickly became a patriotic anthem for all times. In 1916 Sir Hubert Parry set William Blakes's poem *Jerusalem* to music and it has remained a firm favourite with concert-going audiences ever since.

Just as many of the great war poems did not see the light of day until after 1918, much of the music composed by classical writers remained closeted for the war years. Despite an appeal in *The Musical Times*, asking for a composer to write 'the piece of the war', very little was actually made public before the 1920s. Ralph Vaughan Williams's superb *Lark Ascending*, although written in 1914 before he enlisted, was not actually performed until 1921.

The war was an undoubted influence but, unlike poetry which could be scribbled into a notebook, resting on the knee, it was difficult to write music in dugouts and crowded billets. Composers undoubtedly wrote 'in their heads' but, in general, those musicians in the trenches were more than busy just trying to survive.

The concerts that were held in London and other cities tended to rely on old favourites such as Tchaikovsky's *1812 Overture* and Haydn's *Music in Time of War*. The problem was not uncovering music to play but finding musicians who were capable of performing it. By 1915, a large number of composers and musicians had enlisted in the army. More were to follow once conscription was introduced. Some composers, men like Frederick Septimus Kelly and George Butterworth, earmarked as the coming voice of classical music, did not return. Butterworth, like Ralph Vaughan Williams, was a dedicated follower and collector of British folk songs and there was little opportunity for that in the trenches of the Western Front.

Frederick Kelly was one of the few composers able to write while at the front. He produced his *Elegy for String Orchestra 'In Memorium Rupert Brooke'* while sitting in his tent. He had helped to bury Brooke on Skyros in 1915 and was himself later killed on the Somme.

The Gloucester poet and composer Ivor Gurney was another who managed to compose whilst fighting, although he certainly produced more poetry than music during the war years. Some of Gurney's most enduring music was, however, written in the trenches. *By a Bierside* was perhaps the most moving of all. It was recorded on mud-splattered paper while he was sheltering in a mortar emplacement.

Ralph Vaughan Williams was over 40 when he decided it was time for him to enlist. He became a stretcher bearer for the Army Medical Corps, a role where he was continually in danger without any means to defend himself. His musical interests continued throughout his military service, playing the organ in the garrison church and even forming a choir within his unit. Eventually, after a period serving in Salonika, where many of the Welsh regiments like the Cardiff Pals were fighting, Williams was given a commission in the Royal Artillery. Apparently, the roar of the guns permanently damaged his hearing. After retraining he was brought back to France and, finally, was made Director of Music for Haig's First Army.

Ralph Vaughan Williams was probably a far-from-perfect soldier. He had visions of collecting the various soldiers' songs but decided that no publisher would ever publish them! He was not deliberately anti-authority but had little time for mindless orders. While in Salonika he once wrote to his wife: 'From somewhere near the Doiran battlefront, R. VW sent a letter to his first wife Adeline, on which he wrote a musical note in the Dorian scale as a clue to his whereabouts. The censor let it pass.'[2]

One style of music that became exceedingly popular during the war and received regular performances in bars and clubs was jazz. Based on New Orleans ragtime, its first significant proponent was Tom Brown who by 1915 was performing in Chicago with his 'Jas Band'. Jelly Roll Morton quickly became the leading light and helped set the tone for the immense surge of interest in ragtime in the post-war world.

Soldiers' bands were also hugely popular. Initially, bandsmen doubled as stretcher bearers until in 1916 the number of casualties among their ranks caused the high command to rethink. The popularity of the soldiers' bands and their significant role in maintaining morale meant that bandsmen were withdrawn from the front and kept back purely for entertaining the troops.

Theatre troupes were also used, albeit sporadically, to entertain the soldiers. Famous among these were The Balmorals who performed satirical shows for troops out of the line. One of their most renowned sketches showed a German soldier staring down into the wrong end of a British trench periscope, attempting to use it as a mirror to help him shave. It made the soldiers laugh but it was also mocking the intellect of the enemy – propaganda yet again!

With over 800 actors enlisted in the army by the end of 1914 it was inevitable that some of them would be used in entertaining their comrades. The Gaieties was a company of entertainers made up from professional and amateur actors who had enlisted and was just one of several such units that roamed the Western Front performing.

Despite this, entertaining the troops was hardly a considered activity. Indeed, it was almost a secondary consideration, something that happened in spite of the powers-that-be rather than because of them. Even so, the success of the various concert parties and theatre troupes, limited as it might be, and the effectiveness of people like Woodbine Willie, laid the groundwork for a more specific approach during the Second World War when ENSA – Entertainments National Service Association – and other relief organizations would provide much-needed comfort: one of the great tragedies of the First World War was that so little thought was given to taking advantage of such entertainment opportunities. The troops were there, the entertainers were there, it was just that the spirit – or imagination – to do more than play at creating an entertainment service did not yet exist.

Chapter 9

Old Bill

Undoubtedly, the most famous artist/humourist of the First World War was Bruce Bairnsfather, creator of the much-loved cartoon character Old Bill. He was also a primary element in maintaining the morale of people at home and in the trenches. Old Bill was a classic caricature, the vastly experienced old sweat with his walrus moustache, his ever-present balaclava and a battered pipe stuck in the corner of his mouth. Anyone who ever served on the Western Front would have seen men like Old Bill every day.

The true identity of Bill, the man behind the character, has often been debated but he was never just one individual. Rather, he was a composite character, almost a direct lift from the cross-section of men Bairnsfather encountered in his army career, both during his original training with the Royal Warwicks and then later in the trenches of Flanders and France. The soldiers recognized the image but more importantly they identified with the laconic, graveyard wit that Bairnsfather caught so perfectly, both in his drawings and in his caustic bylines that were really titles to each cartoon.

The quality of the drawings, combined with the humour, made Old Bill acceptable to all. He was the epitome of the pre-1914 British regular soldier, a far cry indeed from the happy volunteers who answered Kitchener's call. But even these idealistic young men could see bits of their comrades, even elements of themselves, in the character and took him to their hearts.

Old Bill's first appearance was in 1915. For the rest of the war and in the interwar years he continued to entrance the public – on postcards, in newspapers, in magazines like the famous *Bystander* and on the cinema screen. Even during the Second World War drawings of this long-serving old sweat filled the media and captivated the public in much the same way as Raemaekers' work had done in the previous war.

Until he began drawing cartoons on the Western Front, Bairnsfather's career had been one of great hopes followed by seemingly incessant failures. Thereafter, thanks to Old Bill and his mates in the trenches and shell holes of the Western Front, Bairnsfather's creative life was a litany of unmitigated successes.

*

Charles Bruce Bairnsfather was born on 9 July 1887 in Murree, India (now Pakistan) where his father Thomas was an officer in the Indian Staff Corps. His mother Janie, as she was known in the family, was a more than competent painter, particularly of birds and nature in general.

Related, albeit distantly, to nobility, the young Bruce Bairnsfather spent his first few years in comparative luxury in India. There he was doted on by his two caring and compassionate parents before, in 1898, being sent back to England to be educated and groomed for Empire at the United Services College, Westward Ho!

It was standard practice for the children of the Empire to be dispatched home in this fashion. Most children, unfortunates like Rudyard Kipling, went home at the age of 6. It was a cruel, heartless system but Bairnsfather was lucky, as his mother kept hold of him for two extra years and so it was not until he was 8 that the grief of parting from his parents actually hit him.

Already he was in love with drawing, to the detriment of almost all other subjects. So great was his love of art that he was able to use it almost as a therapeutic tool to keep away the pain of being separated from his family. Bairnsfather was a high-spirited boy who was often in trouble at school and, as was customary at the time, repeatedly caned by masters and prefects alike. But, as with Kipling, his illustrious predecessor at the United Services College, he was determined to endure the harsh regime of Westward Ho! He made a few lasting friendships but found his main solace in his art.

Academically, Bruce Bairnsfather was an undoubted 'no show'. It was not that he didn't have ability; he was just disinterested. He spent much of his time when he was supposed to be studying maths, geography and other necessary evils simply carving holes in his desk and firing pen nibs into the classroom ceiling where they hung like swords of Damocles.

When Thomas Bairnsfather retired and returned to England, he and his wife determined to be as close to Bruce as was possible. They, like him, had hated the separation and wanted to enjoy what little was left of their son's childhood.

The young Bairnsfather had declared an interest in joining the army but his lack of achievement at school was a drawback. In an effort to bring him up to scratch, his parents duly enrolled him at Trinity College near Stratford-upon-Avon. It was what was known as a crammer, the sole purpose of which was to push sufficient facts into its pupils to enable them to pass examinations – in Bruce's case the entrance examination for Sandhurst and Woolwich.

Thomas and Janie Bairnsfather rented a house close to Stratford-upon-Avon and Bruce became a weekly boarder at the school, which meant that he could enjoy those precious weekends at home where he could devote himself to drawing and indulging in his other interests such as amateur dramatics and music. On Saturdays and Sundays and during holidays he learned to play the banjo, using the next-door neighbour as his teacher.

The atmosphere at Trinity College was considerably more relaxed than Westward Ho! Even so Bruce remained far more interested in sketching and enjoying visits to the theatre than he ever did in studying for his Sandhurst exams. When he learned of an evening art class at Stratford Technical College, he persuaded his father to let him enrol. He quickly became something of a star pupil in the art class: 'Bruce's determination to pass the Army entrance examination gradually faded before his burgeoning artistic talent ... Bruce, who was now known as the school's resident cartoonist, also began to sell his drawings to fellow students.'[1]

For a few shillings here and there was how Bruce Bairnsfather's first sales were made. Attempts to sell drawings to advertising agencies were met, however, with repeated rejections. These were the first in a series of failures but he did not give up and eventually found success when he made his first professional sale, an advertising design for Players cigarette and pipe tobacco. It was a seminal moment but soon the spectre of disaster was hovering again.

Failure in the Sandhurst examination was inevitable. The only subject where he did well was art where, as might be expected, he achieved virtually full marks. The rest was an unmitigated disaster. It was time to put Plan B into operation. Another, although less desirable way of obtaining an army commission was to sit a much simpler exam and then undergo an eighteen-month period of basic training with a reserve unit before obtaining officer status. This time, aged 18, Bruce managed to dispense with the spectre of failure and in 1905 passed the exam and began his period of military training.

*

The majority of the soldiers Bruce Bairnsfather encountered during his brief stint as a 'trainee' with the 3rd Militia Battalion of the Royal Warwicks were old sweats who had done their time and had survived with a jaundiced but philosophical view of the army and all its many quirks. He spent some months with these old-timers, drilling, practising bayonet and rifle exercises and sleeping under canvas in the icy cold of a Warwickshire winter.

Finally, he was transferred to the Cheshire Regiment with the rank of second lieutenant. It was his father's old unit but initial pride was soon replaced by boredom and the realization that he had made the wrong career choice. Only the music halls of nearby Birmingham offered any solace. After the regiment relocated to Aldershot, which he considered one of the last outposts of civilization where not even the consolation of the music halls was available to him, he knew he had had enough.

In 1907, Bruce Bairnsfather resigned his commission. After just two, admittedly unpleasant years it was another failure on his record and while his father sympathized with his decision, he must have wondered when, if ever, Bruce was going to settle down to a career. Bruce obliged him by enrolling in the John Hassall School of Art at Earl's Court in London.

He enjoyed the college, working hard to improve his artistic skills. But it was a lonely life, stuck in his bare rented room, the only relief coming when he managed to find the money to visit one of the many music halls of the city.

Owner and principal of the art school John Hassall had made a name for himself designing posters and, perhaps inevitably, this was a genre to which Bruce also turned his hand. The result was more failure, rejection after rejection dropping through his letterbox onto the mat. Finally, he came to realize that things could not continue like this. His only support was from his father who himself was trying to survive on his small army pension and, at the same time, funding his wayward son.

Bruce Bairnsfather might have been serving his artistic apprenticeship, he might even have even deluded himself about his talent but he was not selfish. He knew that he had to find a job and so he became an apprentice at the firm of Spencer's in Stratford, an electrical firm specializing in lighting for private premises.[2]

In his spare time, he continued to paint and draw. Now, finally, when the need was not so desperate, he began to achieve some degree of success, albeit on a small scale. He was soon selling the occasional advertisement to companies like Beecham's Pills and Keane's Mustard. His biggest success came when, for Lipton's the tea distributors, he drew a golfer on top of a packet of their tea. His accompanying joke or byline – always an important part of any sketch he produced – made an enormous impact, playing on the two meanings of tea and tee.

Failure was never far away, however. At one stage he applied for a job, the position advertised in the national newspapers simply as 'Artist Wanted'. It seemed perfect for him but after a wait of many weeks, he received the reply that the firm was 'disappointed' in his work and would not be offering him a job, however nebulous the initial advert might have been. The failure threw Bruce into a fit of depression where he wallowed for some time, convinced that his drawings were poor and that he had no hope of success in the arts.

After time spent as a wireman and then lighting engineer for Spencer's he became something of a commercial traveller, specializing in selling to the gentry. He travelled all over the country and in early 1914 he was even sent on a trip to repair electrical equipment in far-off Newfoundland. The trip was fine apart from the fact that he quickly discovered he was an abominably bad sailor and was seasick the whole way across the Atlantic. It was an affliction that never left him.

He returned home just in time for the outbreak of the First World War, straight into what seemed to be yet another failure. With the advent of war, Spencer's lost a great deal of business and, as a consequence, made him redundant. It was a shock to the young man who had been revelling in his overseas success but his sudden release from the shackles of employment was not entirely unwelcome.

His reaction to being laid off was to visit the headquarters of his old regiment and offer his services. He was already a trained soldier which meant that he was eagerly accepted and within a few days he was back in uniform. Before the year was out, Bairnsfather, at the head of the regiment's machine-gun unit, was in France. And there he discovered the benefits of things like soldiers' songs in keeping up the spirit of the troops. He was later to describe one particular route march, commenting on the wide selection of songs his soldiers knew:

> As I marched along at the rear of the Battalion, at the head of the machine gun section, I selected items from their repertoire and had them sung 'by request'. I had some outstandingly fine mouth-organists in my section. We had 'In the trail of the lonesome pine' sung by half the section with mouth organist accompaniment from the other half; the effect was enormous.[3]

Bairnsfather never forgot the effect of music on his men. Similarly, his own artistic abilities were soon to encourage and fascinate the troops, not just in his battalion but all over France. To begin with, however, he was interested simply in doing his duty and keeping away the dreaded phantom of failure that had seemingly blighted his whole life.

By all accounts he was a good soldier, a caring officer who did his best to look after the interests of his men. It was a new experience for him. Like so many others he was appalled by the mud and filth of the trenches but was fascinated by the robust humour of the working-class warriors under his command. Their ability to laugh in the face of adversity made him feel quite ashamed o his own misery and despair when the inevitable failures came around.

*

The story of how Old Bill and the series of sketches known as *Fragments from France* came about is reasonably well known. It is, however, worth repeating. After spending Christmas 1914 at the front, where he took part in the unofficial Christmas Day Truce, Bruce Bairnsfather and his unit were positioned in front of Nieppe, not far from the famous Plugstreet Wood.

The trenches in that particular region were very wet and he spent several nights sleeping in pools of water. Finally, he and some fellow officers found better accommodation in a half-destroyed cottage in the village of St Yvon, 200 yards behind their particular stretch of trenches.

It was, by his own admission, a troglodyte existence. Bairnsfather and his comrades remained silent and hidden during the day but crept back to the trenches for duty each night. Keeping out of sight of German snipers was crucial and Bruce began filling the empty hours by drawing cartoons of his men at work. He drew his pictures on scraps of paper and then nailed them to the wall, as much to keep them out of the way as anything else. Each drawing was complete with what he called a joke.

To his utter amazement Bairnsfather found that the drawings were soon being 'collared' – his expression – by the men under his command: 'These were the first 'Fragments' and I pinned them up in our cracked shell of a room … I [later] came across them, by then muddy and battered, in various dugouts nearby.'[4]

In an attempt to personalize the cottage accommodation, he then began drawing on the walls. After all, paper was hard to come by and the drawings soon disappeared when spotted by the men. Finding the right materials to draw with was difficult as neither charcoal nor chalk would make any sort of permanent mark on the wall. In the end he used a bottle of Indian ink provided by his batman. The markings took and the legend of Old Bill was born.

When he came across a battered copy of *The Bystander,* a satirical magazine enjoyed by the troops, Bairnsfather transferred one of his drawings entitled *Where Did That One Go?* onto paper and sent it off for consideration. He then forgot about it and returned to the business of soldiering.

A few weeks later, during the fighting around Neuve Chapelle, he received a letter from an unrecognized source. To his surprise it was from *The Bystander*, accepting the cartoon and, just a little later, publishing it. *Where Did That One Go* thus became the first official Old Bill cartoon.

In April 1915, Bairnsfather and his regiment were pitched into what became known as the Second Battle of Ypres when poisonous gas was used by the Germans for the first time on the Western Front. It was a terrifying new development but, in the end, it was a more traditional weapon that 'did for' Bruce Bairnsfather.

At the height of the battle he was seriously wounded, tossed high into the air by an exploding shell before being slammed back into the earth. His hearing was seriously damaged, he was disorientated and soon afterwards was, perhaps inevitably, diagnosed with shellshock. He was promptly hospitalized and then invalided home. Hospitalized again, this time in London, his second drawing – *They've Evidently Seen Me* – was published by *The Bystander* on 21 April. Lying in bed, mind working furiously, he began to think of more cartoons he could draw. His mother brought in materials for him and he drew to his heart's content. At that stage, it was purely therapeutic but then an unexpected visit from a representative of *The Bystander* changed things forever.

The magazine had been inundated with letters about the two published cartoons. It had even received offers to buy the originals. There and then the representative asked Bruce if he would consider drawing a weekly cartoon for the magazine. They would pay him £4 an issue.

After that his recovery was swift and he was soon sent home to recuperate. There he settled down to draw for *The Bystander*. Cartoons – he never referred to them as cartoons, calling them his sketches or drawings – featuring Old Bill and his more naïve pals Alf and Bert were soon appearing in the magazine on a weekly basis.

In December 1915 *The Bystander* used his soon-famous view of Bill and Alf sheltering in a shell hole in no man's land. With Alf grumbling about the state of the hole, Bill's response became a phrase known by every soldier on the Western Front: 'Well if you knows of a better 'ole, go to it.'

The reaction of the public was immediate. They loved it, soldiers and civilians alike, and the Christmas issue of the magazine sold out overnight. The 'better 'ole' comment soon became an accepted response to anyone expressing discontent or unhappiness. Eager to exploit their new discovery, at the beginning of 1916 *The Bystander* put together a collection of forty Old Bill sketches as a booklet under the title *Fragments from France*. Reprinted nine times, *Fragments from France* sold over a quarter of a million copies. Thanks to a photograph published in *The Bystander*, Bairnsfather was now something of a public figure, recognized wherever he went.

He had been returned to duty long before his booklet came out, engaged in what was called 'light duties' on the Isle of Wight before being posted to Salisbury Plain with responsibility for training machine-gun officers and men for his division.

Over the next few months Bruce Bairnsfather spent most of his spare time drawing Old Bill in various dangerous situations. They were situations which, of course, Bill treated with his usual degree of forbearance and the expected wry comment. The soldiers, both at the front and on home service, were increasingly enthralled by the cartoons.

Bairnsfather had a wide range of experience to draw on, his months in the trenches showing him the absurdity and the dangers of war. Anything and everything, whatever he happened across, was fuel for his imagination. He was clear about what gave him the impetus to draw: 'I never went about looking for ideas for drawings; the whole business of war seemed to come before me in a series of pictures.'[5]

A second collection of *Fragments* – forty different views – was soon published, followed by postcards retailing at sixpence for six cards. Bairnsfather's weekly fee had been increased to £20 but in return *The Bystander* retained sole rights over the publication and syndication of his drawings. It meant that reproductions of Old Bill on china jugs, on teapots and as posters brought considerable profit to the magazine but nothing to Bruce Bairnsfather (today what's known as 'merch' or merchandise).

He, of course, was still a serving soldier and it was inevitable that the war would, sooner or later, catch up with him. In late 1916 he was promoted to captain and returned to France, this time to a staff appointment. He was now officially nominated as Officer Cartoonist in the Intelligence Department and was ordered to liaise with and draw cartoons for Britain's allies. It was a task he took to with relish, enjoying the French approach to life and the war. Whether or not this was a War Department move, it is tempting to delve deeper and uncover the hand of Charles Masterman here in this latest exploitation of Bairnsfather's unique talent.

Between 1916 and the end of the war Old Bill, became something of a cult – and not just in the pages of *The Bystander*. Bruce contributed a short humorous play about Bill and his mates Alf and Bert to the revue *Flying Colours* which ran for some time in the West End. He even made a gramophone recording of the sketch. Then he worked with Ivor Novello on the show *See, Saw* and in 1916 even wrote his own book, *Bullets and Billets*. It was a first-hand account of the war as he saw it, illustrated with a number of his Old Bill cartoons.

The families of soldiers bought the book in their thousands, thoroughly enjoying Bairnsfather's light touch with prose. Critically, it was well received but only in some quarters – in others the book met with strong objections. The comment that he was a better artist than he was a writer was one that rankled. The jury, as they say, remains out on that particular judgement.

It is easy to see the positive effect on Britain's 'brutal and licentious soldiery' of Bruce Bairnsfather's cartoons. Each issue of *The Bystander* was eagerly anticipated and then passed from hand to hand – not only in the trenches but also back home in England. Old Bill was hugely popular with men in training and with the families of the fighting men. As with the criticism of Bairnsfather's book, however, it was not a case of universal approval. In some sections of the army his drawings were regarded as vulgar caricatures. Old Bill was not the sort of character the high command viewed as a representative of the army. He was scruffy, jaundiced and curmudgeonly in his opinions and exactly the type of old soldier that generals and staff officers hated on sight.

However, the success of the cartoons with the troops overrode any criticisms that were levelled at Bairnsfather. Old Bill became an essential part of Britain's war effort, symbolizing the stoicism and the inbred gallantry of the British Tommy. As far as Masterman and the other propaganda chiefs at Wellington House were concerned, Bruce Bairnsfather was an important element in their fight to raise and sustain morale. They were not about to sacrifice his popularity on the altar of snobbish posturing and phoney attitudes.

Forget his political incorrectness, not that the term was known back then; it was what the character could provide that was important. Old Bill was popular with the people, he made them laugh and forget their worries for a moment. Old Bill's popularity was not just a flash in the pan. It continued long after the war ended. In the 1930s and 1940s he was portrayed many times on film and on stage and, it has been argued, the popularity of the walrus-style moustache with the British police even led to the nickname Old Bill being given to Britain's fourth official paramilitary force.

During the first few years after the war Bairnsfather continued to write, diversifying into films and directing the 1928 Canadian talkie, *Carry on Sergeant*. He was even involved with early television broadcasts from Alexandra Palace. And, of course, he continued to draw.

During the Second World War Bruce Bairnsfather was the official cartoonist for the American forces in Europe and contributed to US magazines such as *Yank* and *Stars and Stripes*. He was even rumoured to have provided some of the famous 'nose art' on American bombers, although no one seems certain about the exact extent of his involvement.

He died of cancer at Worcester on 29 September 1959, his obituary in *The Times* of 30 September perfectly catching the character of the man and his place in British society: '[He was] fortunate in possessing a talent which suited almost to the point of genius one particular moment and one particular set of circumstances.'[6] That moment was the First World War and the set of circumstances was the raising of morale among the troops and their families back home. For both, Bruce Bairnsfather was certainly the man of the moment.

Chapter 10

A Canadian Genius

Rivalling Bruce Bairnsfather for popularity, particularly among the families waiting at home for the return of their loved ones, was Canadian artist Fergus Mackain. Mackain is now something of a forgotten figure but for the second half of the war he was a postcard artist of considerable influence, a man whose importance as a provider of morale-boosting images cannot be ignored.

Mackain's work had an altogether softer and less dramatic appeal than Bairnsfather's. His colouring was more pastel with often the hint of hope in the images. However, in many respects, his drawings were far more realistic than Bairnsfather's and any of the other artists who attempted to catch the mood of the trenches in their work. If Bairnsfather's characters were caricatures – in the way that Dickens's famous Pickwick, Jingle and Micawber were grotesque representations of real people – Mackain's were more identifiable with the British public. The soldiers depicted on the cards could have been a brother or a husband, a friend or a lover. They were real. Many, in particular people around the fireside at home, found that they could relate to the new recruits of Mackain far easier than they could to Old Bill. They could laugh at Bill's antics, smile at his asides, but they would feel anguish, affection, even love when they stared at one of Fergus Mackain's works of art. The reason for his popularity among the families of serving soldiers can be traced almost directly to the location of his publishers.

Many, if not most of Mackain's postcards were produced by the firm of P. Gaultier of Boulogne-sur-Mer. The thriving seaside town was a major cross-Channel port for the transportation of British troops, either returning to 'Blighty' on a short spell of leave or coming the other way. Good marketing at the quayside and in the town shops ensured that the departing or arriving Tommies would buy complete sets of the Mackain postcards and either post them or take them home to their families. Such cards would never be written on but were preserved, pristine and virginal, in the soldiers' homes.

Another reason for the success of the cards was the accuracy of Mackain's illustrations and the almost light-hearted approach he took to difficult situations. There was no undue brutality and no broken bodies on his cards but there were delicately coloured and beautifully drawn images depicting things with which the soldiers could relate – the delight of the daily rum ration, the sheer slog of carrying supplies up to the lines at night, puttees that persisted in coming undone, dropping a newly cleaned rifle into the mud and so on.

Mackain did not hide the horrors of war. Several of his drawings showed the blasted terrain around the trenches but invariably the centre of attention in each drawing was the soldier. And that was a figure with which most men could relate. All of the usual bugbears of a soldier's life were shown, from screaming sergeant-majors to endless drilling in the rain. Good or bad, the cards showed the experiences that men at the front endured but did so in a way that would engage rather than repulse or upset whoever was looking at the image.

More than anything it was the sympathy of the artist for the Tommy that came through. And that was how it should have been because, after all, Mackain was one of them. He was a serving private in the British Army.

*

Fergus Herbert Elgin Mackain was born on 28 March 1886 in the Canadian province of New Brunswick. Despite his Scottish name, his father, also called Fergus, had his roots in England but had moved the family to Canada some years before Fergus was born. Canada was fine but Mackain Snr had a large family to support, seven children in all, and in an effort to seek a better life, in the early 1890s he relocated to the USA.

The Mackain family spent time in several different US states. Little is known about what they did or how they earned a living. Apart from, that is, the most memorable member of the family, the young Fergus. By 1910, the year he was married, he was residing in New York City where he worked as an advertising illustrator and artist. He lodged at 86 West 14th Street but according to the 1910 Federal Census of New York, his wife does not seem to be listed as living at the same address, even though by that time they had been married for a month.[1]

When war broke out, Mackain decided that rather than sit in comfort and safety in the USA, he wanted to contribute to the war effort. He could not deny his English heritage – nor did he want to. It was time to help. Consequently, in 1915 he worked his passage to 'the old country' on a horse transport vessel and, after a period of calling on various extended family members, enlisted in the British Army. He gave his address as the home of one of his relatives. On his enlistment documentation his next of kin in England is shown as the Reverend W. J. Mackain. In November 1915, he was enrolled as a private in the 23rd Battalion, Royal Fusiliers, known as the Sportsman's Battalion.

By early summer 1916, Mackain was in France preparing, like the rest of the army, for the Big Push. His battalion fought at Delville Wood, one of the many actions that made up the Somme offensive. The battle around the wood lasted from 14 July until early September and was a bloody, hard-fought affair.

At some stage, although the exact date is unclear, Mackain was wounded and either because of this or due to a subsequent illness, he was transferred to the Army Service Corps.[2] Out of the trenches Mackain began to think again about his art. Drawing and sketching had been shelved and forgotten about in the chaos of enlistment, training and trying to survive, but now the urge to draw began to emerge once more.

Like other soldiers he had seen the postcards available to buy from shops and vendor stalls and decided that he could do just as well. In fact, he could do better. He began drawing the images that were soon to become famous and loved throughout the army. The difference between Fergus Mackain and other 'doodlers' was that he had already worked as a professional artist and had a clear eye for a business opportunity. That did not make him particularly mercenary but even Bruce Bairnsfather looked to make money out of his skill. The workman is always worthy of his hire, as they say. Not only that, as a serving soldier he could relate to the difficulties and problems all Tommies faced and that gave his drawings an edge of reality. It was an edge that so many other cards of the time lacked. The series of postcards that he now produced were to become known as *Sketches of Tommy's Life*.

Delicately coloured and immediately appealing to the eye, there were four different series, each of which perfectly captured the important elements of a soldier's life. These were In Training, At the Base, Up the Line and Out on Rest. The two earlier series, In Training and At the Base, were published by the firm Gaultier of Boulogne, the second series coming from another company known as Savigny which was based in Paris. The reason for the change of publisher is not known but the Gaultier cards were printed on high-quality card, the Savigny ones on a lighter and more flimsy material.

After 15 September 1916 British postcard producers were forced to submit their product to the Press Bureau for examination and possible censorship. This was a reaction to the debacle of the Somme battle but as Mackain's cards were published in France, they escaped this particular obstacle. There is no record or reasoning about how and why Mackain chose a French publisher. It remains one of those unanswerable questions – did he approach the publishers or did they come to him?

The horrors of trench life might have been eased over or ignored in Mackain's drawings but he was well able to use irony and even satire in his productions:

> Up the Line card No. 9, for example, has two Tommies in separate shell holes as bullets and shells whistle overhead. Between them in the open lies a tin of jam. The caption reads, 'When you are in one hole and your pal is in another. He had the jam and at dinner time tried to chuck it to you but missed fire. And the machine guns are not likely to miss fire if you get out just now!'[3]

The line could have come directly from Bruce Bairnsfather. Every soldier could relate to the dilemma of men in shell holes, a dilemma which tapped on the two basic elements of life in the trenches – food and safety.

The style and subject matter of Mackain's cards made them perfect for collecting by non-combatants and soldiers alike. Everyone could laugh at the antics of the soldier – invariably the same hapless individual each time – and not worry too much about the reality of the situation which the real man and his comrades were facing every day at the front. In effect, what the Mackain drawings offered was a form of escapism, momentary as it might be, for men and women who worried and wondered every day the war continued.

The central character on each of the cards was a figure that was probably based on Mackain himself. Standing over six feet tall with fair hair and blue eyes, he would have made a perfect artist's model. Unlike Bairnsfather's Old Bill, this character was young and fresh faced, just the type of man now serving in Kitchener's New Army.

Fergus Mackain went on to draw and produce other cards although they do not seem to have been produced in quite the same quantities as the *Sketches of Tommy's Life* series. A number of greeting cards – celebrating Christmas, summer and the like – were published towards the end of the war. One of them showed British soldiers painting 'Merry Xmas' onto a shell while another centred on a German infantryman about to be struck by a hand grenade: 'I feel that I am a nice present to get soon,' he declares. Yet another card shows a Tommy with his head projecting out of his dugout. 'We had our tea out in the garden today,' he says as he drinks from his billy can, 'just as we used to do at home.' The caption at the top of the card reads simply 'Your Health'.

Mackain also drew a number of cards during 1917 and 1918 showing an American soldier, a Sammy as the newly arrived Yanks were called, experiencing life in France, meeting French soldiers and women. How many of these 'Sammy cards' were published is not known but as they were aimed at the American soldiers, it is highly likely that a large number of them were quickly sent back across the Atlantic.

It is also possible that he illustrated a French phrasebook for the newly arrived American troops during the final year of the war. The drawings, unlike his postcard views, were unsigned but they were clearly in the Mackain style. And there is an advert for his *Sketches of Tommy's Life* series of cards on the back cover.

None of Mackain's later work was ever as popular as *Sketches of Tommy's Life*. With that series of postcards, he seemed to have tapped into a rich vein of humour and sentiment, ideal for the essential purpose of maintaining morale, both in the trenches and at home.

Mackain's work was never commissioned by Wellington House and he never obtained official standing like Bruce Bairnsfather as an army cartoonist. But until the end of the war, he retained not just his popularity but also a certain standing as one of the troops, albeit one with a specific and much-valued talent.

*

It took some time for Mackain to be allowed out of the army once war ended, presumably because of his work in the Service Corps. There might be no longer any need for infantry but men who controlled supplies and equipment would always be needed, in France, in Britain and in an impoverished Germany.

Fergus Mackain finally returned to America in 1920, sailing from Liverpool on the curiously named *Kaiserin Augusta Victoria* – probably a German liner appropriated by the Allies after the war – and arriving in New York on 9 September. Presumably his wife was waiting for him, although nothing is known about his personal life at this time. After demobilization he resumed his career as a freelance artist and illustrator. Unfortunately, once again, little is known about his activities over the next few years.

Soon after his return to America, a children's book entitled *Buzzy: The Story of a Little Friend of Mine*, written and illustrated by a certain F. E. Mackain was published by a Philadelphia publishing company.

The name and initials on the title page fit but there is no further biographical information about the author/illustrator and whether or not it was the same man remains unclear. It would be nice to think that after years of death and destruction, Fergus Mackain had been able to turn his hand to a more passive subject. We will never know. Fergus Mackain remained a man of mystery until the very end.

That end was not long in coming. In 1923, he was diagnosed with pulmonary tuberculosis, probably a result of his war service but, inevitably, it proved fatal. He died at the Oteen Veterans Hospital in North Carolina on 3 July 1924 and was buried at Riverside cemetery.

By his skill as an artist and illustrator Fergus Mackain provided an invaluable record of life in the trenches. It was a different view from the reality of the photographic images offered by the *Daily Mail* and other official sources but it remains, nonetheless, equally as valid and equally as effective.

As far as morale was concerned Mackain's drawings did more than any of the more shocking photographic images of the conflict. And for that he deserves to be remembered.

Chapter 11

A Touch of Satire

The First World War is not a conflict you normally associate with satire. There are many reasons for this, not least because the events of the war were too violent, too depressing and too close at hand for many of those involved to do little more than endure them.

Where there was humour, as with Mackain's *Sketches of Tommy's Life*, it was a case of laughing at what was going on rather than taking an ironic glance at the causes of the situation. Asking readers to dig deep into their subconscious to see what was really being said was an intellectual exercise that was beyond many – or so thought most of the publishers of the time.

Those who did possess the intellect to examine hidden meanings behind words and images, the publishers felt, were usually too ingrained and established within the system to take real notice – in other words, the privileged classes. Most of the country's publishers were men of the establishment and to allow too much questioning of the status quo might, when all was said and done, lead to some hideous outpouring of anger like the two Russian revolutions of 1917.

All of this was in total contrast to the Second World War where satire and irony were more commonplace, so much so that the humour of that second great war of the twentieth century, bitter and bleak as it was, led directly to an explosion of 'underground' comedy that was equally as bleak and bitter. The link to radio and TV programmes like *The Goon Show*, *That Was the Week that Was* and the satirical nihilism of the 1950s and 1960s is not difficult to trace.

As an aside worth considering, there was much to be satirical about. Churchill, Hitler, military blunders, bleak postings to the back of beyond – they were all grist to the satirist's mill during the Second World War. When Lady Astor accused the Eighth Army of malingering in order to avoid the D-Day landings, her comments were met with, among other things, the song *D-Day Dodgers*. That hugely effective soldiers' song not only accused Lady Astor of having a somewhat oversized mouth but offered listeners a distinctly ironic view of what the politician was clearly missing in her view of the Italian campaign:

Look around the mountains in the mud and rain,
You'll find the scattered crosses, some that have no name,
Heartbreak and toil and suffering gone –
The boys beneath them slumber on.
They are the D-Day Dodgers who stay in Italy.[1]

Apart from the later poems of Siegfried Sassoon there is nothing from the First World War quite so evocative and yet so simple as that song; intended to be sung to the tune of *Lili Marlene*, it was a seminal piece of satirical writing.

To return to 1914–18, there *was* satire of a sort at work during what was originally called the Great War. You have to look for it but it was there. After all, what was that label 'The Great War' if it was not a satirical dig at those in power? *Great* War, indeed!

Arguably Bairnsfather and Mackain came close but both were far better at showing life on the Western Front in picture form than in words. And that limited the amount of satirical content they were able to get into their cartoons.

John Hassall, the artist and former tutor to Bruce Bairnsfather, managed to produce a modern version of the Bayeux Tapestry, a thirty-six-panel folding cartoon showing German soldiers engaged in barbarous deeds at the beginning of the war: Prussians tearing up peace treaties, Belgian cities on fire, troops shelling hospitals, Hassall's drawings had them all. He even portrayed Germans inventing poisonous gas by eating vast quantities of sauerkraut and Lemberger cheese. It was an idea that Charlie Chaplin took a stage further in his 1918 film *Shoulder Arms* when the little tramp and his mates could not stand the smell of a cheese they had been sent from America and hurled it at the German lines! Hassall's effort was a one-off success, however. For real First World War satire you have to look at the pages of *The Wipers Times*.

The story of how the most significant of all the trench newspapers came into existence is fascinating. The name of the journal came from the British soldiers' pronunciation of Ypres. They never could get their tongues around it and gave the city a wide variety of titles. Wipers was the one that stuck.

There were twenty-three issues of *The Wipers Times* during its three-year existence. It was irregularly printed because of various battles and offensives but, even so, the publication has been described as the most perfect trench magazine of the war. It began life as something of a trial issue, a single-page news sheet with a print run of just 100 copies, published on 6 February 1916. After that the magazine increased its size to twelve pages per issue.

Members of the 12th Battalion Sherwood Foresters had come across an abandoned printing press in a bombed-out house on the Ypres Salient. One of the men, a sergeant, had been a printer in civilian life and reckoned he could get the press working again.

The magazine was the brainchild of Captain Frederick Roberts with Lieutenant John Heskith Pearson as his sub-editor. The title of the paper changed several times as Roberts' and Pearson's pioneer unit was posted from one location to another along the front. Sometimes it was known as *The BEF Times*, sometimes *The Somme Times* and the final edition even went into print as the *Xmas, Peace and Final Number*. It finished production at approximately the same time as the war ended, there being no need of such a journal after 1918. Sometimes a single issue had two or even three titles. Volumes and issue numbers also replicated themselves. It hardly mattered; always known by the troops as *The Wipers Times*, the journal was loved by everyone who picked up a copy.

From the beginning the magazine/newspaper was intended as a satirical look at life in the trenches. It was not meant to be taken seriously but by poking fun, some gentle, some more challenging, at what the soldiers were enduring, it was able to bring home the reality of the situation and help people cope with the horrors of twentieth-century warfare.

Interestingly, while the paper contained considerable criticism of the way the war was being conducted, there was never any 'finger pointing' either at or, in return, from the high command. Field Marshal Haig, in particular, seems to have escaped condemnation, something that continued after the war when many of his colleagues were heavily criticized. Despite his lack of thought, his continual and sole tactic of hurling men at the enemy lines, you would have to look long and hard to find criticism from soldiers who served under Haig. War profiteers who never ventured far from home, on the other hand, were fair game.

Mock advertisements were a staple part of *The Wipers Times*. For example, in each issue of the magazine The Wizz Bang, Menin Gate and Dead Cow cinemas offered adverts and reviews for several different films, notably one called simply *Inferno*, complete with a cast of 50,000 extras.

Then there were the for-sale adverts. The Complete Ypres Salient Front Line, a *Flammenwerfer* (a German flamethrower), a building site known as No Man's Land and even brothels like The Plug Street and The Poplar Tree all came up for purchase or rent at one time or another, at least according to *The Wipers Times*. Personal column adverts included appeals for wire cutters, offering good openings for 'sharp young men'.

The pages offering the Ypres Salient Estate for sale, Issue No. 4, 21 March 1916, were particularly notable. According to the advert the shooting on the estate was perfect and the fishing very good. Applications were to be made to Messrs Thomas Atkins, Sapper & Co. of Zillebeke & Hooge.

'Things We Want to Know' was always a popular column, although the questions were so obtuse as to defy any form of answer. No one expected an answer anyway.

The regular column attributed to Mr Teech Bomas (a lampoon on the name of William Beach Thomas, an arrogant and self-important journalist from the *Daily Mail*) was invariably a model of purple prose. 'How could Anyone fear anything in the belly of a perambulating peripatetic progolodymythorus?' the editors once had him declare about an imagined journey in the belly of one of the new giant tanks. The man himself could not have done better.[2]

The notable engraver E. J. Couzens provided a striking image of a rather 'chinless' senior commander standing bemused and clutching his officer's cane, wondering, 'Am I as offensive as I might be?' The engraving was so popular with readers that it became the motif for the paper.

Articles in the style of writers like Hilaire Belloc (Belary Helloc as his pieces were bylined) as well as genuine contributions from a then unknown – but a future celebrated writer – Sapper Gilbert Frankau were standard fare. Long-running diary entries by a certain Lt Samuel Pepys and stories about the detective Hermlock Shomes were augmented by a great deal of ironic poetry, most of it submitted by readers but some emanating from the agile minds of the editors:

> *The world wasn't made in a day*
> *And Eve didn't ride on a bus*
> *But most of the world's in a sandbag,*
> *The rest of it's plastered on us.*[3]

Anything subversive was fair game for Roberts and Pearson, both believing in the cathartic nature of humour. They felt that to be able to laugh in the face of adversity, when assailed by terrible stress and tension, was nothing short of a gift.

The main theme was 'dark humour,' the darker and more sardonic the better. As all the articles were published anonymously there was no fear of reprisal and, remarkably, *The Wipers Times* had precious few run-ins with the censor. Death was never far away from the pens of the editors but it was something to be laughed at, not feared:

> *There was a young gal of the Somme*
> *Who sat on a Number Five bomb.*
> *She thought 'twas a dud 'un*
> *But it went off sudden –*
> *Her exit she made with aplomb.*[4]

The magazine was immensely popular with the troops but very few copies ever found their way back to Britain. The reason was simply their popularity in the trenches. It was, after all, a trench newspaper, aimed at the soldiers and was full of trench humour, which would have had little or no meaning back home. And of course, each copy changed hands so many times that it is doubtful there were any copies in a fit enough state to send back to Britain. Mud, water and the general filth of the trenches would have made each copy virtually unreadable after twenty-four hours.

Even so a facsimile reprint of the various issues was put together in 1918 and sold to the British public. Another complete facsimile edition came out in 1930 and then again in 1988. The early facsimile editions were aimed at old, retired Tommies who eagerly snatched up the copies they remembered so well. The later editions have now become museum pieces.

Copies and print runs of the original magazine were small, due mainly to the lack of paper, with the result that each copy of *The Wipers Times* was repeatedly and eagerly passed from hand to hand in dugouts and on firing steps.

Eventually, muddy, stained and torn, the copies would have fallen apart, have been consigned to the trench floor or used to stuff up cracks in windows and floorboards. Or possibly for more basic needs. Then it was a case of simply waiting for the next issue.

The Wipers Times was an attempt to help Tommies cope with the challenges of a new style of warfare, something they had never expected to encounter. It was a combination of *Punch* and the later *Private Eye* or, as the Navy and Army Museum called it 'A cross between a parish magazine, a school magazine and the illustrated magazines of the day'.[5]

Its main purpose was to make people laugh, to laugh at their own misfortunes and to laugh at the foolishness of the situation in which they found themselves. There is no doubt that in that particular aim the two editors succeeded admirably.

*

The Wipers Times was not alone. There were dozens, possibly hundreds, of other attempts to create and distribute trench or unit magazines. Some lasted only a short time, others a somewhat longer stretch.

The Waitemata Wobbler was created on a troopship carrying New Zealand soldiers to France while *Aussie* was an Australian trench magazine devoted to jokes, poems and, like *The Wipers Times*, to spoof adverts. Even the German Army, not normally noted for its humour, managed to produce a journal entitled *Simplicissimus*. The Royal Naval Division produced its own magazine, *The Mudhook*, which had its origins in *Dardanelles Dug-Out Gossip,* written and published by members of the division fighting on the beaches at Gallipoli. Rupert Brooke of the Naval Division never made it to the Gallipoli beaches but his skill with comic verse does make you wonder what he might have contributed had he lived.

There were so many trench magazines like *The Bird* and *The Balkan News*. Not to be left out, the Royal Air Force, which only came into existence in April 1918, published *Clickety Clack* soon after the RFC and the Royal Naval Air Service were amalgamated into the RAF.

Humour was an essential element. The parody was a particularly effective tool; parodies, unlike the originals, could be resonant with satire and irony. *The Fifth Glo'ster Magazine* of February 1917 included a take-off of W. B. Yeats's poem *The Lake Isle of Innisfree*, a parody which began with the lines:

> *I will arise and go now to Picardy*
> *And a new trench line hold there,*
> *of clay and shell-holes made.*[6]

Kipling, of course, was an obvious target but so, too, was anyone who the editors of the various magazines felt was standing on their dignity and taking themselves too seriously. Nursery rhymes were easy meat for the trench poets:

> *Little Jack Wrench*
> *Sat down in a trench*
> *With a 'pork and some beans' and some bread*
> *When an Allemande shell*
> *On the parapet fell*
> *So 'e got iron rations instead.*[7]

Rations were a staple of the trench journals – no pun intended – with everyone bemoaning the lack of certain essentials like strawberry jam and the inevitable presence of Maconochie's stew. As one short poem in *The Wipers Times* began, 'Maconochie, Maconochie, bully beef and biscuits.'

Satirical comment was not just the preserve of soldiers. Commercial magazines like *The Bystander* and, in particular, *Punch* also had an eye for subversive black humour. *Punch* had been founded in 1842, its editors firmly believing in the rejuvenative quality of humour. However, *Punch* first published John McCrae's *In Flanders Fields* in 1915, proving that the magazine could also be serious if the editor chose.

Occasional serious poetry in *Punch* or any of the trench magazines was one thing, but for the readers of *The Wipers Times* and the other trench papers it was the humour that kept them going. And as the war went on and there seemed to be no end to the casualties and the inane orders 'from above', the laughs became increasingly satirical and pointed: 'Is your life miserable? Are you unhappy? Do you hate your company commander? Then buy him one of our own patent tip duck boards. You get him on the end, the board does the rest.'[8] There would have been many war-weary Tommies who related to that and wished that something like a tip-up duckboard really had been available.

What made the poems, the articles and the parodies so effective was the fact that the writers had experienced the horrors of war: 'For an outsider, anyone who had not known the full horror of war, to attempt a humorous interpretation of its experience would have been a gross insult. For the men themselves, however, such humour was a lifeline, but one established on their own terms.'[9]

Put simply, you had to have been there in order to make sense of what went on in the trenches of 1914–18. Only then could you laugh at it.

*

Satire and irony were ever-present, if you cared to look for them, in almost every part of the soldier's daily existence. Having said that, it is doubtful that too many of those serving in the trenches would have realized it or acknowledged it as satire at the time.

Every trench system on the Western Front had homemade or hand-drawn signposts giving the name of each trench and pointing the way to the front line and to no man's land – not that anybody apart from raw recruits had any real need of such directions. Many of the names awarded to the trenches, names such as Piccadilly Circus, Leicester Square and Watling Street, were direct lifts from soldiers' experiences and were ironic references to the condition and situation of a particular trench. Even Charlie Chaplin in *Shoulder Arms* has soldiers sheltering in dugouts cut into the side of a long trench named Broadway. The more derelict and dangerous the trench, the grander its name. So, Hell Fire Corner and other places were named and quickly passed into legend. Irony was rife so that nowhere was safe from the ribald comment. Rat-infested dugouts might be christened Park Lane or The Palace or Home from Home, the very opposite to the way they really were. Little things, maybe, but ironic enough to raise a slight smile, no matter how many times you saw them. Others signs were considerably more sarcastic. Any unexploded shell lying at the side of the road was labelled 'Iron Rations' or something similar. Meanwhile a half-destroyed house behind the lines would very quickly have some wag painting 'Hotel for Sale' on its broken-down door. Shells waiting to be fired were chalked on by the artillery gunners 'A Present for Willie' or 'Happy Christmas, Kaiser Bill'. Crudely drawn signs that declared 'No hawkers or salesmen' were everywhere. 'No German bands' was a particularly popular message. It was all fairly basic humour but it was also a satirical response to what were decidedly unpleasant situations.

And it was not just signposting or chalked-up messages. Soldiers' language, so long affected by the experience of the Indian Army, was also undergoing a change. Much of the new slang came from contact with the French – 'We're all tres bon' and the like. Much of it was affected by the new-born love of imagery, satire and irony.

Hunting for lice in your clothes was an interesting experience. Lice were an occupational hazard for men who spent their days scrambling around in water and mud, and the regular attempt to hunt them down was soon being universally referred to as 'reading your shirt'. It was a clever comment that fitted the experience quite perfectly. Men would spend hours cleaning lice from their clothing but no matter how long they spent 'reading their shirts', the creatures, attracted by body heat, would return as soon as the clothing was put back on.

From the early days of the war anti-aircraft fire was known as Archie – by ground forces as well as RFC pilots. It acquired its name after one early aviator, whenever the German guns opened up on him, began to sing a well-known song of the time, *Archibald, Certainly Not*.

Confusion and chaos, in the ranks or at HQ, elicited a more basic response. Everything, according to the Tommies, was not confused but 'arse about face'. That undoubtedly had and still has a more than satirical quality to it.

Many soldiers turned their hands to poetry, so many that it is tempting to misquote Napoleon and declare that every soldier had a book of poetry and a pencil in his haversack. Some soldiers' poetry was published in the trench journals, some was sent home to local newspapers and magazines (more of this particular aspect of morale boosting later) and some was simply kept with the soldier's personal belongings and equipment. Surprisingly, much of this outpouring of verse was satirical.

Winston Churchill's brother John, or Jack as he was known, fought at Gallipoli where the narrow invasion beaches were each given a code number – X and Y and so on. The beaches were totally inappropriate for landing troops but still the Allied commanders insisted on deploying troops from rowing boats – yes, rowing boats, not landing craft – onto these scraps of sand. Jack Churchill was so moved by what he saw that he decided to put pen to paper:

> *Y Beach, the Scottish Borderer cried*
> *While panting up the steep hillside,*
> *Y Beach!*
> *To call that thing a beach is stiff*
> *It's nothing but a bloody cliff.*
> *Why Beach?*[10]

Woodbine Willie, the Anglican clergyman who served as an army chaplain, was equally as direct in his views of the war. Never one to pull his punches, he was adamant that war and all the horror which came with it, was an abomination that had to be condemned. In the final few lines of his poem *Waste* he took a more ironic stance, even questioning God and his role in the slaughter. It was a viewpoint that would have appalled many of the more traditionalist clergy and churchgoers but, from a satirical point of view, it was a statement that made people stop and think. It was all the more powerful because Woodbine Willie had been enormously supportive of the war in its early stages:

> *Waste of Blood and waste of Tears,*
> *Waste of Youth's most precious years,*
> *Waste of way the Saints have trod,*
> *Waste of Glory, waste of God –*
> *War!*[11]

Satire, someone once declared, is the lowest form of wit. In fact, it is quite the opposite. Satire requires intelligence and the ability to see beyond what is immediately apparent. It is the ability to look beneath whatever superficial meaning there might be, to get to the metaphorical level and not take everything at face value. Letting your audience know that you, like them, can see profound absurdity in the trials and tribulations you both face is only the start. While seeming to accept it at face value, the ability to use language and visual art to incite thought and even condemnation, is a hugely difficult thing to achieve. The poets and humorists of the First World War were not there yet but they were well on the way.

*

One other aspect of the war is well known but is rarely associated with satire. It is, of course, the soldiers' songs, pieces of music and humour that were warbled incessantly when troops were on the march or lying in their dugouts. Thanks to theatre productions like Joan Littlewood's *Oh! What a Lovely War* and Richard Attenborough's film adaptation of the same, we are now well versed with the songs, perhaps almost as familiar with them as the soldiers themselves.

Most of the soldiers' songs took popular pieces of music, hymns in particular, and simply added their own lyrics. These efforts, pieces like *When This Bleedin' War is Over* from *What a Friend We Have in Jesus*, or *John Wesley Had a Little Dog*, sung to the tune of *O God, Our Help in Ages Past*, were acceptable outbursts of anger that provided a few moments of amusement. Yet they were hardly satirical, more banana-skin laughs than any cerebral taxing of the brain:

> *John Wesley had a little dog,*
> *He was so very thin.*
> *We took him to the gates of Hell*
> *And threw the bastard in!*[12]

For satirical troop songs you have to look at what were probably, to us at least, the less familiar examples. They might be less well known now but they were hugely popular with the troops and they did not rely on hymns to make their point. Songs like *Two German Officers Crossed the Rhine* and *I Don't Want to Join the Army* were regularly sung in the estaminets behind the lines when the decidedly risqué words gave an added appeal to those rare off-duty moments.

The satire and irony might have been a little heavy-handed but there was no mistaking the target in songs like *I Wore a Tunic*. The stay-at-home civilians, men who had not risked everything by joining up, increasingly became figures of hatred for those in the trenches as the war went on. Back in Blighty such people were safe in their 'cushy billets', often making fortunes for themselves through work or investments, or even dabbling in the black-market economy. It was something which not only angered the troops but caused great bitterness that took years to dissipate:

> *I wore a tunic, a dirty khaki tunic,*
> *And you wore your civvie clothes.*
> *We fought and bled at Loos*
> *While you were on the booze,*
> *The booze that no one here knows,*
> *You with the wenches*
> *While we were in the trenches*
> *Facing an angry foe.*
> *Oh, you were a-slacking*
> *While we were attacking*
> *The Germans on the Menin Road.*[13]

There were many more examples of songs like these. Some, such as *I Want to Go Home*, were perilously close to the mark but were tolerated by the officers because they felt exactly the same. Everyone wanted to go where 'The Allemand can't get at me', but equally everyone knew there was a job to be done first. Bravery might not be expected of everyone but the solid, easily demonstrated job of doing one's duty certainly was.

Officers and NCOs accepted the fact that they were often the target for satirical humour from the troops under their command. It had been that way for many years and so they did not react when the soldiers sang songs like this example which was performed to the tune of the ever-popular *My Bonnie Lies Over the Ocean*:

> *Last night as I lay on my pillow,*
> *Last night as I lay on my bed,*
> *I dreamed our old Sergeant was dying,*
> *I dreamed that the old sod was dead.*
> *Send him, oh send him,*
> *Oh, send our old Sergeant to Hell – to Hell.*
> *Oh, keep him, oh keep him,*
> *Oh, keep the old bastard in Hell.*[14]

Perhaps one of the most satirical songs of the trenches was sung to the tune of the sickly sentimental *My Little Grey Home in the West*. The contrast between the words of the original, which made even the most sentimental of the New Army men blanche, and the soldiers' more bitterly decisive invention is what makes the front-line version so powerful. It is all there, the filth and the mud, the terrible conditions, the potential for disease or death, all expressed in a few taut words, so powerful and emotive and about as far removed from the sentimentality of the original as you could get:

> *In our little wet home in the trench*
> *That the rain storms continually drench,*
> *There's a dead cow near-by with its hooves in the sky*
> *And it gives off a terrible stench.*[15]

Humour was clearly the main element in these songs, but there was also pathos. That emotion needed to be closely monitored by the powers-that-be. In war-battered, mud-encrusted trenches those powers-that-be were usually the trench officers and the NCOs who watched carefully to see that things did not boil over into any kind of anti-war sentiment.

Even here the satire of the soldiers is apparent, the strong sense of men laughing at themselves coming through in pieces like *They Wouldn't Believe Me*:

> *And when they ask us,*
> *And they're certainly going to ask us*
> *The reasons why we didn't win the Croix de Guerre,*
> *Oh, we'll never tell them, no we'll never tell them*
> *There was a Front – but damned if we knew where.*[16]

Laughing at the officers, laughing at the NCOs, it is easy to see the roots of a powerful stream of sarcasm, and eventually satire, in songs like this. It would take time to develop, time that many of the soldiers simply did not have. However, in the interwar period, in the six years of conflict against Hitler and in the post-war austerity of the 1950s, the use of sarcasm and satire grew into one of the most significant forces ever seen in popular culture. And it began in the First World War.

PART V

Using What We've Got

*'Growing up in an age of security, we showed a yearning for
danger, for the experience of the extraordinary.'*
Ernest Jungen, *Storm of Steel*

Chapter 12

Heroes, Villains and Victims

All wars throw up heroes, an inevitable result of pitching man against man in deadly combat. However, the First World War was probably the first time that such individuals were picked out and set on pedestals as morale-boosters – not in retrospect but while the war was still raging.

Wellington House, realizing that fate had given them an exceptional opportunity to secure men of bravery and dedication, were quick to react. The country needed heroes and they would provide them. They had a lot to choose from.

Huge casualty figures from the first few days of the conflict, culminating in nearly a million British dead by the war's end, meant that this was the costliest war in history, eclipsing by far the 1939–45 conflict. The horror of the trenches has never yet gone away. Nor is it likely to. From the beginning of August 1914 through to 11 November 1918, deeds of great bravery were happening every day. Not all heroes were winners of the Victoria Cross, Britain's highest award for gallantry although, of course, many of them were. In all 628 VCs were awarded to 627 recipients during the war, one man receiving the medal twice. The pool from which Wellington House could choose seemed to grow wider and deeper with each passing day.

It is said the true heroes were not the medal winners at all, but the ordinary soldiers, sailors and airmen who simply did their jobs to the best of their ability. Most volunteers and conscripts were content to simply go home at the end of war with little or no fuss and with precious few honours to mark them out as being different from any of the other 'hostilities only' warriors. That may have been what the soldiers wanted but a great number of the men and women waiting at home had a rather different point of view. They wanted to celebrate the return of their loved ones, their very own special heroes. It didn't stop the discharged soldiers from playing things low key and many of them refused to even talk about their experiences at all. When they did speak it was usually self-deprecating:

> My uncle Glover Griffiths was in the Royal Artillery and went out to France in 1914. He was captured, held prisoner till the end of the war. When he came back, we'd ask him, us kids, how it had been. He wouldn't reply so we kept pestering him. 'Well,' he'd say eventually, 'we fired our guns until they were red hot. Then the officer told us to rip up everything we had, letters, photographs and stuff. We were prisoners.' And that was it, that's all he'd say.
>
> Another local man I remember was Jack Duckett. He was taken prisoner right at the beginning of the war. When he came home, we gave him a procession through the village. I must have been seven or eight and I can remember making dip sticks, dipping the ends into tar, then setting them alight. We paraded along, pushing Jack – he didn't really want any part of it – in front of us, flames from our sticks billowing into the night sky. You could never get much out of Jack, no matter how hard you tried. Just one story, that's all: 'I remember treading on my own hair, it was that long!'[1]

Wellington House stood squarely alongside the families. Regardless of what the soldiers said or felt, it needed stories of bravery and courage, not just for enlistment purposes but for the vital business of keeping up morale. One of the earliest national heroes was Lieutenant William Leefe Robinson of the Royal Flying Corps.

On the night of 2/3 September 1916, Leefe Robinson destroyed the first German airship to be shot down over British soil. The airship, a wooden structured Schütte-Lanz machine on a bombing mission to attack London, was brought down over Cuffley in Hertfordshire. It was a very public demise. Thousands watched the combat as it unravelled above their heads. They then rushed to view the charred remains of the burnt-out airship that had plummeted down to earth from a height of several thousand feet. Perhaps more than anything, it was this personal involvement that made the incident such a matter of national pride.

Ordinary members of the public could see and, if they managed to elude the protecting arms of the hastily assembled police cordons, even touch the war! This was real, this brought the combat they had previously only read about in the papers right into the orbit of each and every one of them. Charred bodies of the Zeppelin crew and indentations in the ground where those who had jumped to their deaths rather than stay on board and burn simply made the experience more real. Zeppelins had been terrifying the country since January 1915, seemingly impervious to all attempts at destroying them. Anti-aircraft fire, machine guns from RFC planes, even naval gunfire from ships moored in the Thames – nothing seemed able to stop the airships. The image of giant Zeppelins nosing silently through the clouds, appearing without warning over towns like London, Great Yarmouth and Southend brought the war home to the civilian population. It was the stuff of nightmares. Nobody knew when Zeppelin bombs might suddenly drop from the sky but it was a fear that everyone carried with them, day and night.

While Sub-Lieutenant Reginald Warneford was the first man to destroy a Zeppelin in the air, bringing down *LZ 37* in June 1915, he achieved his victory over French soil. Leefe Robinson was the first flyer to destroy an airship over Britain and that feat demanded he be awarded a special place in wartime history. The Propaganda Bureau seized on the event and almost overnight the airman was turned into a national figure. Wellington House had been unable to make much profit out of Warneford's success as he had been killed in a flying accident just a few weeks after bringing down his airship. Leefe Robinson was different; he was alive and kicking! Both men were awarded the Victoria Cross, however, Warneford being honoured by George V just a few days before he died.

Both Warneford and Leefe Robinson destroyed their airships in night attacks, Warneford by dropping bombs onto the flammable gas bag of the Zeppelin, Leefe Robinson by pouring incendiary bullets into its flank. Leefe Robinson's victory was the beginning of the end for the Zeppelins. Their supposed invulnerability had been exposed as a myth and the giant airships were revealed as unwieldy and dangerous machines – for their own crews rather than the British public – which had proved totally unsuited to aerial warfare. It took time for the message to penetrate the minds of the German high command who had placed such value on the giant airships but eventually the Zeppelins were removed from active service and replaced by more reliable Gotha bombers. These massive fixed-wing aircraft ensured German attacks on Britain would continue almost to the end of the war.

With Leefe Robinson safe on British soil, the propaganda machinery quickly began to roll. Photographs, postcards, artistic interpretations of his action were soon on sale everywhere and the city of Newcastle even awarded him a sum of £2,000 in recognition of his achievement. He could not even walk down the street without hordes of girls, not to mention their mothers, throwing themselves at him, desperate just to touch his arm or exchange a few words. It was mass hysteria, on a massive scale.

For the first time the British public felt that their armed forces were finally gaining the upper hand over the Zeppelins. And it was all down to one man, they felt, William Leefe Robinson. In actual fact there was another, perhaps more significant element to the emotion. It was, of course, none other than Charles Masterman, whose instinctive grasp of the value of publicity and the public need for heroes in times of crisis was nothing short of sublime. Regardless of who was the guiding force behind the acclaim, the propaganda value of Leefe Robinson's achievement was enormous. Masterman and his colleagues marked down the remarkable effect of a man who had achieved greatness simply by doing his duty. When Leefe Robinson went back to the war, they realized that he was now in a position, once more, of great danger. With that in mind they had to start looking for their next hero.

As Wellington House suspected, their hero's position at the front was tenuous and the acclaim for Leefe Robinson did not last. Flying one of the new Bristol fighter aircraft he was soon to be shot down by Manfred von Richthofen, the infamous Red Baron, and spent two years in a German prisoner of war camp. As far as possible that fact was kept from the British public who still viewed him as a hero who had now gone on to carry out other duties for King and Country. Sadly, the Zeppelin destroyer did not enjoy a long and happy life. Several escape attempts and harsh treatment because of his accomplishment weakened Leefe Robinson's constitution and he died during the flu pandemic just two weeks after being released from the PoW camp in 1918.

Captain Albert Ball, one of the early air aces, was a distinct possibility for exploitation by Wellington House. Young, good looking and with forty-four confirmed kills plus over twenty probables to his name, he was everything the Propaganda Bureau could hope for. After some initial press coverage things were brought to a dramatic halt, however, when Ball was killed in action. And that caused Wellington House to rethink the advisability of using flyers as morale-boosting resources.

Combat flying was a dangerous business. Wooden aircraft, their wings and fuselage covered with highly flammable dope, were lethal machines, both to the enemy and to those who flew them. An airman's life expectancy was short and as the French ace Georges Guynemer once declared, the only award they could all be sure of earning was a wooden cross in the cemetery. When, inevitably, men like Guynemer and Ball were shot down, it was difficult to admit that they had been killed by someone who had outflown and outfought them. The Propaganda Bureau declared that Ball had just disappeared, flown into a cloud and not emerged on the other side. He was, they later announced, probably brought down by mechanical failure. Guynemer, the French told the world, had simply flown so high he could not come down again! Thousands of French schoolchildren sat crying at their desks, believing implicitly in the story about their great hero.

Partly as a result of all this, a decision was made to take a backward step where airmen were concerned. In future they would be anonymous – so, airman X or pilot Z had just shot down another half dozen enemy planes. Consequently, people like James McCudden and Edward 'Mick' Manock, high-scoring aces and VC winners both, remained virtually unknown until their deaths.

Private Billy Sing, an Australian sniper who killed at least 150 Turks during the Gallipoli Campaign was a possible alternative hero but his nickname – Murderer – gave some indication of how he was perceived even by his colleagues. Sniping was necessary but not quite 'gentlemanly' and so Murderer was relegated to the sidelines.

Then there was Captain Dr Noel Chavasse, the only man to win two Victoria Crosses during the war. Undoubtedly brave, almost to the point of foolishness, he was eventually killed at Passchendaele in 1917. He had put himself at such risk, many said, that it was bound to happen sooner or later. Nobody doubted the courage of this former Olympic athlete but he was a medical man, devoted to saving lives, the very antithesis of Billy Sing. And that ruled him out as well.

*

The Battle of Jutland in 1916, when the fleets of Britain and Germany finally went head to head, provided Wellington House with the best possible morale-booster of the whole war. Boy Seaman John Travers

Cornwell was just 16 years old but despite being mortally wounded in the opening hours of the battle, stayed at his position as a gun layer on the cruiser *Chester* when the rest of his gun crew were dead or seriously injured. His chest virtually torn open by shrapnel, Cornwell died in hospital soon after the battle. *The London Gazette* for 15 September 1916 gave the sombre announcement that Jack Cornwell had become the youngest VC winner of the whole war:

> The King has been graciously pleased to approve the grant of the Victoria Cross to Boy First Class John Travers Cornwell … for the conspicuous act of bravery specified below. Mortally wounded early in the action Boy First Class Cornwell remained standing alone at a most exposed post, quietly awaiting orders, until the end of the action, with the gun crew dead and wounded all around him. His age was under sixteen and a half years.[2]

The Propaganda Bureau eagerly seized on Boy Cornwell, as he became known, and made sure his story was front-page news all over the country. Cornwell was immediately hailed as a young man who had stuck to his post and done his duty, even unto death. He became the epitome of British soldiers and sailors, an ideal everyone should strive to emulate. A more cynical view is that Jack Cornwell's sacrifice was an ideal way of deflecting attention from the fact that the German High Seas Fleet had outfought the Royal Navy at Jutland, sinking more British ships than they lost and inflicting over double the number of their own casualties on the enemy. Admiral David Beatty had been in command of the battlecruiser squadron which bore the brunt of the casualties and, it has to be said, endured most of the action during the battle. His practice of leaving the magazine doors of his battlecruisers open in order to facilitate faster fire – as well as stacking cordite in any open space – was certainly the cause of three of his capital ships exploding and going to the bottom, taking most of their crews with them. Beatty was more than happy to approve the award even though his reckless tactics greatly contributed to the British losses. Anything to deflect blame being attached to him. As a tactic there can be little doubt that Beatty's deflection worked perfectly.

The public quickly identified with young Jack Cornwell. There were memorial funds created in his honour and the Boy Scouts – Cornwell was a scout before enlisting in the navy – created the Cornwell Scout Badge to be awarded for brave deeds and devotion to duty. Schools organized Jack Cornwell Days, streets and houses were named after him, posthumous portraits by artists like William Wyllie and Frank Salisbury were commissioned and his name quickly became a byword for courage. The young man was exactly what the propaganda chiefs had been looking for. Sadly, the fame and glory of young Jack did not extend to his family. When his father and brother were killed fighting in France, it left his mother destitute. None of the memorial funds was willing to help out and she ended her days in poverty soon after the Armistice of 1918.

One hero that Wellington House missed was T. E. Lawrence, the famous Lawrence of Arabia. A seminal figure in the Arab Revolt, his exploits remained largely unknown until after the war. Then the American journalist Lowell Thomas, who had spent a few weeks with Lawrence's Arab forces during the campaign, began a series of lecture tours. Showing several of the films he had made of the Arab Revolt and Lawrence's part in it, the lecture tours were wildly successful. Much to his annoyance, Lawrence, always a difficult man who wanted fame and yet deplored it, became an instant star.

Local heroes were something of a speciality for the propaganda men of Wellington House. One example was Sergeant-Major Fred Barter, a reservist from Cardiff who was recalled to the colours when war broke out. He won his VC at Festubert on 15 May 1915 when he led a group of just eight men to capture over a hundred enemy soldiers and 500 yards of trench.

Wellington House immediately sent him back to Cardiff to 'show the flag,' raise morale and help in recruiting. When he arrived in the forecourt of Cardiff Central Station, he was seen to be sporting a grazed nose, which was not as a result of enemy action but from a poorly aimed box of chocolates thrown to him by an admiring young lady on the platform.

*

If there were heroes there had, of course, to be villains and Wellington House quickly cottoned on to the fact that they could get as much publicity and mileage out of these enemy individuals, albeit carefully reconstructed into what were virtually pantomime villains, as they could out of the more heroic members of their own armed forces.

German soldiers and airmen were an obvious source of material. That meant Manfred von Richthofen, the famous Red Baron and the top-scoring air ace of the war with eighty confirmed kills, was public enemy number one. Forget his bravery, ignore his very real skill as a pilot and marksman, the Red Baron was portrayed as a cold-blooded killer who deliberately hung around the fringes of a dogfight and picked out only on the weakest of his opponents. When, in November 1916, von Richthofen shot down the British ace Major Lanoe Hawker the national press made much play out of the fact that Hawker had been trying to return to his own lines after running out of ammunition. Richthofen, it was said, had no compassion and no understanding of gallantry. This was just another potential victory for him, even if it was over an unarmed man, and he promptly moved in to kill the hapless Hawker. Similarly, the Red Baron's habit of commissioning a silver goblet in order to mark every enemy plane he shot down did not exactly endear him to the British or French. Such a practice was hardly the mark of a gentleman.

In Germany there were no such concerns and von Richthofen was quickly caught up by the cult of hero worship that engulfed the country. There were, however, fears of what his death might do to German morale. Von Richthofen refused a take a home posting, out of the firing line, and the German propaganda machine began to circulate stories that the British had put a price on his head. They had, it was stated, also assembled a squadron of aces just to shoot down von Richthofen and take him out of the war. When the Red Baron was finally shot down and killed in 1918 – by groundfire, it now appears – the British newspapers were quick to jump on the story. Machine-gunners firing from the ground would not do; he had to have been downed by a pilot, someone who had outgunned him, and so the Canadian ace Captain Roy Brown was given the credit.

More reviled than von Richthofen, however, were the Zeppelin crews who with their bombing campaign prayed on defenceless civilians and thought nothing of killing fifty or a hundred people in one go! Masterman and Wellington House made sure that the press was given exact details of casualties and the damage inflicted in the bombing raids – over 1,000 fatalities attributable to Zeppelins and bombers during the course of the war. Never hugely destructive in terms of people killed and property destroyed, it was the psychological effect that these raids had on the people of Britain that was important. The Zeppelin crews did not exactly help themselves much and Masterman and his staff must have laughed out loud when, on 31 May 1915, the following message was discovered, hurled from the gondola of *LZ 38* by its commander Eric Linnarz as the airship passed over Southend-on-Sea: 'You English, we have come and will soon come again. Kill or cure. German.'[3]

It was perfect propaganda material, guaranteed not to frighten the British people but to stiffen their resolve. The emotion that caused Linnarz to drop the message was undoubtedly fuelled by the British naval blockade that was already causing great hardship in Germany but it was still an ill-judged thing to do. As long as the Zeppelin crews were willing to make such comments, Wellington House had no need to resort to black propaganda.

There was little sympathy for the crews of downed airships. When Leefe Robinson shot down the first 'English' Zeppelin in September 1916, his success brought thousands to the scene of the crash where there was almost manic gaiety. Highly flammable, the Zeppelins burned when hit by incendiary bullets and the crews knew that their lives were hanging by a thread. When Warneford dropped his bombs onto the Zeppelin and sent it hurtling to its destruction, some of the debris from the blazing airship fell onto a convent, killing two nuns. A German crewman, however, had a lucky escape, falling from the airship, crashing through the convent roof and landing on a bed just vacated by one of the nuns. He survived the fall. Most of those who fell from the Zeppelins, people like the famous commander Heinrich Mathry who leapt from his blazing airship over Potters Bar, knew that their end was just as certain had they stayed on board. Falling several thousand feet was deadly but it was a lot quicker than waiting to be burned to death.

U-boat crews were equally as reviled, particularly by those citizens living near the coast or having relatives serving in the Merchant Marine. The U-boat campaign was a long, drawn-out battle against British and neutral shipping so essential in supplying goods and provisions to Britain. It was a highly effective blockade, so effective in fact that in 1917 the submarines almost brought the country to its knees. For a brief period, the whole island was on the verge of starvation.

By the end of the war nearly 5,000 merchant vessels had been sunk by the U-boats, some 13 million tons of shipping sent to the seabed. Altogether 15,000 sailors, British and neutral, were killed. In addition, 104 warships were also sent to the bottom. It was a terrifying total, achieved for the loss of just over 200 U-boats. Only Lloyd George's decision to adopt the convoy system and the development of reliable anti-submarine weapons ended the U-boat threat and prevented mass starvation in Britain. It had been an incredibly close-run thing where for a brief two-week period in the middle of the year Britain almost ran out of food.

Where possible, U-boats operated on the surface and attempted to give advanced warning to the merchant ships before firing their torpedoes. Such a tactic was not always feasible, however, and the inevitable losses created huge feelings of animosity towards the German submariners. Killers and murderers, that was how Wellington House described the U-boat crews and that was how the majority of the public perceived them. Attacking warships was one thing; cargo vessels were a different matter altogether. It is interesting to note that despite hundreds of merchant vessels lost to U-boats, sailors refused to give in or abandon the sea. There was a job to be done and within days of coming ashore, most had signed on with another vessel for another cruise.

It was not just enemy villains that the propaganda men used. There were also more than enough 'bad eggs' on their own side, people who needed to be exposed as charlatans. On 10 November 1915, the *South Wales Echo* gleefully announced that a certain Sergeant-Major White was currently recuperating at the home of his father in South Wales, waiting to be called to London to receive the Victoria Cross. He had won it, the paper said, by rushing out into no man's land to rescue a wounded officer who had been shot in both legs and was unable to move. A few days later the newspaper was forced to make a humiliating announcement: 'Yesterday Company Sergeant Major Mouser and Farrier Sergeant Spiller arrived in Cardiff from the Curragh with orders to escort White back to his regiment. It is a fact that White had not been in France since the outbreak of war.'[4] White was duly reduced in rank, confined to prison and later sent to a mental hospital. Occasional stories like that put the record straight and ensured that men like Sergeant-Major White were kept well away from the gullible public. It was also a little bit of light relief!

Wellington House made sure that the Zeppelin bombs and the U-boats torpedoes were weapons and actions that were well publicized. With their links to national and regional newspapers it was only a matter of a quick telephone call or hurried memo and the news would be in the public domain within hours of an attack. If they couldn't stop the air raids from the sky and the U-boat attacks underwater, Wellington House could at least ensure that the activities of the German air force and navy were noted and regarded by the British public almost as acts of murder. What the Germans were doing was underhand and uncalled for. Britain's bombing campaigns and the Royal Navy blockade, on the other hand, were an acceptable part of modern war. Nothing could be guaranteed to fuel anger quite as quickly as yet another Zeppelin raid or the sinking of another unarmed merchant ship. It was simply a matter of balancing the losses with the hatred of the enemy that the attacks produced. Wellington House clearly believed that the attacks were more than compensated for by the subsequent raising of public morale

*

The last element in the hero and villain concept, something closely linked to both, was that of the victim. And once again the propaganda machine had plenty to choose from. One of the earliest victims, her story caught and circulated around the world by Wellington House, was the British nurse Edith Cavell.

A native of Norfolk, Edith Cavell had been working for some time as a nurse in Belgium when the Germans invaded. As matron of the new Saint-Gilles Hospital, she was clear that she would use her position to help stranded Allied soldiers – and more than a few Germans as well – who might otherwise have fallen into enemy hands. With her assistance, she decided, they could be returned to their own lines rather than vegetate, hiding out in German-occupied Belgium. In one year, from the beginning of the war to the summer of 1915 she helped over 200 Allied troops escape to safety, despite the very real danger to herself and her assistants. Cavell was an undoubted patriot but was also a devout Christian who saw what she had to do as being driven by God and her religious beliefs: 'Patriotism is not enough. I must have no hatred or bitterness to anyone.'[5]

She was eventually betrayed and on 3 August 1915 was arrested by the German occupying forces. She was accused of treason and while there have been suggestions that she was also engaged in espionage for MI6, there is no proof that she did anything other than assist soldiers to their freedom. That alone was a serious offence. It was enough to consign her to prison and have her put on trial where she had to answer the charges of breaking German martial law. There was no real trial: Edith Cavell admitted her guilt.

Inevitably, she was found guilty and despite worldwide appeals for clemency, she was shot by firing squad on 12 October. The execution caused a huge upsurge of anti-German feeling and Wellington House exploited her fate to the full. Newspaper articles, postcards, books Cavell's life and death were all produced, thanks to the efforts of the British propagandists. In a very short space of time, they turned Edith Cavell into an iconic figure and reinforced the negative opinion of German barbarity. The propaganda campaign, well orchestrated and brilliantly run, made Edith Cavell the most prominent female casualty of the war. More importantly, her death was used to increase voluntary enlistment – the final throw of the dice in this area – and, in particular, as a morale-booster. The whole affair, Wellington House declared, showed the utter contempt held by the German race for any of the normal and accepted values of life.

Both before and after her execution there were public meetings and rallies in support of Cavell and, equally, in support of the British war effort. The message was simple and was accepted by everyone – this is the reason why we are fighting, people declared, to eliminate German barbarism.

Soon after Edith Cavell was shot, the French executed two German nurses who, like Cavell had helped prisoners of war escape. The Germans chose not to exploit the incident, feeling that more publicity would do them no good whatsoever.

*

Perhaps the most notable of all the victims of the war were the passengers and crew of the Cunard liner *Lusitania*. Popular myth has it that her destruction brought the USA into the war. That is not so, but the torpedoing of the liner and the consequent death of many American civilians on board did harden US attitudes so that two years later, when unrestricted submarine warfare was introduced by Germany, the Americans were ready to take up arms.

The facts behind the sinking are simple. On Friday 7 May 1915, the *Lusitania*, en route from New York to Liverpool, was torpedoed by *U 20*, just eleven miles off the Old Head of Kinsale in Ireland. As Kapitänleutnant Walther Schwieger, commander of the *U 20*, recorded in the logbook: 'Torpedo hits starboard side right behind the bridge. An unusually heavy detonation takes place with a very strong explosive cloud.'[6]

Within eighteen minutes the *Lusitania* had slid beneath the waves, taking 1,198 passengers and crew with her. There were just 761 survivors, eleven of them American citizens. Of the other American passengers 139 died. Repercussions were huge. Wellington House was quickly on the case and within weeks, if not days, postcards and newspaper reports condemning the attack were circulating. The most famous recruiting poster of the war – after Kitchener's 1914 appeal – declared, 'Take up the Sword of Justice', showing the female figure of justice in the centre of the drawing, sword unsheathed and the *Lusitania* sinking in the background.

Germany, inevitably, defended the action, declaring that the torpedoing of the liner was a justifiable act of war. There were many reasons for that stance. In response to the Royal Navy blockade of German territory, ranging from her European homeland to her African colonies, Germany had recently announced that all the seas around Britain would henceforth be regarded as a war zone. From 18 February 1915, any vessel encountered in the zone would be regarded as a legitimate target that could be attacked without warning. That was the German view. The opinion of the rest of the world – including Germany's allies, Austria-Hungary and Turkey – was very different. This, the world declared, was a war crime, with innocent men, women and children being killed in the most diabolical manner. Condemnation in the USA was particularly virulent and for a brief while there was even a possibility that America might declare war. It did not happen and, of course, the German government immediately hit back at their critics.

The particularly heavy explosion immediately after the torpedo struck was, they said, an indication that there was ammunition on board. Several survivors reported a second explosion, almost immediately after the first, thinking it was a second torpedo. It wasn't – the *U 20* had been on patrol for some time, had used up most of her ammunition and fired only one torpedo at the *Lusitania*. If the *Lusitania* was carrying ammunition for the British war effort, that would have made her an acceptable target. Though quite how the captain of the U-boat was supposed to know what was on the ship's manifest was not made clear but it was at least some sort of defence for the German Navy.

There was another point in the German favour. The building of the *Lusitania* had been partially funded by the Royal Navy. She was built with the intention of converting her into an armed merchant cruiser should the need arise. *Jane's Fighting Ships* for 1914, the classic reference book and one that Schwieger would have had in the control room of the *U 20*, did in fact list her as an armed merchant cruiser.

In fact, although gun mountings had been installed on deck, the Royal Navy had not taken up the option of bringing her into naval service, feeling that she would use too much valuable coal from their already dwindling stocks. Schwieger, like other U-boat commanders, would have been unaware of this.

In the weeks before she sailed, the German embassy in New York had taken the unusual step of posting adverts in over fifty US newspapers advising people not to travel on the *Lusitania*. Many heeded the warning, others did not, believing that this was just German scaremongering.

In the wake of the sinking, debate continued for several months. After initially trying to distance themselves from the event, the German government began to see that perhaps there was value in the sinking. Schwieger became a German war hero and the Munich sculptor Karl Goetz even struck a limited-edition medal commemorating the sinking. It was so popular that the German government decided to produce several thousand copies for sale across Germany. Even the British got in on the act. The Foreign Office and Wellington House decided they would also produce a copy of the Goetz Lusitania Medal and after negotiating with Harry Selfridge, the attractively boxed medal was sold through the same Selfridges store that was still operating its War Window. Selling for a shilling apiece, complete with a propaganda leaflet deploring the sinking, the reproduction medal was an immediate success. It was exactly the same medal even if the message on the accompanying leaflet was contrary to that on the original.

No matter how much the sinking was condemned, it was later revealed that the *Lusitania* was in fact carrying significant quantities of ammunition. In her hold were five million rounds of small-arms ammunition, 5,000 shrapnel shells and a large number of brass percussion fuses. Walther Schwieger could not possibly have been aware of this but it was some form of justification for Germany.

*

Heroes, villains and victims were all part of the propaganda campaign of Wellington House; it was clever manipulation of the media but, perhaps inevitably, such practices eventually came in for a fair degree of criticism.

In February 1918 parliament actively accused Lloyd George – the only public figure MPs knew to be involved with propaganda – of using too many Fleet Street contacts. This would, it was said, increase Lloyd George's control over the press and so decrease the long-held and widely respected independent stance of the media. The little Welshman observed and listened, and then appointed another press baron, Lord Beaverbrook, to run the new Ministry of Information. Lloyd George knew that the war was in a state of delicate balance. He would do nothing that might damage the chances of Allied victory. And anyway, he was more than happy to have the media beholden to him.

In the immediate post-war years, the heroes and the villains returned home, content with their glory or even vilification. The ones who remained without any support were the victims of the conflict.

The most undervalued and underrated victims of the war were the front-line troops who spent their time in the trenches battling in the mud and filth. That was something to which the Propaganda Bureau had never been able to admit to, as the conditions of the Allied trenches were, to a large extent, down to the General Staff. Britain and her allies fought an offensive war. They were always intending to push forward, dislodge the Germans and set free the cavalry to chase them back over the Rhine. It was a policy that did not work until 1918 and, even then, only partially but it resulted in British and French generals viewing their trench systems as temporary accommodation. Why spend time and effort digging permanent fortifications if tomorrow or next week they might be vacated and left behind? When they did occasionally manage to capture them, British soldiers were amazed at the quality of the German trenches. They were permanent structures which had been built to withstand bombardment and assault from both infantry and artillery. In complete contrast to their own accommodation, they found that the Germans had deep dugouts and wood-lined trench walls. There was virtually no mud or filth and the duckboards were not submerged in three feet of water. Most German entrenchments occupied the higher ground which meant that water from the shattered drainage systems of Flanders ran downhill into the British lines.

After failing to take Paris in 1914, the German Army was intent on waging a defensive war. They had conquered large parts of Belgium and France and were not going to give them up easily. It meant that their trenches, particularly in the much-vaunted Hindenburg Line, were built to last and where possible provide a degree of comfort.

It was only after the war that the true horror of conditions on the Western Front were fully realized. By then, of course, it was all immaterial. The war had been won, the Ministry of Information had been disbanded and the future was one of glorious peace and prosperity. It didn't quite happen like that. It would take another forty years, another world war and the rigours of yet another period of post-war austerity before that particular dream could be realized.

Chapter 13

People's Poetry

There is a school of thought that says more poetry was written during the First World War than in any other conflict ever fought. Generalization or not, it is probably true as the war did, indeed, throw up huge amounts of poetry and verse. Most of the poetry written between 1914 and 1918 was not the product of professional or well-established writers but belonged to the ordinary man or woman. In the main it came from people who fought their war in the armament factories, in the family home or in the trenches. A great deal of it originated with men who were too old or infirm to fight but were not too old to venture their opinions.

It has to be admitted that much of what was produced and published was not great poetry, a large portion of it being mere doggerel, but it was certainly heartfelt. If there was one general motivating factor, it was simply that the poetry – verse would probably be a more accurate word – was the result of much soul-searching by haunted individuals who were trying desperately to express their feelings in a time of crisis.

It is unusual to find efforts at boosting morale that had little or no connection with Charles Masterman and Wellington House. But with the poetry of the ordinary people that is clearly the case. Such poetry was not elicited by the Propaganda Bureau or by its successor, the Ministry of Information but, rather, was a spontaneous outpouring of emotion. That spontaneity was to remain with these people's poets right to the end of the war. The individual writers obviously gained pleasure, relief or whatever they were trying express. People had been doing that for years but what made these efforts different was the simple fact that they were shared with the rest of the country, by publishing them in the national and local papers of the time. Soldiers in the trenches might send their efforts home, to their parents or wives. The families would then pass them on to the papers. Or the soldiers might send them directly to the editors of their local news-sheets. It was clearly a matter of choice but from the beginning of the war newspapers made it clear that they would welcome any sort of communication, poetry or prose, from the men at war.

Similarly, many people on the home front also sent in their efforts. These tended to be more patriotic, more gung-ho than those of the Tommies, many of them urging men to enlist and join their friends on the Western Front.

The Times of London estimated that during the month of August 1914 alone, they received a hundred poems a day. That was not exceptional; provincial and local papers were receiving even more. By the end of the war, it is highly likely that tens of thousands of pieces of verse had been sent to the various newspapers. They were not all published – that would have been impossible – but a significant number did appear in print, which were read by thousands of eager, sympathetic patrons. The readers may not have known who the writers actually were but that did not prevent them gaining solace from the verses before them.

Simple rhythms, simple ideas, simple language, that was the pattern of verse from these people's poets. Metre varied, some with no notion of metre at all, but the important thing was the emotion and the joy that creation, and then publication, provided. It is easy to see why poetry was so popular at that time. Poems had always been a vehicle for deep emotion and contemplation. Throughout the Victorian age people had regularly sent verses to their loved ones. A poem for Christmas, a set of verses for St Valentine's Day, or even just an excuse to express your love, it was common practice in pre-1914 society.

Music halls and hymns provided excellent examples of good-quality poetry. Then there were the postcards that everyone loved, cards that were often ordained with poetry. It meant that verse, comic or serious, was in everyone's mind, day and night. But love of poetry went a lot deeper than that.

The coming of war sharpened feelings. Fear of loss, the pain of parting, an almost overwhelming sense of loneliness and a longing for home, these were the subjects of the people's poetry. And, as the papers and the individuals themselves discovered, it was natural for men and women to turn to verse in an attempt to ease their desperation. The obvious question is why.

Formal education for everyone in Britain had been introduced with Forster's Education Act of 1870. It took time to create an educational system and establish the new schools that the Act had ordained, but by the turn of the nineteenth century almost every man and woman in Britain under the age of 40 had attended school of some sort and, more importantly, were able to read and write.

The men – and it was largely men – who took up teaching positions at the new Board Schools were themselves products of the public school system where the emphasis on the arts had always been significant. A little maths or science and a lot of Milton and Coleridge, that was the mantra that dominated Britain's public schools and was now to be the guiding factor of the country's educational system up to and beyond the Great War. It was a fairly logical development, one that was only to be expected. When it came to creating a curriculum for the new schools the teachers and administrators turned to what they knew best and drew unashamedly on their own experience. The emphasis therefore was quite naturally on the arts. What that meant was that the product of these schools, wherever they were based, inner cities or rural hamlets, were well versed in poetry to the detriment of the sciences.

Pupils could recite page after page of Wordsworth and Tennyson – sometimes even Homer and Shakespeare – but had little idea of quadratic equations or the laws of physics. For such youngsters the practice of reading and then writing their own verse stayed with them long after they had left school. Social and working conditions mattered littel. It was as common for the builder's labourer to express himself in verse as the lady's maid or the bank clerk. It was a significant factor that was to be crucial in the development of people's poetry.

*

Philip Knightley, writing in *The Guardian*, recently declared that there were four initial stages in any propaganda campaign during times of war. These were recording the crisis, demonizing the enemy leader, demonizing the enemy as a whole and, finally, highlighting any atrocities that might have been carried out by him.[1]

That was certainly the case during the war. In early August 1914, the crisis in Europe dominated the papers and everyone's thoughts were on war which loomed large and more certain with every passing day. It did not take long for hatred of the Kaiser and, consequently, the whole German nation to develop. As news of the atrocities in Belgium spread, horror stories soon came to dominate the headlines.

The people's poets, eager to get their views out into the open, unknowingly followed the formula. It was done without question or even realizing what it was they were trying to achieve. To begin with, their poems were about the progress of the war, descriptions of battle that were resonant of Tennyson's *The Charge of the Light Brigade* or Wolfe's *The Burial of Sir John Moore*. It was a traditional view, expressed in traditional fashion, and was to be expected from people who had not seen modern warfare at first hand.

That was soon replaced by verses about Kaiser Wilhelm's towering ambitions before the people's poets turned their attentions to the Teutonic nature of the German nation:

> *Oh, coward, mean, contemptible,*
> *You thought to subjugate*
> *Nations stronger than your own.*
> *Oh, what will be your fate?*
> *You led your army Paris-bound,*
> *What were your evil plans?*
> *Ah, slayer of defenceless ones*
> *Who'd scorn to touch your hands.*
> *Your soul shall always tortured be,*
> *It cannot be at rest.*
> *The awful tortures wrought by Thee*
> *Can never be redressed.*[2]

It was inevitable that when news of the Belgian atrocities began to emerge, the people's poets would write about them. Many other topics naturally followed but that was how people's poetry of the war began life.

One of the interesting aspects when looking at examples of the people's poetry is the way the overarching themes evolved as the war progressed. The 'school' of popular poetry, if that is not too grand a title to bestow upon it, began in 1914 with an explosion of unadulterated patriotism. Many of these early patriotic poets were women, people like Jessie Pope with her poem *The Call*:

> *Who's for the trench ...*
> *Are you, my laddie?*
> *Who'll follow the French ...*

Will you, my laddie?
Who's fretting to begin?
Who's going out to win?
And who just wants to save his skin ...
Do you, my laddie?[3]

The 'dig in the ribs' or the sting in the tail comes in the final two lines of Pope's poem, beautifully handled if not quite politically correct for these days. The closing months of 1914 were the time of the white feather, of accusations of cowardice and back-sliding. Reading such lines in the local paper would undoubtedly have affected some of those who had not yet joined up.

Highlighting the quality of the British soldiers was one sure way of denigrating the enemy, as with this anonymous verse from the early weeks of the war. The metre is clumsy and uneven but the message is clear: the British Tommy is always worth at least two or three Germans:

He's the pepper and the mustard and the salt you see,
And the Germans they will rue it.
He isn't only one of them but all the blessed three –
He's a perfect breakfast cruet.
He'll eat the German sausage with his mustard
And the salt cellar he won't spare,
The pepper he has sprinkled where they've clustered
And Tommy Atkins he's all there.[4]

The Christmas Truce of 25 December 1914 was a rare phenomenon when soldiers of both sides, with no prompting, laid down their arms for the day – two or three days in some cases – and banded together in no man's land to chat and play football. News of the unofficial truce was quickly squashed by the high commands of both sides who could not have rank and file troops, let alone junior officers and NCOs, thinking for themselves and consorting with the enemy.

Learning of the truce, the generals, from Sir John French to 'Papa' Joffre, from the Crown Prince of Germany to Douglas Haig, were afraid that front-line troops would join together in universal solidarity with their comrades on the other side of no man's land. Surely no one could wage a war like that? Almost without thinking, the generals ordered the guns to fire again and tried their best to say that the truce had never happened.

Even so, some writing about that truce did manage to find its way into the British papers. Mostly this was in the form of letters but sometimes as poetry. This vibrant account written by a soldier, sent home to his family and then published anonymously in the *South Wales Echo* is a cross between prose and free verse. It predates much of the experimental poetry of the 1920s and remains a compelling observation:

From our trenches –
Good morning, Fritz.
No reply.
Good morning, Fritz.
Still no reply.
GOOD MORNING FRITZ.
From the German trenches, guardedly,
Good Morning.
From our trench – How are you?
All right, Tommy.
Come over here, Fritz.
No. If I come, I get shot.
No, you won't. Come on.
No fear, Tommy, I stay here.
Come and get some fags, Fritz.
No. You come half way and I'll meet you, yes?
All right. Here I come.[5]

The writer ignores the fact that the impetus for the truce came largely from the Germans who, to the amazement of the British, held lighted Christmas trees above their parapets and sang Christmas carols. Even so, the two men apparently met in no man's land. They were soon joined by soldiers from both sides, all heartily sick of the war.

Patriotism continued into 1915 but the Allied defeat – perhaps stalemate might be a better word – at Loos was beginning to make people question what was happening. Poetry from the trenches at this time tended to be mainly descriptive. It centred on tales of honour and bravery with just the faintest hint of criticism beginning to nudge its way through:

In a dirty ditch I'm lying, midst
The dying and the dead

With a piece of shrapnel sticking in
My dazed and aching head.
For I've been sorely stricken
In the carnage that befell
Among the Seaforth Highlanders
That day at Neuve Chapel.[6]

It took 1916 and the massive casualty lists from Battle of the Somme to really get people questioning the running of the war. And that was where Masterman and his Propaganda Bureau stepped in. They could not allow outright criticism of government policy in the newspapers and so a system of rigid censorship was established. Letters from the front were now read and alterations or omissions were made as the officers saw fit. Newspapers were told, categorically, that nothing in any way critical of the war effort must be allowed to find its way into print. It was doing little more than reinforcing the Defence of the Realm Act which regulated newspaper content and which had been law since the autumn of 1914. Now it was enforced with a vengeance.

And yet, despite censorship, some criticism did manage to find its way into the papers. However, this was invariably guarded and the modern reader has to almost read between the lines to see what the writer was really trying to say. The following example, written in 1916, is part of a much longer poem by a private in the South Wales Borderers, a young man by the name of Tom Parton. He was killed in action the year after he wrote his poem but he had managed to survive the earlier slaughter on the Somme. And that became the underlying theme for his piece of verse. The poem is, on the surface at least, mainly about the horrors that faced the South Wales Borderers as they charged across open ground before throwing themselves at the heavily defended German positions in Mametz Wood:

We marched from North to South, Sir,
Not a mile did we ride on the way.
It took us quite six solid weeks, Sir,
To help get the Big Push away.

We took it at terrible cost, Sir,
The wonderful woods of Mametz,

Every man that went down was a soldier sound
And deserved what a soldier gets.

And now a word for the survivors,
You would think we were entitled to rest
But we are still in the war, Sir,
Fighting that strange German fest.

In a well-known place called Ypres
Again, we are holding the Line,
In one of the saddest places
Wherever the sun did shine.[7]

Parton's poem is naïve in its structure and faulty in its metre, but it certainly makes its point – no rest for the wicked, as the soldiers would say. And getting that message across, that was what Parton was trying to achieve, not write a literary masterpiece. The men of the Welsh Division were criticized for taking five days to capture Mametz Wood rather than the twenty-four hours that the high command had expected. And then, when victory was achieved, rather than come out of the lines to rest, the battered division was sent to Ypres for the next piece of action.

Poetry flowed freely in 1916, perhaps as much as in the first year of the war. Even the editor of *The Wipers Times* was moved to make a point, albeit humorous, about the propensity and ease with which soldiers could turn their hands to verse:

> An insidious disease is affecting the Division, and the result is a hurricane of poetry. Subalterns have been seen with a notebook in one hand and a bomb in the other, absently walking near the wire in deep communion with the muse. The Editor would be obliged if a few of the poets would break into prose as a paper cannot live by poems alone.[8]

One change that remains noticeable is the heightening of a different type of emotion. Glorification of war and the nobility of an honourable death were gone. Death now was rotting corpses hanging on the wire or lying in no man's land. There was still honour, there was still bravery, but now no one celebrated them in quite the same way.

163

By 1917 there was a distinct sense of anger in the poetry that was being produced by the people's poets. It reflected the feelings of a war-weary nation and some of it was markedly good:

> *What's in the air? Oh, strategic plans*
> *And banquets for men in corned beef cans.*
> *Oh yes, there's fever and dread disease,*
> *Mosquitoes, bluebottles, lice and fleas.*[9]

The war had reached out beyond Europe and was now a truly global conflict. New experiences, new countries and different cultures were all augmented by the taste of blood and a war that somehow never seemed to go away.

The disaster on the Gallipoli Peninsula in the Dardanelles remained in the minds of anyone who had served there and fought on the beaches. It was inevitable that some of the emotions should surface in the work of the people's poets. The short, four-lined stanza below is about the effect of Gallipoli. It came from a writer by the name of P. McGill and surely has to be one of the finest efforts from any of the so-called people's poets. It is taut, without a wasted word, and it captures the mood precisely:

> *Above your graves no wattle blooms*
> *Nor flowers from English dells,*
> *You men who sleep uneasily*
> *Beside the Dardanelles.*[10]

Egypt, Mesopotamia, Syria and the Holy Lands of Palestine – by 1917 the war was taking men everywhere. Wherever they were sent death and destruction continued to hover. Inevitably, it began to have an effect. To begin with there was excitement and wonder. But men's pleasure and raw excitement at suddenly experiencing places they had previously only read about or heard the vicar mention at Sunday service did not last for long. Exotic, even erotic, encounters in the bazaars, camel rides across the desert and swimming in the Nile quickly became commonplace. Even the joy of simply walking past the pyramids and the sphinx, new and exciting as it had been at first, soon became more of a battle to beat off the hawkers who infested the tourist sites than any sort of cultural expedition.

It was perhaps inevitable that the discomforts and hardships of these eastern lands should soon hit home. The troops, most of them now young volunteers rather than the Old Contemptibles, were not prepared for prickly heat, sunburn, dysentery and other unpronounceable fevers. Forget the enemy, disease and illness were what made countries like Egypt uncomfortable, even a little dangerous. In the days before penicillin, it did not need much to remind the soldiers that Rupert Brooke had died, not from a bullet but from the effects of a mosquito bite.

The noble Tommy Atkins, with his usual phlegm and wit, met the occupational hazards of serving in foreign climes head on. He would deal with disease as and when it came. The one thing he had not counted on and had no possible way of avoiding was sand. All that he could do was laugh at it:

> *There's sand and sand for miles around,*
> *It clogs yer mouf and eyes*
> *And when yer aint a chewin' sand*
> *You're chewin' bags o' flies.*
> *Blokes say this place aint arf so bad,*
> *Some say yer cannot beat it;*
> *I like old Egypt a bit myself*
> *But, blimey, not enough to eat it.*[11]

By the middle of 1918, the war was clearly nearing its final stages. Yet the German Army was far from beaten. At home, things like the U-boat blockade with its dire consequence of food shortages and rationing were causing major discontent. While still attempting to say how they felt, the people's poets, of course, faced it all with sarcasm and humour.

A new phenomenon now began to affect the British way of life. With food shortages impacting every section of society, people found that they were being expected to form queues and wait in line, sometimes for long periods, in order to get what they needed. Frustrated housewives turned, again, to the old faithful – the humorous ditty. And surprisingly some of these satirical or humorous poems did manage to find their way into the papers:

> *Oh margarine, oh margarine,*
> *Thy absence causes many a scene.*
> *I stand in queues mid snow and rain*

To get some more of Thee again.
Fed up with jam and bloater paste,
Oh margo, come to me in haste![12]

Inevitably, people began to cast about for culprits. They were only too well aware that there was a submarine blockade of the British Isles and that they could not, in all honesty, criticize the merchant seamen who were still dying in order to bring food and raw materials into the country. But everyone also knew that there were others, people who presented much easier targets. Shopkeepers were one group open for attack. And then there were the farmers. Always viewed with suspicion, never really trusted, farmers were another group who by the very nature of their role were clear targets:

Oh, where and oh where can our taters be?
We've none for dinner, and no sugar for tea.
The farmer has plenty, we know full well,
But the shops are empty, there's no taters to sell.[13]

It was, perhaps, a combination of jealousy and envy. The thought that farmers were holding onto their crops, keeping them for their own use, struck at the heart of the nation. It was, of course, a notion that was largely unfounded. That did not make emotions any less virulent.

*

When peace finally came in November 1918, the people's poets had done their job and done it most effectively. Never before and never since have amateur poets achieved such success, both in getting their work published and in having it read by the public. The people's poets did not exactly 'hang up their pens' in 1918 but the soldiers' relief of no longer having to worry about making it home or, at the other end of the spectrum, of families waiting for loved ones to return, seemed to deaden the need to write.

Apart from an initial and short-lived surge celebrating the Armistice, people's poetry seemed to have hit something of a wall after 1918. Judging from the newspapers of the time, there was an immediate falling away in the number of poems being produced – or, at least, being sent off for publication.

In the days, weeks and months after the conclusion of the war, people found that there were other ways of expressing themselves. A more frivolous era dawned with new fashions, music and dancing to experience, even trips out to Flanders to view the graves and battlefields of the Western Front. Soldiers out, entrepreneurs in – trips and excursions to the battlefields of France and Belgium began almost as soon as hostilities ended.

The Second World War did not produce quite the same volume of poetry. One newspaper in the first few weeks of that war was moved to ask, 'Where are all the war poets?' They were there, just not in the same numbers as in the previous war.[14] By 1939 there were other ways of expressing concern or demonizing people like the Nazis, ways that had not been available in the First World War. They were many and varied, film in particular, both animated and real, but also stage shows and revues specifically for the troops, plus wireless, books and music.

The people's poets of the Second World War might have been fewer in number than their Great War counterparts but, in general, their offerings were markedly superior. The formal educational system had been in existence for a further twenty years, hence the improvement in quality. Despite this it remained a minority interest.

Mass production of and interest in poetry had to wait until the late 1950s/early 1960s before it became really popular again. Poetry and even intellectual prose became largely the preserve of college academics and their protégés. Then, in the wake of the Beatniks and following the path set by the Beat Generation of American poets and writers like Alan Ginsberg and Jack Kerouac, it seemed as if every second person was either an 'underground' poet or in the process of using the office duplicator to create a small-press magazine.

The people's poetry of the First World War had been something of a phenomenon. It was not a movement or anything that was deliberately contrived. It just happened because there was a need.

Now that the need no longer existed, it was right and proper to leave the creation of poetry to the specialist. It was the end of a brief but unique period in English literature.

Chapter 14

Shoulder Arms, Mr Chaplin?

In the third part of the satirical television series *Blackadder Goes Forth* there is a remarkable comment on cinema and film history. Towards the end of the episode entitled *Major Star*, the audience is treated to a brief exchange between General Melchett, Captain Darling and Blackadder himself. With his overriding desire for self-preservation Blackadder has been directing a morale-boosting variety show for the troops, something that he hopes will take him out of the trenches and return him to London. He has, however, overstepped the mark:

> Darling: So the show's cancelled. Permanently.
>
> Blackadder: But what about the men's morale, sir? With the Russians out of the war and everything …
>
> Melchett: For goodness sake, Blackadder, have you been living in a cave? The Americans joined the war yesterday.
>
> Blackadder: So how is that going to improve the men's morale, sir?
>
> Melchett: Because, you jibbering imbecile, they've brought with them the largest collection of Charlie Chaplin films in existence![1]

By 1917, when the exchange quoted here was meant to have occurred, Charlie Chaplin was the most famous movie actor in the world. Although not normally or obviously associated with the soldiers of the First World War, his work was immensely popular both with the men in the trenches and with their families on the home front. By 1917 Chaplin's name had become a byword for entertainment, in particular for pathos and humour, something that had an immense appeal for almost all British soldiers. Conscription had been introduced twelve months before and men torn from their homes were vulnerable to stress, no matter how much they agreed with the cause. Sent into a war zone where imminent death hung permanently over their heads, they were destined for nervous exhaustion – unless something was done about it. The troops needed succour, something that would ease their tension. Charlie Chaplin, with his antics that were more resonant with the circus than the cinema, provided exactly the right sort of relief. More importantly, he not only offered escapism that was immediate but it was entertainment that required little thought.

Cinema was a relatively new art form, still viewed by many of the 'top brass' with a degree of suspicion – unlike General Melchett in the *Blackadder*. The success of films as entertainment during the First World War has never really been acknowledged and the industry never credited with the acclaim it deserves. It was hugely significant but it was also a two-way process.

Apart from documentaries like *The Battle of the Somme*, cinema was never an official part of the propaganda war, much to Charles Masterman's regret. Even so, people, soldiers and civilians alike, gained a great deal of comfort from watching the offerings from the various film studios of Hollywood, London, Paris and Moscow. At the same time, it must be remembered that the war played a significant role in the development of the film industry and of cinemas in general. There are many strands to that progress.

To begin with, cinema was used as a tool for recording what was going on in the war. That was an obvious role, one that even the 'powers that be' understood and appreciated. But there was also a less obvious benefit. From the beginning of the conflict cinema quickly became a means of assisting with public motivation. During the four years of war, huge steps were taken in many aspects of film. In particular, the use of animation and of camera panning became commonplace. Also, for the first time, the concept of the 'movie star' began to take hold. Such developments would have occurred anyway, it was simply that the war – by the necessity of its requirements – accelerated it all.

By the end of the war, cinema, which had been developing its popular appeal over the previous dozen or so years, had become socially acceptable. It had become a cultural force that was an upholder of social mores. It would be wrong to say that everyone went to the cinema for their entertainment but by the 1920s, in Britain, France and the USA, it was rapidly coming to that.

*

Cinema, as an art form and as entertainment, had been around for some years before the war. A product of nineteenth-century scientific experiment, in 1895 the Lumière Brothers were the first to show short films to a paying audience. Thereafter the Kinetoscope, as it was then known, developed quickly. The early films were shot from a fixed camera and were restricted to human-interest items such as trains emerging from tunnels, horses galloping across fields and beaches, workers pouring out of factories at the end of a shift, and so on. Despite the seemingly low interest value of the subjects, the sheer novelty of seeing moving motion pictures on the screen ensured success and the medium rapidly expanded.

Georges Méliès – with his short multi-scene documentaries like *The Dreyfus Affair* and the animated take on Jules Verne's *A Trip to the Moon* – famous for its image of a rocket embedded in the eye of the man in the moon – was hugely influential. His work led on to Edwin Porter's *The Great Train Robbery* (1903) and to the epoch-marking *The Birth of a Nation* which came out in 1916.

By 1914 there were several national film industries in existence. Europe – in particular Scandinavia and Russia – took the lead. Only as longer films involving plot and story line became popular with audiences, did the USA start taking over as the leading player in the cinema world – witness D. W. Griffith with his ground-breaking but clearly racist *The Birth of a Nation*.

Despite the fact that the USA was seeming to drag its feet, the first ten years of the twentieth century was a crucial decade for the cinema. It saw the essential founding of a base line for the film industry and that applied both in the quality of the films and the outlets where they could be seen by members of the general public. Initially, films were shown almost anywhere that could be darkened and which had facilities for a screen to be set up. Village halls, libraries and Workers' Institutes all played their part. Travelling showmen at music halls and fairgrounds were soon offering mixed media programmes to anyone who would pay their shilling for an hour's entertainment. These shows consisted of talks, dancing girls, even short plays before the unveiling of the main feature, movies as they were already being called. It was an effective start but cinema wanted and needed more.

By the time war broke out, purpose-built cinemas were increasingly to be found on the high streets of most major cities and towns. At the beginning of 1914 Britain could boast almost 5,000 permanent cinemas.

Russia had 200 in St Petersburg and Moscow alone while there were over 1,200 in the rest of Tsar Nicholas's sprawling empire.

No one had yet worked out how to add sound to the moving images but that did not seem to matter to the audiences who flocked in droves to the new picture houses. They came to be entertained and to be informed. The two big hits of the pre-war cinema were both Italian productions, *Quo Vadis* in 1912 and *Cabiria* in early 1914.

Early in the war Charles Masterman, understanding the value of film and cinema, proposed the use of films as a morale-booster. The Propaganda Bureau, he believed, should make films of their own.

In particular, Masterman noted how the director D. W. Griffith had manipulated his audience with *The Birth of a Nation*, a film which centred on the policy of Reconstruction following the American Civil War. Griffith's portrayal of the Ku Klux Klan as a powerful, independent militia with the good of all America at heart, was sheer nonsense but it made good cinema and it was hugely influential. Its inherent racism propelled much of the country firmly to the right and ensured that anti-black values remained in place across the southern states.

If Griffith could use cinema to propound such a sordid view, then surely Masterman and Wellington House could use the same medium for more noble purposes altogether? Masterman's proposal was howled down by people like Joseph Brooke Willinson. The British Board of Film Censors had been founded in 1912 and with Willinson as its first director, it was a powerful force. Willinson apparently greeted Masterman's suggestion with the throwaway line 'What, has the country now come to that?'[2]

Willinson's curt dismissal of the idea meant that Britain's Propaganda Bureau could not make anything other than basic information films – for a while at least – and would have to rely on independent filmmakers for anything that might be regarded as 'entertainment value'.

There was plenty to choose from. In particular, two British films produced in 1914 were ideal for entertainment and morale-boosting purposes. These were *England's Menace*, which was concerned with espionage and a potential enemy invasion – a perpetual theme for British writers and artists – and *An Englishman's Home.*

From America came a number of pacifist films like *Civilization* which has often been credited with helping Woodrow Wilson into the White House, and *War Brides*. The latter was actually withdrawn in 1917 when the USA entered the war on the side of the Allies but both films were, on release, hugely popular at box offices on both sides of the Atlantic.

Gradually British and American filmmakers moved into the realms of escapism, a far more subliminal approach to keeping people's spirits up and was something that Masterman had kept in mind, despite Brooke Willinson's disparaging remarks. Masterman's view was that the great British public could sit in a cinema for a few hours believing that the sole purpose of the film they were watching was to entertain them, little realizing that they were being fed propaganda that would ensure their continued support in the fight against Germany. He was not wrong.

The Bully Boy and *The Clutches of the Hun* were British productions that came out in 1915. The next year saw D. W. Griffith's *The Birth of a Nation*, a classic example of how to pass on a subliminal message. America took it a stage further when Cecil B. de Mille came up with pure escapist movies such as *The Little American* and *My Four Years in Germany*, both dating from 1918.

It quickly became apparent that even the newsreels which now accompanied every showing of *The Little American* and other entertainment movies were not actually breaking news. Newspapers traditionally brought vital, up-to-date news to the people, usually within hours of the event, not films. With morning and evening editions of most papers, they were better geared than the cinema in keeping the public aware of what was happening. Film – even rough and ready newsreels – might take weeks to bring items and stories before the public. With such a time delay they could not hope to break news stories. What they could do, however, was to provide an overview or a summary, reflecting on things people had already learned about from the papers.

With the newsreels able to deliver only so much information, it was inevitable that the filmmakers should turn their minds to feature-length documentaries which could explore issues in some depth. Masterman's commissioned product, *The Battle of the Somme*, was one of the early successes of this type of film. It was quickly followed by others like *Pershing's Crusaders* and *America's Answer to the Huns*. Such films could hardly be called relaxing but they were hugely informative, reinforcing the initial news items gleaned from the papers.

The real success of the war years, however, came from the feature films that kept the public smiling, forgetting their troubles for a few hours. Featuring actors like Mary Pickford and Douglas Fairbanks, cinema-going had become something of a cult. Britain had its own stars in people like Chrissie White and Henry Edwards. But in particular there was one man who could claim the crown on both sides of the Atlantic. That was, of course, the inimitable Charlie Chaplin.

*

Despite living and working in America, Charles Spencer Chaplin was British, born in poverty in London in 1889. As a child he was twice committed to short spells in the workhouse system because of his father's prolonged absence from home and his mother being sent to an asylum. He left school at the age of 13 and began his career on the Music Hall stage, as a way of earning money for the family. His big break came when he was signed by the famous Fred Karno Company and taken to the USA for a series performances.

In America Chaplin quickly graduated from Fred Karno to film work in Los Angeles. His first film, for Mack Sennett's Keystone Studio, came out in January 1914. Chaplin did not like it but there was a quick turnaround in the shooting of films in those days and only a month later his second film, *Mabel's Strange Predicament*, was finished. Its release was delayed, however, only appearing in movie theatres after *Kid Auto Races at Venice*. Although *Kid Auto* was technically Chaplin's third movie, the delay in releasing *Mabel's Strange Predicament* meant that it was credited as his second.

Mabel's Strange Predicament was more acceptable to Chaplin than his first screen effort. It also gave him the chance to put on the costume and persona that were soon to become famous – baggy trousers, tight jacket, oversized shoes and a tiny black moustache.

His classic role of The Tramp – a role that he guided through a whole string of movies – first saw the light of day in *Kid Auto Races at Venice* which appeared on cinema screens at the end of February 1914. That made it three films in one year for the boy from London's East End.

Worldwide acclaim followed quickly and after a disagreement with Mack Sennett over money, Chaplin moved to the Essaney Film Manufacturing Company where he was paid the enormous fee of $1,250 a week. Sennett had, supposedly, refused him a weekly salary of $1,000.

Chaplin's creation of The Tramp (alternatively The Little Tramp) was what really made his name. People were able to relate to the little man who was picked on and derided by society but was always willing to come back for more, time and time again. It was slapstick humour but it was wildly successful on both sides of the Atlantic. In particular, Chaplin's antics were considered something of a miracle cure for wounded soldiers on the Western Front. Projectionists even managed to show his films on the ceilings of hospital wards so that men who were confined to bed or, because of their wounds, lying flat on their backs could watch in comfort. Believing the old cliché that laughter is the best medicine, doctors and nurses unashamedly used Chaplin's films as a way of helping patients forget their pain and trauma. The films were silent with the benefit that Chaplin's antics transcended the barrier of language. British, Belgians, French, even Germans could appreciate this very visual form of comedy without any reference to translation.

Audiences, civilian and military, screamed with laughter at The Tramp's adventures, totally forgetting things like the possibility of Zeppelin raids or gas attacks. Time to consider those once more when the film had ended and the cinema had turned everyone out onto the streets. For many of those living in the inner cities of London, Manchester or Birmingham, Chaplin through his inimitable Tramp was nothing short of a lifesaver.

And yet it was not all plain sailing for the film star. Led by the eternally disgruntled Lord Northcliffe of the *Daily Mail*, there was an immediate outcry when Chaplin did not enlist in the British Army when war was declared. He was vilified in some quarters, the critics somehow forgetting that he was providing a better service by making films than he could ever have done in uniform. Northcliffe, vitriolic as ever, demanded that Chaplin return immediately to Britain and get himself enrolled in the army. He totally disregarded a clause in Chaplin's contract with his film company, for whom he was now directing as well as starring in movies, that he should not return to his native country while war was still raging. Chaplin, said Northcliffe, was nimble on his feet, which was an ideal skill for mounting trench ladders when going over the top!

It was all puerile stuff but it rankled with Chaplin. When the USA entered the war in 1917, there was a second, similar furore in America. Once again Chaplin was sent dozens of critical letters and even the odd white feather or two. Again, Northcliffe was at the helm, mobilizing the opposition. Finally, in an attempt to put an end to Northcliffe's bullying, Chaplin registered for enlistment with the US Army. It was probably the best move he could have made. He was rejected as being underweight and undersized.[3]

Northcliffe finally shut up, found other victims for his malice, and Charlie Chaplin went back to doing what he did best – making movies.

*

Towards the end of 1918 Charlie Chaplin made a unique contribution to the history of film as an art form. That spring he wrote, produced, directed and starred in what, at nearly an hour's length, was the longest movie of his career up to that point. Length of the film was not the real issue. Significantly, the film was about the war, making Chaplin the only Hollywood star to take on and deal with the issue of war while the conflict was still raging. *Shoulder Arms* may well have arrived too late to be of much direct use in raising morale but in the final months of the war and in the immediate post-war years it was instrumental in helping people cope with loss and with the realities of a world that was really no better than it had been in 1914. The film was an anti-war comedy using a watered-down version of Chaplin's Little Tramp character as the central figure. As an awkward, unkempt recruit who has to battle army routines, the Germans and conditions in the trenches, the film was one of his better and more compelling performances.

Shoulder Arms was originally intended to be much longer but scenes of Chaplin's home life, in particular featuring a domineering wife who throws things at him and makes his life unbearable, were cut from the finished product. It was probably a wise decision as those snippets which survive show that this earlier section was out of character with the rest of the film and were really quite unnecessary.

Shoulder Arms begins with Chaplin and his unit in training, something that allows him to make full use of his clowning techniques as an inept, ham-fisted recruit trying to come to terms with drill. The action then moves to France. There the new American unit is beset by mud and water, by German attacks and by the reality of trench warfare. The main body of the story concentrates on Chaplin, disguised as a tree, venturing out into no man's land and finally capturing Kaiser Wilhelm who is on a morale-boosting visit to the front. At that point, Chaplin wakes up to find that the events of the previous forty-six minutes have all been a dream – a device much used in later TV and film.

The film was a huge success, both with the public and with the critics who were unstinting in their praise, even those who really did not like Chaplin's on-screen antics:

> 'The fool's funny' was the observation of one of those who saw Charlie Chaplin's new film *Shoulder Arms* – and apparently that was how everyone felt. There has been learned discussion as to whether Chaplin's comedy is high or low, artistic or crude, but no one can deny that when he impersonates a screen fool, he is funny. Most of those who find fault with him remain to laugh.[4]

Soldiers, or ex-soldiers as most of them were when they were finally able to see the film, found so much they could relate to. The scenes of the dugout quickly filling with water were played for laughs but they were real enough to cause many a shudder. The German trench raids were all too familiar, the presence of bad food was guaranteed to have all front-line troops nodding their heads in agreement and even Chaplin made up like a tree had tinges of reality. Snipers and observers regularly used a tree disguise to carry out their work.

Chaplin was totally opposed to war, a fact later confirmed by his renowned 'Hitler impression' in his satirical effort, *The Great Dictator*. In *Shoulder Arms* it is the hardships that he and his comrades have to endure that underline his opposition to war and demonstrate his pacifist views. In many respects *Shoulder Arms* was a precursor to the anti-war films of the 1920s and 1930s. It certainly led the way and while it was a comedy, in contrast to the dramatic offerings that were to come, it laid the ground for the enormous raft of serious war films that derived their impetus from a somewhat different base line.

Chaplin undoubtedly subscribed to the Shakespearean concept of all drama needing a comedic element, and vice versa. The way that the war, the most dramatic event in recent history, was being run by the various generals was surely comedy enough. The great war films such as *Wings*, *Journey's End* and *All Quiet on the Western Front* were very different from Chaplin's effort. And yet without *Shoulder Arms*, it is doubtful that any of those more serious later films could ever have been made.

The films of the First World War, specific or subliminal in their message, were enough to confirm the value of cinema as an important element in establishing and maintaining morale. It was something that was remembered in the Second World War when films like *Casablanca* and *In Which We Serve* were some of the most popular movies of the time. More subliminal escapist offerings from the 1939–45 war, films such as *The Wizard of Oz, Fantasia* and *Gone With the Wind* were also well received. For soldiers in the depths of the Burmese jungle or for their families back home, those less obvious movies took them, for a few moments at least, out of the tense reality of the war. It was such a significant factor that it is almost impossible to measure its value. Of course, there was a message in most of the escapist films from the period but it had to be looked for. The subliminal messages were straightforward enough: good triumphs over evil, never give up, keep right on to the end of the road and so on.

Charles Masterman, dead for nearly twenty years when the war against Hitler broke out, had laid the ground well but it remains doubtful if any of the renowned films of the Second World War would have achieved the success that they did had it not been for the antics of The Little Tramp.

*

Renowned film actors like Charlie Chaplin, Gerald du Maurier and Douglas Fairbanks had all made their professional debuts on the stage, either in Music Hall or at the supposedly more refined theatres of London's West End or New York's Broadway. Treading the boards was considered good training for any film star and many performers preferred the close relationship with their audience in the theatre to the anonymity of the cinema experience. The screen actor had no idea if people in the auditorium were laughing, crying or hurling abuse at their image on screen. Not so with live theatre. Feedback, good or bad, was immediate and to most performers that was highly desirable.

In London, apart from an initial two-month ban imposed by the government in August and September 1914, theatres were open and continued to run throughout the war. It was a significant effort by theatre owners and managers but it was not achieved without difficulty. Zeppelin raids, the blackout, poor public transport and a strong anti-theatre lobby that insisted it was not right for civilians to enjoy the theatre while men in the trenches could not enjoy the same luxury, all caused major difficulties.

Yet the theatre managers persevered, firmly believing in the pride and quality of the British stage and the right of everyone to a little escapism.

Plays were produced at places like the Adelphi, the Theatre Royal on the Haymarket and at the Savoy as well as at regional venues across the country. Gerald du Maurier, father of the novelist Daphne, managed and acted at Wyndham's Theatre throughout the war. He was just one of many famous faces that audiences might hope to see on stage.

Dozens flocked to enjoy a brief respite from anxiety, at least for a few hours, and to see what was on offer. Theatre was in many cases something they had taken for granted in the days before war broke out. Now attendances had never been higher. This was despite an exorbitant entertainment tax that was levied in 1916, resulting in a large increase in ticket prices. The plays varied in length and quality but the essential message was the promotion of British identity. It was a clear case of British values above all things.

Shakespeare was an obvious choice for performance, which suited the martial mood of the country, particularly in the early days of the war, and there was an almost immediate revival of the most obvious of all Shakespeare's works, *Henry V.* The recruiting scenes from *Henry 1V,* featuring the ever-popular Falstaff, were also well received. Louis Parker's *Drake* was another patriotic offering that played to full houses.

What the public seemed to want more than anything else, however, were revues and musicals. It is easy to see why. Musicals were light and cheerful and allowed no time for deep reflection, offering instant enjoyment and relief. *Pell Mell, Shell Out* and *Bubbly* were all popular but the real success of the war years was *Chu Chin Chow* which opened at His Majesty's Theatre in August 1916.

Loosely based on the legend of Ali Baba and the Forty Thieves, *Chu Chin Chow* was a lavish musical which even featured live animals such as camels and donkeys. It quickly became a must-see production for all soldiers at home on leave.

Marie Lloyd and Harry Lauder were the best-known stars at this time, dominating the Music Hall scene for most of the war years, but French dancer and actress Gaby Deslys also held centre stage for a while. As exotic and as mysterious as the famous spy and courtesan Mata Hari – as well as being a considerably better dancer – Gaby was the former mistress of the king of Portugal. Her fame, transient as it might have been, attracted large audiences wherever she performed.

It is estimated that around 3,000 new plays were written during the war. Not all were produced but among those that did see the light of day were two by J. M. Barrie, creator of Peter Pan. One of these was *The Old Lady Shows Her Medals*, a strange effort about the conversion of Mrs Dowey from a self-centred liar into a caring and compassionate woman. The other Barrie offering, an equally strange play, was *A Well-Remembered Voice* which emerged at the end of 1918. It deals with people attempting to get in touch with loved ones in the after-life, a process which was fairly common in the post-war world and led to a sudden surge in seances and other out-of-body experiences.

Night Watches by Alan Monkhouse appeared on the London stage in 1916. It was a black avant-garde comedy dealing with the issue of shellshock and, interestingly, the nurse in charge of the hospital ward where the action takes place only ever refers to her patients as 'boys'. There are no names for the male players, simply First, Second and so on.

Anything remotely anti-war was immediately pounced on by the censors. Miles Malleson's *Black 'Ell*, for example, dealt with the issue of self-defence and the guilt felt by the central character after he has killed a German soldier. Although written in 1916 it was banned under the Defence of the Realm Act and did not premier until 1925.

Delay had become an occupational hazard for the London stage. Some of the more truly great representations of combat and its effect had to wait until after the war. R. C. Sherriff's *Journey's End* made its debut in 1919 and continued to appear regularly in new productions until the 1930s. Even now the play still makes the occasional appearance and has been hailed as the original source for many war films about the Western Front.

Other playwrights quickly found that their progress as writers might be better served in different areas. J. B. Priestley, the author of the phenomenally successful *An Inspector Calls*, was just one who made his name as a novelist rather than a dramatist. He did not turn to theatre until the 1930s.

It is relatively easy to see where Priestley, himself a serving soldier during the war, was coming from. For many writers who were considering writing about the war, the depictions of reality needed in good visual and dramatic representations of the recent conflict were far too close for comfort. Best stick to fiction! That at least gave writers the opportunity to deploy their imagination rather than fall back on the harsh reality of the Western Front.

One of the most interesting theatrical developments was something of a sideline or at least a sideways move away from theatrical productions. The Shakespeare Hut was officially opened in August 1916. Situated on an empty lot in Bloomsbury, it provided refuge for soldiers making their way to the front or on the way back home, offering a meal, a bed and a warm, welcoming environment. Perhaps most strikingly, The Shakespeare Hut also boasted a purpose-built stage. It was made by actors and many productions – free of charge – were staged. Once Ellen Terry played the lead in an all-female version of *Henry V* – to rapturous applause from the troops. One of the aims of the Hut was to keep men out of the bars and brothels of nearby Soho. The warmth of the welcome and acts like Ellen Terry went some way in achieving that.

PART VI

Shrines for the People

'If any question why we died, tell them because our fathers lied.'

Rudyard Kipling

Chapter 15

A Forest of Flowers

Nearly three-quarters of a million British people died in the First World War. The addition of Commonwealth dead brings that number to well over a million. In some respects that may not seem a great many, not when you are talking about a war that has since dominated twentieth-century history. It remains an emotive subject, one that is almost too painful to talk about. In whatever way you look at it, three-quarters of a million is an enormous total but it remains small when compared to the sixteen million deaths worldwide that occurred in the same conflict.

That total of British deaths includes casualties on the home front, victims of Zeppelin and Gotha bombing raids and of shelling by German warships. But by far the greatest number of British and Commonwealth deaths, obviously, took place on the battlefields of France, Belgium, Turkey and the Middle East. Whether you believe British deaths in the First World War to be enormous or not hardly matters. Even one death was a death too many and for a small country whose army and navy were dwarfed by the gigantic forces of Russia, France and Germany a million casualties was a hugely significant figure.

The war marked, as the tabloid press later had it, the death of a generation. When you break down that rather glib comment and look at the individuals who perished, their future prospects, their characters and their personalities, their individual tragedies were something that had a dramatic effect on the economy, the social life and the well-being of the whole nation.

As the war progressed and casualty figures mounted, there was a growing feeling that the dead needed to be publicly commemorated in some way. When it became clear that government policy was not to bring back the bodies of those killed but to allow them to lie peacefully in war cemeteries in France and Belgium, most could understand the logic of the decision. Even so, it left a void in people's lives. The public's need to remember their dead, at home and in their own way, was something that rapidly gained momentum.

Where the idea of people's shrines originated is not clear, although the idea might have come from similar floral tributes laid at the roadsides behind the lines in France. Soldiers would have seen these and brought the idea back home when they returned to Britain on leave or on admission to hospital to recover from serious wounds. The first recorded instance of such a British street shrine – little more than bunches of flowers at that stage – was at South Hackney in London. That was in 1916, letters in the *London Evening Standard* drawing the public's attention to its existence. Selfridges gave tacit approval to the idea as did many wartime evangelists.

After that the creation of people's or wayside shrines as they were also known became a popular movement in a war-ravaged Britain. Within months, a whole raft of shrines had come into existence, most cities, towns and villages quickly seizing on the idea. The visit of Queen Mary to the East End shrines gave official credibility to the idea and merely advanced the concept so greatly that it was not long before the basic materials required for standard shrines became commercially available. At this time there were no parish and civic war memorials and although the idea of formal memorials had been mooted, the concept of people's shrines was something totally separate.

The people's/wayside shrines were exactly what the name suggests, wreaths or bunches of flowers cut and laid at the roadside. They were usually situated away from places of worship and were often in the very streets where the men who were now being remembered once lived. The idea of community memory was strong and so the shrines were invariably created by a particular community or a specific street rather than a whole town. The local community funded the shrine, made all the arrangements and ensured that it was well maintained with flowers being regularly refreshed. A roll of honour was an important part of each shrine, listing the men who had died, and Union Jacks or other flags were also used to adorn the site. Sometimes each shrine would also boast a small, homemade wooden cross.

The shrines were a popular and spontaneous phenomenon. They were almost always the responsibility of the women from the community and many believed that they were tapping into long-gone superstitions such as the placing of flowers alongside holy wells. Their origin hardly mattered: the shrines gave comfort, even a degree of spiritual protection, to the families of the dead and to the men still at the front.

People's shrines might seem to have been a harmless phenomenon but that was not how some sections of society viewed them. There were those who violently disagreed with the whole idea. And they were not exactly backward in making their views known. In 1916 a people's shrine at Ilford was desecrated by an unknown vandal. It was followed a few days later by a letter to *The Christian Recorder* expressing support for the action. The writer, who may or may not have been involved in the vandalsim, put forward the view that the shrines were nothing more than symbols of latent Catholicism, papal superstition, more akin to ritual than to Anglican or non-conformist religious views. Further desecration and letters to the papers continued.

Despite opposition, the shrines also continued to appear. The movement finally culminated in the Great War Shrine in Hyde Park where, between 4 and 5 August 1918, it was claimed that over 200,000 attended to view the floral display.

There was also an exhibition of war shrines at Selfridges in central London and the Civil Arts Association, a voluntary organization formed in 1916, gave its approval to the movement. The CAA was insistent, however, that any shrines erected must be tasteful, well designed and made from good-quality material.

The whole idea of people's or wayside shrines has remained part of British culture ever since that first example was created in London. The funeral of Princess Diana in 1997 was marked by an enormous upsurge of floral tributes when thousands of wreaths and bunches of flowers were laid in front of Kensington Palace and along the route of her funeral cortège. Even now, road deaths from accidents are often marked by bunches of flowers laid at the place of death, along with a small cross. And it all began in the First World War.

*

People's shrines were destined to be just the start of commemorating the war dead. Anyone who has ever visited Flanders or any part of northern France will have seen the colossal war cemeteries filled with thousands of white headstones. The creation of such burial sites began before the war ended but gathered pace after November 1918. The cemeteries are controlled by the Commonwealth War Graves Commission and are still visited by thousands every year.

There are 1,620 war cemeteries in France and 372 in Belgium, all containing the remains of British, Allied and Commonwealth troops. There are also 203 German cemeteries in France, Belgium and Luxembourg. The cemeteries remain the ultimate commemoration of soldiers killed in the Great War. Initially marked by wooden crosses, the graves are now headed by white stones that are inscribed with the man's name and date of death.

For those who have no known grave – and there are thousands of them – the huge memorials at the Menin Gate in Ypres and at Thiepval on the Somme act as a significant but strangely surreal memorial. The playing of *The Last Post* at the Menin Gate each evening is one of the most profound symbols of commemoration ever practised.

A national symbol of commemoration was, it was felt, still required and so the Cenotaph Memorial was commissioned by Lloyd George and erected at Whitehall in London in time – just – for the nation's peace parade. Designed by Sir Edward Lutyens there were only two weeks between the commissioning and the formal parade, with the result that the memorial was originally made out of plaster and wood. It was intended to last for only the immediate parade but it was so popular that Lutyens was asked to create a permanent structure. This was done, Lutyens creating an exact replica of the original but made now from Portland stone.

The London parade was a huge affair, led by American General John Pershing, French Marshal Ferdinand Foch and Britain's Field Marshal Douglas Haig. In addition, 15,000 Allied troops from America, France, Britain and the Commonwealth marched through the city. The government had declared a bank holiday to commemorate the victory – formally recognized by the Treaty of Versailles rather than the Armistice of the previous November – but again time was short and many communities were forced to delay their holiday and their parade for a brief period. The government was clear that the July date should be met, announcing the fact with typical portentous language: 'It is desirable that Saturday the nineteenth day of July should be observed as a Bank Holiday and as a Public Holiday throughout the United Kingdom.'[1]

Whether on 19 July or later, victory or peace parades to mark the coming of peace were held in almost every town in Britain. Even those communities that had suffered no fatalities – Thankful Villages as they were known – organized some type commemoration. In many respects a gesture of thanks from a community that had got through the bloodiest war in history without losing a man was as poignant as that from a city that had lost thousands.

*

Three further examples of commemoration are worth recording. All three were then, and still remain, hugely significant in post-war Britain. Each was a way of giving thanks for the sacrifices made during the conflict. They may not have been morale-boosting exactly but they certainly allowed the country to know that their loved ones had not been forgotten.

The idea of 'an unknown warrior' had been first conceived by the Reverend David Railton in 1916. Serving as an army chaplain in France, he had come across a simple, homemade cross in empty land behind the trenches. It was battered, sagging into the mud with the inscription 'An unknown British soldier' pencilled onto its crossbar. Railton was moved by the simplicity of the monument and by the fact that this marked the last resting place of a soldier whose name and unit were unknown to everyone but God. An act of true compassion, the cross had obviously been made and placed there by people who had found the body, rather than allow it to lie and decompose in the mud. Surely, the chaplain thought, there was a message here? Railton immediately contacted the Dean of Westminster Abbey and suggested the concept of an unknown warrior, as a memorial to the fallen. The dean was in favour, David Lloyd George gave his unqualified support to the idea and arrangements were put into motion.

On 7 November 1920, almost exactly twelve months after the Armistice, the bodies of a small number of unknown men – some reports say four, others six – were exhumed from four of the pricipal British battlefields in France and taken to the chapel at St Pol near Arras. That evening a representative group of senior officers – Lieutenant-Colonel E. A. S. Gell, the Reverend George Kendall and Brigadier-General L. J. Wyatt – entered the building. With his eyes closed, General Wyatt approached the bodies and chose the unknown warrior by randomly placing his hand on one of the coffins. It was immediately taken to Boulogne for transportation to England. At Boulogne the coffin was placed in a casket of oak made from the trees at Hampton Court Palace and loaded on board the destroyer HMS *Verdun*.

Escorted by a number of other warships, the *Verdun* immediately left for England, with Marshal Foch standing on the quayside to salute the departure. The other bodies were quickly reburied by the Reverend Kendall, secrecy over the identity of the men being preserved until the last.

On the morning of 11 November, the coffin was placed on a gun carriage and with George V and members of the royal family walking behind, it was solemnly transported to Westminster Abbey. The procession was accompanied by a number of VC winners and by 100 women, randomly selected because they had lost husbands in the war. The body was interred at the western end of the nave in earth brought from the battlefields of France and Belgium. In the week following the ceremony, is estimated that a million people visited what was now known as the Tomb of the Unknown Warrior. It has retained its significance for the British people: symbolizing the sacrifice of so many British soldiers, the tomb is still visited by thousands every year.

A similar ceremony was held at the Arc de Triomphe in Paris at the same time as Britain's warrior was placed in the tomb at Westminster Abbey. Most other countries involved in the war have now followed suit in creating a similar resting place for an unknown soldier.

The second act of national commemoration concerns something that many people have now rather taken for granted. It is the sale and subsequent wearing of poppies on and around Remembrance Day, 11 November, each year. The idea was simple. The battlefields of Europe were, by the end of the war, a series of blasted, desolate wastelands. Mud, bomb craters, barbed wire and corpses – the sum total of the fields of Flanders. Nothing grew there, nothing except the blood-red poppies that Canadian poet and doctor John McCrae wrote about:

> *In Flanders Fields the poppies blow*
> *Beneath the crosses, row on row.*[2]

The idea of using poppies to commemorate the war dead came from America. Academic Moina Michael conceived the idea after reading McCrae's poem and listening to the words of survivors from the trenches. She campaigned tirelessly in order to get the poppy recognized as a symbol of remembrance across the US and before long the idea caught on. In Britain, France and the dominions enthusiasts began similar campaigns.

In 1921 a Frenchwoman by the name of Anna Guerin was in London selling paper poppies to the public, when she met Field Marshal Haig. Eloquent and determined, she convinced Douglas Haig to adopt the poppy as the symbol of the Royal British Legion which had just come into existence that year. The rest, as they say, is history. Now, over a century later, hundreds of thousands of poppies are still being made and sold each year.

And that brings us to the third commemorative gesture, war memorials. There is now hardly a town or village in the country that does not have either its own or a shared memorial related to the two great conflicts of the twentieth century. That, if nothing else, speaks volumes about the effect of the Great War – and the subsequent Second World War – on the communities of Britain.

Of course, there had been memorials before. The early Victorians saw it as a Christian duty to erect tablets or free-standing tributes to those who had fallen in the course of establishing the empire. In the main, however, those being commemorated were unnamed – unless they were the sons of the great families.

The First World War was different. Those who had died were not faceless warriors whom no one would mourn; they were either enthusiastic volunteers or conscripted men and the sheer volume of the casualties meant that precious few families across Britain and the Commonwealth had not suffered loss of some sort. Something had to be done to ease the pain of loss, particularly as government policy was to bury men as close to the field of battle as possible. The decision was understandable but there was still a desire to create local memorials in the hometowns and communities of the dead:

> The Imperial War Graves Commission was constituted in 1917 with a remit to design and construct military cemeteries, and later to commission the building of monuments for the 'missing', those with no known grave. The government encouraged local communities to form committees to raise funds for their own memorials but offered little advice and imposed few restrictions.[3]

What resulted was a mix of memorials ranging from classical crosses and stained-glass windows to single or group statuary. There were also cricket pavilions, memorial arches and schools, all dedicated to men who had died. For most communities, however, it was a case of a simple stone monolith and, more importantly, a list of those who had died. Sculptors and artists like Eric Gill, Albert Toft and Goscombe John were employed to produce the memorials which have now become works of art in their own right.

The first war memorial to be erected after the Great War was a 14-foot obelisk in Etherley near Bishop Auckland. It was unveiled on 7 August 1920. It may have been the first monument but many other working memorials were already up and running. Working memorials, many felt, were a particularly appropriate way of commemorating the dead.

In 1917 Gladys Gibbs of the Cardiff ship-owning family purchased the old Taff Vale Railway Hotel in Penarth, determined to see it opened as a memorial to her husband John who had been killed on the Menin Road earlier that year. Strong Methodists, the Gibbs family was dedicated to the creation of a memorial that was not simply a lump of stone but something that would help children, many of them orphaned by the war, to make good in the world. Barely a year after it was purchased, the huge building was opened as a nautical training school, training deprived boys for careers at sea. It ran under the name the J. A. Gibbs Home and the first pupil was admitted on 24 October 1918, before the war had even ended. The school still exists on the same site although its purpose is now to educate and care for emotionally disturbed children and young people.

Perhaps the most moving of all the memorials has to be the statue of a British Tommy standing solemnly, reading a letter from home. Designed by Charles Jagger, the memorial stands at Paddington Station, having been commissioned by the Great Western Railway Company to commemorate the men from the company who died in the war.

People's shrines, war memorials, the Tomb of the Unknown Warrior and selling poppies are still significant acts of commemoration. They undoubtedly gave comfort to those who had lost loved ones and are still in use today. They may not have been intended as a way of boosting morale but that, in effect, is exactly what they did. They gave, and continue to give, reason for the sacrifice and you are left with the question: could there be any better way of sustaining the morale of the people?

Chapter 16

An End

When the end of the war came suddenly in November 1918, it caught many by surprise. It shouldn't have done; the writing had been on the wall ever since the failure of Germany's Operation *Michael*, the Spring Offensive, earlier in the year. And yet, while the German Army was retreating, they were not broken but were fighting every inch of the way. Morale in the German military was still relatively sound; it was only back in Germany where the effects of the British naval blockade were becoming more telling by the day that gloom and despair were prevalent.

The terms of the Armistice were dictated by Marshal Ferdinand Foch, the supreme commander of the Allied forces, and were laid out for the Germans at a meeting in a railway carriage at a siding in the forest of Compiègne. The Germans had little alternative but to accept and sign the document.

In the British ranks, despite the mud and the blood, despite the casualties and the seemingly never-ending nature of the war, morale was surprisingly high. In all fairness, it had been throughout the war despite catastrophic defeats like the opening hours of the confrontation on the Somme or at Passchendaele where Douglas Haig commented that 35,000 casualties on the first of the battle was 'a good day's work'. Nothing seemed able to dampen spirits and for that Wellington House must take a great deal of credit.

The level of morale had been set high and there was little that seemed likely to change it. Compared to what was happening in the French Army it was nothing short of miraculous. The Nivelle Offensive of April 1917 had cost the French 96,000 men and, despite another bloodthirsty diversionary attack at Arras in the north by Haig and the British New Armies, Nivelle's assault made absolutely no headway. If the Battle of Verdun in 1916 had virtually crippled the French Army, Nivelle's battleplan and the subsequent offensive took it to breaking point.

The result was mutiny. All along the French lines soldiers laid down their arms and refused to fight. Fifty-four divisions were involved and even those who did not join in the mutiny marched towards the front bleating like sheep. Others sang, sadly and almost under their breath, what quickly became known as *The Song of Despair*:

> *Goodbye life, goodbye love, goodbye all women.*
> *It is well finished, it is for always,*
> *This infamous war.*
> *It is in Caronne, on the plate,*
> *Where one must leave his skin*
> *Because we are all condemned,*
> *We are sacrificed.*[1]

Nivelle was sacked and replaced by Marshal Philippe Pétain, later the villain of Nazi-occupied France during the Second World War. Pétain instituted a clever combination of harsh punishment for some of the major offenders and conciliatory treatment for others. It solved the problem before the Germans learned of the mutiny, before they could exploit the situation.

Of course, there were mutinies in the British ranks but never to such an extent as this and when they did occur, they usually occurred well behind the front. Out of the three recorded British mutinies during the war by far the most serious was the well-reported event at the Etaples training camp in September 1917. The camp, twelve miles along the coast from Boulogne, was a brutal place, run by NCOs and officers who had had no experience of front-line conditions and were therefore incapable of relating to the men under their command. In August and September 1917, a number of riots, originating in the unhappiness of ANZAC troops about living conditions and treatment, saw several army units brought in to deal with the situation which had got out of control. Many arrests were made and long-term prison sentences liberally dished out. Two of the mutineers were executed by firing squad but order was eventually restored. Out of 1,800 British servicemen who were court-martialled for mutiny during the war, only forty-two were based on the Western Front. Just three were executed, two of them from the Etaples disorder. This was in complete contrast to the French Army where 40,000 soldiers were court-martialled in 1917 alone.

There were several reasons for this. Most of the British Army during the war was made up of volunteer regiments who had a clear moral code and would do nothing that would likely bring shame on their families back home. But another vital factor was high level of morale.

All the tactics employed by the propaganda men, combined with the fact that Britain, unlike France, was never occupied by the enemy, went some way to ensuring the quality of the British military response. The availability of leave on a fairly regular basis was essential to the efficiency of the troops. With Britain just a short hop away, men granted leave could often be home with their families within twenty-four hours. In contrast, leave was uncommon in the French Army, at least until Marshal Pétain introduced a regular rotational process as part of his cure for the 1917 mutinies.

Regular leave for the British was matched by a steady delivery of post. Mail could be handed to the troops on the Western Front within days of posting. Locations like the Middle East obviously took longer. It is estimated that over 2,000 million letters and parcels were delivered to British troops during the conflict, an amazing total that had a profound effect on their morale and well-being. Having regular access to mail reduced feelings of isolation that all soldiers away from home were bound to feel. French post was neither as regular nor as effective.

Two items, delivered free to the troops, were hugely important in keeping up spirits and morale: alcohol and nicotine. All front-line troops were issued a daily rum ration – whisky being substituted for rum as far officers were concerned – and this was eagerly anticipated. It was doled out in more than liberal quantities when an attack was imminent or when a trench raid was in the offing. Cigarettes were also issued on a regular basis. If nothing else tobacco calmed the nerves and helped keep men content. No thought was ever given to the harmful effects of tobacco and many who entered the army as non-smokers ended the war addicted.

And then there was the little matter of new equipment. Strange as it may seem, the regular issuing of new equipment, particularly the supply of rubber boots and waders to soldiers in the most waterlogged sections of the line, helped British troops feel that somebody out there cared about them, even a little. It was the same with the issuing of warm sheep- or goatskin coats for the winter months. Traditional army greatcoats were issued to officers only but goatskins were welcomed by the rank and file. Unfortunately, it was quickly discovered that the coats trailing on the ground picked up heavy clods of mud which made them weigh a ton. The solution was simple: take your bayonet, saw off the bottom portion and turn the coat into a jacket. As the war went on goatskin coats were replaced by leather jerkins with the wool on the inside – more effective all round.

The regular supply of three hot meals a day was crucial. If the soldiers had to cook their own food that was fine, they did it on trench cookers cut into the side of the trench. It was not a universal response but it was felt ungentlemanly to be fired upon whilst cooking a meal. When out of the line, battalion cooks produced the meals. The fare might be boring – stew, stew and more stew – but at least it was hot and filling. If tea was the opiate of the masses, it quickly became a staple for British troops. A brew of hot tea, topped up with condensed milk and sometimes even a splash of rum, was the answer to all kinds of problems, from nerves down to minor wounds.

These might have been little things but they all helped keep British morale high. In their own way they were each as important as *The Wipers Times* or the advent of a new song from Ivor Novello to warble out around the dugout at night.

*

News of the Armistice, effectively a temporary ceasefire which would end hostilities until a formal peace treaty could be negotiated, was greeted rapturously. There was no thought that this was only a temporary arrangement and that fighting could begin again. It was the end of hostilities, that was all that mattered.

Church bells rang out and there were parades and parties in almost every street of every town. Homemade flags and bonfires, dancing and singing, that was what everyone seemed to want. There appeared no end to the celebrations. For children, who were now able to anticipate the return of fathers and brothers after years of worry, it was a particularly poignant moment:

> On Armistice Day I was ill in bed. You were usually confined to bed when you weren't well in those days. Anyway, I heard a lorry coming down the road. It was full of airmen and they were going into town to celebrate. I grabbed a flag.

193

We always had lots of them in the house as my mother was commander of the local VAD [Voluntary Aid Detachment that provided nursing care] in the town and we always had them in case they were needed. I ran to the window, stuck my head out and started to wave the flag. The men in the lorry waved back, cheering and laughing. And then I realized I'd been waving a Russian flag. I told my mother but she just laughed. 'I don't suppose they minded,' she said. There was great cheering and excitement everywhere all day, all over the town. Everybody was so happy.[2]

Morale had never been higher or was never seen to be higher than on that very special day. And yet it was, for many, a day tinged with sorrow. So many men had died and for those who had lost friends or relatives it was a bitter-sweet experience. And, of course, the War Office telegrams continued to arrive for several weeks, the gap between death and notification to the family taking several days to bridge. The family of poet Wilfred Owen, for example, killed just a week before the Armistice, heard the news of his death as the bells of victory echoed and rolled around the streets of his native Oswestry.

News of the ceasefire was treated a little more cautiously by the soldiers of both sides. Although the Armistice agreement had been signed the night before, hostilities were not due to end until 11 a.m. on 11 November and consequently, on many parts of the front, fighting continued until the very last moment.

George Edwin Ellison was the last British soldier to be killed, at approximately 9.30 that morning. None of the British troops were keen to expose themselves to enemy fire and apart from the German and British/French artillery barrages which continued almost to the end, it was a case of 'Keep low, keep close'.

The very last man to die on Armistice Day was an American, Henry Gunter who was killed just sixty seconds before 11 a.m. Gunter had apparently been recently demoted and in an attempt to redeem himself charged at the amazed Germans who had already downed their rifles, waiting for the end of hostilities. They had no alternative but to pick up their weapons and fire at the crazed man charging across no man's land.

Altogether 2,738 men died on that final day of the war, mostly as a result of artillery fire; many more were wounded and incapacitated while waiting for the 11 a.m. deadline. The ceasefire itself was something that could and should have taken place several hours before. But somebody, somewhere, had wanted that alliterative ending – the eleventh hour of the eleventh day of the eleventh month of the year, and as a result, nearly 3,000 men died to allow him his poetic finale.

When the last shot had been fired, the German troops simply stood up, saluted or bowed towards the Allied lines and then turned round and headed back across the Rhine. That was what the terms of the Armistice had demanded and carefully the Allies watched them go.

Over everything there lay an air of stillness, an uncanny atmosphere covering the fields and trenches where just minutes before shot and shell had dominated. It was a terrible anti-climax for the victorious Allies who had been dreaming of this moment for many months. But now, finally, it was over; the war had ended, and that took some time for the men in the trenches to comprehend.

Silence was the only real tribute to those who had died. It was something that was implemented at the first Remembrance Day service, at the regular evening commemoration at the Menin Gate and at all memorial services ever since. Silence: the ultimate tribute.

Conclusion

The First World War has often been called the first modern war. In terms of new technology used in warfare, it is probably an accurate comment but it was also the first war where propaganda was deliberately and clinically used to vilify the enemy and, at the other end of the spectrum, increase the morale of the home side.

Britain, Germany, France, the USA, all the warring nations were highly conscious of the value of propaganda. It was, therefore, a technique that they all used but during the course of the war nobody did it better than the British.

Keeping the fires of home burning brightly, ready for the return of the country's victorious soldiers, was an integral part of the process. People who had been constantly fed with the need to stay happy and expectant, ready for a better world, might have been excused for their moments of jollity when peace finally came. Soldiers who had endured the mud and filth of the Western Front for four horrific years might equally have been content to go home to what David Lloyd George had called 'a land fit for heroes'.

It was not to be. The Great Depression soon bit into whatever vestiges of relief the end of war might have brought. And just over twenty years later everyone would have to do it all again as Hitler's panzers rolled across Europe.

The First World War had been 'marketed' as a just war, a war to stop the advance of the Teutonic hordes of Kaiser Wilhelm. That was probably so far from the truth as to be laughable but thousands of willing volunteers fell for it and, still believing in the validity of their actions and the nobility of the cause, went to their deaths in the fields of Belgium and France.

The war demonstrated, as never before, the power of propaganda. There can be no doubt about its effectiveness, so much so that propaganda can, even now, probably be classified as the fourth offensive arm.

That was a lesson quickly learned by the men of Wellington House and its successors during the First World War. The War Propaganda Bureau was dissolved almost as soon as hostilities ended but when conflict returned to Europe in 1939, the value of effective propaganda was immediately apparent and politicians and civil servants alike turned instantly to founding another bureau. In fact, discussions about founding another propaganda bureau had begun as far back as October 1935. The perceived need for such an organization mirrored the Nazi build-up in Germany, shadowing the war clouds that were slowly but surely gathering over Europe in the closing years of the decade. However, nothing formal was put into place.

The war changed everything and a new ministry of information was created on 4 September 1939, the day after Britain declared war. It was not a day too soon. Its purpose was to promote the cause of countering Nazi aggression. It would do so by issuing national propaganda and by controlling news and information both at home and abroad. Once learned, never forgotten.

Sources

Primary Sources

The Wipers Times, 12 February 1916–December 1918
Diary of Gwennie Thomas, unpublished, 1917 (copy held by author)
various newspapers *see* periodicals

Books

Anon, *Blackadder: The Whole Damn Dynasty*, Penguin, London, 1999
Bairnsfather, Bruce, *Bullets and Billets*, Grant Richards Ltd, London, 1915
Baker, Richard Anthony, *British Music Hall*, Pen & Sword, Barnsley, 2014
Brooke, Rupert, *1914 and Other Poems*, Faber, London, 1941 edition
Buchan, John, *Memory Hold the Door*, Hodder & Stoughton, London, 1941
Carradice, Phil, *The Great War*, Amberley, Stroud, 2010
_____, *An Illustrated Introduction to the First World War*, Amberley, Stroud, 2014
_____, *Cardiff and the Vale in the First World War*, Amberley, Stroud, 2014
_____, *People's Poetry of World War One*, Cecil Woolf Publishing, London, 2007
_____, *The Zeppelin*, Fonthill, Stroud, 2017
Corke, Jim, *War Memorials in Britain*, Shire Library, Oxford, 2011
Earl, John, *British Theatres and Music Halls*, Shire, Oxford, 2005
Fussell, Paul, *The Great War and Modern Memory*, Oxford University Press, Oxford, 1977
_____, *Wartime*, Oxford University Press, Oxford, 1989
Gardner, Brian (Ed.), *Up the Line to Death*, Methuen, London, 1976
Geraghty, Tony, *Rendezvous with Death*, Pen & Sword, Barnsley, 2017

Harris, John, *Covenant with Death*, Sphere, London, 2014

Hewison, Robert, *Under Siege*, Readers' Union, Devon, 1978

Holman, Bob, *Woodbine Willie*, Lion Hudson, Oxford, 2013

Holt, Tonie & Valmai, *In Search of a Better 'Ole*, Pen & Sword, Barnsley, 2001

Hoover, A. J., *God, Germany and Britain in the Great War: A Study in Clerical Nationalism*, Praeger, London, 1989

Masterman, Lucy, *C. F. G. Masterman: A Biography*, no publisher listed, London, 1939

Noakes, Vivien (Ed.). *Voices of Silence*, Sutton Publishing, Stroud, 2006

Phillips, Robert, *The Battle of Mametz Wood*, C.A.A., Aberystwyth, undated

Press, John & Roger, *Trench Songs of the First World War*, Cecil Woolf Publishing, London, 2005

Raemaekers, Louis, *Cartoons of Louis Raemaekers*, Holgate, London, 2018

Ratcliffe, T. P., *The News Chronicle Song Book*, News Chronicle, London, undated

Roberts, John Stuart, *Siegfried Sassoon*, Cole Books, London, 1999

Sassoon, Siegfried, *The War Poems*, Faber, London, 1983

Studdert Kennedy, Rev G. A. *Peace Rhymes of a Padre*, Hodder & Stoughton, London, 1922

_____, *Rough Rhymes of a Padre*, Hodder & Stoughton, London, 1918

Tate, Trudi, *Women, Men and the Great War*, Manchester University Press, Manchester, 1995

Viney, Nigel *Images of Wartime*, David & Charles, Newton Abbot, 1991

Webb, Paul, *Ivor Novello: Portrait of a Star*, Haus Books, London, 1999

Wilson, Sandy, *Ivor*, Michael Joseph, London, 1975

Periodicals

Barry Dock News, 18 January 1918

The Penarth Times, 1914–20

The South Wales Echo, January 1915

The London Gazette, September 1916 and July 1919

The New York Times, 21 October 1918

The Times, 27 August 1916, 27 July 1956, 30 September 1959
Siegfried's Journal, winter 2020 (Journal of the Siegfried Sassoon Association)
Sub Rosa, 1917 (55th West Lancs trench paper)
Picture Postcard Monthly, July 2008
BBC History Magazine (various issues, 2010–20)

Interviews

(all copies/transcripts held by author)
August Clubb 2006
Harry Griffith Jenkins 2006
Anne Hughes 2020
Dilys Hughes 2006
Roger MacCallum 2020
Ronnie Phillips 1973
Megan Rees 2006

Media

BBC Wales History Blog, 2010–14
BBC Wales radio programme *The Past Master*, 2007
The Chaplin Revue DVD (Fusion Media)

Websites

bbc.co.uk/blogs.waleshistory
bl.uk/world_war_one/themes/propaganda
bl.uk/world-war-one/article/classical-music
en.wikipedia.org/wiki/Charles_Masterman
en.wikipedia.org/wiki/Sinking_of_the _RMS_Lusitania
encyclopedia.1914-1918-online.net/article/filmcinema
firstworldwar.com/source/brycereport.htm
globalissues.org/article/157/war-propaganda-and-the-media
independent.co.uk/arts-entertainment/art/features

mayhum.net/mckain_fergus_h_e.html
spartacus-educational.com/FWW.wtp.htm
spartacus-educational.com/FWWmail.htm
traditionalmusic.co.uk/folk-song-lyrics/When_This_Bloody_War_is_
  Over
worldwar1postcards.com/louis-Raemaekers/disable_mobile_true

Unpublished Thesis

Compton, Norma Ruth, 'Propaganda and Poetry During the Great War',
  MA thesis, East Tennessee State University, 2008

Notes

Introduction

1. Paul Fussell, *The Great War and Modern Memory*, OUP, p. 9
2. Isaac Rosenberg quoted in Tony Geraghty, *Rendezvous with Death*, Pen & Sword, p. 63

Prologue

1. Ivor Novello, song lyrics *Till the Boys Come Home*, 1914

Chapter 1: To Have and Have Not

1. John Buchan, *Memory Hold the Door*, Hodder & Stoughton, p. 171
2. www.spartacus-educational.com/FWWwpb.htm
3. Buchan, p. 170

Chapter 2: Daddy, What Did You Do in the War?

1. Fussell, p. 151
2. Ford Madox Ford, *The Scaremonger*, included in *Women, Men and the Great War*, edited by Trudi Tate, Manchester University Press, p. 269
3. Rupert Brooke, *1914 and Other Poems*, Faber, 1941 edition, p. 15
4. John Heath Stubbs quoted in Robert Hewison, *Under Siege*, Readers' Union, 1978 edition, p. 96
5. *The Times*, 27 August 1916
6. www.firstworldwar.com/source/brycereport.htm
7. Fussell, p. 119

Chapter 3: Music Halls and Home Entertainment

1. Popular Music Hall/Nursery Rhyme – in common use
2. https://en.wikipedia.org/wiki/Your_King_and_Country_Want_You
3. Richard Anthony Baker, *British Music Hall*, Pen & Sword, p. 123
4. Ibid., p. 147
5. Interview with Anne Hughes, 1 December 2020, transcript held by author
6. T. P. Ratcliff, Introduction to *The News Chronicle Song Book*, News Chronicle Publications, undated, p. 2
7. Interview with Roger MacCallum, 1 December 2020, transcript held by author
8. Quoted in *British Music Hall,* p. 123
9. Siegfried Sassoon in *The War Poems*, Faber, p. 61

Chapter 4: The Church Has One Foundation

1. Interview with Megan Rees, August 2006, transcript held by author
2. www.traditionalmusic.co.uk/folk-song-lyrics/When_This_Bloody_War_is_Over
3. A. J. Hooper, *God, Germany and the Great War*, Praeger, p. 24
4. Phil Carradice, *Cardiff and the Vale in the First World War*, Amberley, p. 24
5. Interview with Ronnie Phillips, summer 1973, transcript held by author
6. Carradice, p. 23
7. John Harris, *Covenant with Death*, Sphere, p. 366
8. Interview with Dilys Hughes, August 2006, transcript held by author
9. Sassoon, p. 68
10. Ibid., p. 57

Chapter 5: Is There Really a Price on His Head?

1. www.worldwar1postcards.com/millicent-sutherland.php
2. Tony Allen, foreword to *Cartoons of Louis Raemaekers 1914–18*, Holgate

3. Tony Allen quoting *The Times*
4. Obituary in *The Times*, 27 July 1956

Chapter 6: Gathering Lilacs, Keeping the Fires of Home Burning

1. Phil Carradice, article in *Siegfried's Journal*, winter 2020
2. John Stuart Roberts, *Siegfried Sassoon*, Cole Books, p. 195
3. Paul Webb, *Ivor Novello: Portrait of a Star*, Haus Books, p. 17
4. Carradice in *Siegfried's Journal*
5. Lena Novello quoted in Sandy Wilson, *Ivor: Biography of Ivor Novello*, Michael Joseph
6. https://en.wikipedia.org/wiki/Ivor_Novello

Chapter 7: Woodbine Willie

1. Worcester Cathedral Archives quoted in Bob Holman, *Woodbine Willie*, Pen & Sword, p. 31
2. Rev G. A. Studdert Kennedy, *Peace Rhymes of a Padre*, Hodder, p. 11
3. Holman, *Woodbine Willie*, p. 39
4. Studdert Kennedy, p. 14

Chapter 8: Art for the People

1. Nigel Viney, *Images of Wartime*, David & Charles, p. 53
2. Tony Geraghty, *Rendezvous with Death*, Pen & Sword, p. 121

Chapter 9: Old Bill

1. Tonie & Valmai Holt, *In Search of a Better 'Ole*, Pen & Sword, p. 19
2. Ibid., p. 36
3. Bruce Bairnsfather, *Bullets and Billets*, Grant Richards Ltd, p. 240–1
4. Ibid., p. 119
5. Ibid., p. 220
6. Obituary, *The Times* 30 September 1959

Chapter 10: A Canadian Genius

1. www.mayhum.net/mckain_fergus_h_e.html
2. Ibid.
3. Phil Carradice, article in *Picture Postcard Monthly*, July 2008

Chapter 11: A Touch of Satire

1. Phil Carradice, quoted/collected in *People's Poetry of World War Two*, Cecil Woolf
2. *The Wipers Times*, 1 December 1916
3. Ibid., 12 February 1916
4. Ibid., 31 July 1916
5. www.nam.ac.uk/explore/wipers-times
6. Quoted in introduction to facsimile issue *The Wipers Times*, p. xii
7. *Sub Rosa*, trench newspaper of 55th West Lancs
8. *The Wipers Times*, various issues
9. Vivienne Noakes, introduction to *Voices of Silence*, Sutton Publishing, p. xii
10. Jack Churchill in *Voices of Silence*, p. 112
11. Rev G. A. Studdert Kennedy in *Voices of Silence*, p. 137
12. Phil Carradice, *The Great War*, Amberley, p. 135
13. John & Roger Press, *Trench Songs of The First World War*, Cecil Woolf
14. Soldiers' song of the First World War, in common usage
15. John & Roger Press
16. Ibid.

Chapter 12: Heroes, Villains and Victims

1. Interview with Harry Griffith Jenkins, August 2006, transcript held by author
2. *The London Gazette*, 15 September 1916
3. Phil Carradice *The Zeppelin*, Fonthill, p. 24
4. Phil Carradice, *Cardiff and the Vale of Glamorgan in the First World War*, pp. 69–70
5. From memorial to Edith Cavell in St Martin's Place, London
6. https://en.wikipedia.org/wiki/Sinking_of_the_RMS_Lusitania

Chapter 13: People's Poetry

1. www.globalissues.org/article/157/war-propaganda
2. BBC Radio Wales series *The Past Master*, 2010
3. Jessie Pope in N. P. C. Leadingham, 'Propaganda and Poetry During the Great War', 2008, MA thesis
4. *Soldiers Poetry*, BBC Wales blog, 2014
5. *The South Wales Echo*, January 1915
6. Phil Carradice, *People's Poetry of World War One*, Cecil Woolf
7. Robert Phillips, *The Battle of Mametz Wood*, CAA
8. *The Wipers Times*, 20 March 1916
9. Ivor Morgan in Phil Carradice, *Cardiff and the Vale in the First World War*, p. 60
10. Carradice, *People's Poetry of World War One*, p. 54
11. Ibid, pp. 38–9
12. Ibid, p. 55
13. *Barry Dock News*, 18 January 1918
14. Hewison, p. 95

Chapter 14: Shoulder Arms, Mr Chaplin?

1. Anon, *Blackadder: The Whole Damn Dynasty*, Penguin, p. 400
2. Lucy Masterman, *C. F. G. Masterman: A Biography*, 1939, p. 283
3. https://en.wikipedia.org/wiki/Charlie_Chaplin
4. *The New York Times*, 21 October 1918

Chapter 15: A Forest of Flowers

1. *The London Gazette*, July 1919
2. John McCrae, included in *Up the Line to Death*, Methuen, p. 49
3. Jim Corke, *War Memorials in Britain*, Shire, p. 11

Chapter 16: An End

1. Anon quoted in Phil Carradice, *The Great War*, Amberley, p. 108
2. Interview with Augusta Clubb, August/September 2006, transcript held by author

Index